Mahatma

G A N D H I

and His Apostles

Books by Ved Mehta

FACE TO FACE

WALKING THE INDIAN STREETS

FLY AND THE FLY-BOTTLE

THE NEW THEOLOGIAN

DELINQUENT CHACHA

PORTRAIT OF INDIA

JOHN IS EASY TO PLEASE

THE NEW INDIA

THE PHOTOGRAPHS OF CHACHAJI

A FAMILY AFFAIR

THREE STORIES OF THE RAJ

RAJIV GANDHI AND RAMA'S KINGDOM

CONTINENTS OF EXILE

DADDYJI

MAMAJI

VEDI

THE LEDGE BETWEEN THE STREAMS

SOUND-SHADOWS OF THE NEW WORLD

THE STOLEN LIGHT

UP AT OXFORD

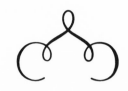

Mahatma
GANDHI
and His Apostles

VED MEHTA

YALE UNIVERSITY PRESS

NEW HAVEN & LONDON

ACKNOWLEDGMENTS

During the more than five years that this book was in the making, I relied for support on the John Simon Guggenheim Memorial Foundation, which appointed me a Fellow (1971–1972), and on the Ford Foundation, which awarded me an extended Travel and Study Grant (1971–1976); presumed upon the good will of hundreds of Gandhi's disciples and followers, all of whom contributed to my knowledge but only a few of whom could be directly introduced in the text (some—Rajagopalachari, M. A. Abdullah, Nirmal Kumar Bose, Sucheta Kripalani, Raihana Tyabji—have since died); enlisted the aid of a phalanx of readers, amanuenses, typists, and editorial assistants, notably Doreen Beck, who helped me revise and distill the week's work every Saturday; benefitted from the comments of, among others, Judith M. Brown, of the University of Manchester, and Hugh Tinker, of the University of London, each of whom read sections of this book in proofs; and freely called upon the grammatical expertise of Eleanor Gould Packard and—for want of a better phrase—the editorial guidance of William Shawn. To all of them:

> I thank you for your voices, thank you,
> Your most sweet voices.

Ved Mehta
New York City

CONTENTS

FOREWORD

The life of Mohandas Karamchand Gandhi (Mahatma, meaning "great soul," was an honorific title) is abundantly documented; perhaps no life in any period has been more so. Certainly it was an extraordinary life, fusing, as it did, ancient Hindu religion and culture and modern revolutionary ideas about politics and society—from any viewpoint, a strange combination of perceptions and values. There are at present about four hundred biographies of Gandhi, yet, as Jawaharlal Nehru wrote in the foreword to one of the weightiest of them, D. G. Tendulkar's eight-volume work "Mahatma," "no man can write a real life of Gandhi, unless he is as big as Gandhi." In Nehru's view, the best that anyone could hope to do was to conjure up some pictures of that life: "Many pictures rise in my mind of this man, whose eyes were often full of laughter and yet were pools of infinite sadness. But the picture that is dominant and most significant is as I saw him marching, staff in hand, to Dandi on the Salt March in 1930. Here was the pilgrim on his quest of Truth, quiet, peaceful, determined, and fearless, who would continue that quest and pilgrimage, regardless of consequences." Leaving aside the riddle of who but Gandhi could write his "real life," the writer's task would have to be to discover and truthfully portray the heroic but human pilgrim amid the myths that began proliferating around him when he started his quest and that have inevitably become more numerous because the quest ended in martyrdom. In fact, the very core of Gandhi's thought, presented and developed in tens of thousands of his writings and speeches—his search for God through celibacy and cleanliness, through mastery of all human needs and functions, mental and bodily, and through insistence on personal hygiene and public sanitation—has been obscured by mythologizers fearful of debasing and sensationalizing their martyred hero. Perhaps because Indians rely for information more on the spoken than on the written word, and because they still live close to the soil, with an awareness of the mystery of the land, myths can become established in India as truths, sometimes within only a few years. In "A Passage to India," E. M. Forster touched on this aspect of Indian reality when he described how in India the death of a character "took subtler and more lasting shapes" than the actual facts warranted:

> A legend sprang up that an Englishman had killed his mother for trying to save an Indian's life—and there was just enough truth in this to cause annoyance to the authorities. . . . Nonsense of this type is more difficult to combat than a solid lie. . . . At one period two distinct tombs containing Esmiss Esmoor's remains were reported. . . . Mr. McBryde visited them both and saw signs of the beginning of a cult. . . . "There's propaganda behind all this," he said, forgetting that a hundred years ago, when Europeans still made their home in the country-side and appealed to its imagination, they occasionally became local demons after death.

Forster's Esmiss Esmoor and his "demons" were only local manifestations. Gandhi was a national manifestation. He himself invested many of his gestures with special symbolic meaning, and at one point or another somebody has sanctified his every action and utterance, so that today in India—and elsewhere—there exists not one Gandhi but hundreds of Gandhis. An eyewitness on the BBC once recalled a day when he and Gandhi and some friends were out for a walk and suddenly a tree sprang into bloom out of season and a cobra bent its hood at Gandhi's feet as if in salutation.

Because I was interested in exploring the "subtler and more lasting shapes" that Gandhi has assumed, and because it is in the memories of his closest followers that the pictures live, the myths take their shape, and his message is propagated, I travelled through India, beginning in 1971, and I visited Afghanistan, Bangladesh, Japan, England, and Austria, in order to collect the views of various specialists and the oral testimony of Gandhians in a cross-section of society. I have also made use of recordings, memoirs, and press clippings, and of Gandhi's own writings and speeches, in an effort both to demythologize Gandhi and to capture something of the nature of his influence on his followers and the nature of the influence of their interpretations of his life on India. Indeed, the use of the facts and myths of Gandhi's life may help to determine the future not only of India but of numerous countries that have a stake either in India's well-being or in Gandhi's thought; in a time of widespread corruption and of ruthless political opportunism and repression, people have increasingly been turning to Gandhi for inspiration and an understanding of the role of principles in democratic government. His ideas have application wherever there are poor, op-pressed people—even in the richest country in the world, as has been demonstrated by, for example, Martin Luther King, Jr., and Cesar Chavez. What follows, therefore, is as much about how Gandhi affected and animated others, how his ideas are now understood and applied, how he is enshrined and remembered, how he lives on, as it is about Mahatma Gandhi himself. It necessarily portrays at the same time his closest disciples and relatives, who are now mostly very old men and women, and in some cases are quite eccentric and enfeebled by their age. For a number of these people who had the opportunity of knowing him and of living in his presence, Gandhi was Christ, and they them-selves are now his apostles, trying to spread his word through an indifferent world.

I

Subtler and More Lasting Shapes

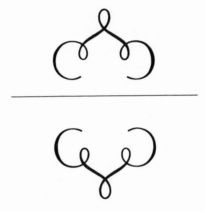

Bapu

HERE ARE THE RECOLLECTIONS OF AN APOSTLE WHO CONVERSED with me for several days as she travelled through the villages of Central India doing Gandhi's work:

"It is said that the Taj Mahal looks different to different people, depending on where they're standing and particularly on what time of day it is. I feel rather like that about Bapu. [Gandhi was affectionately called Bapu, which means "father."] Sometimes I remember him as small and unimpressive-looking, other times as a tall silhouette. Sometimes I think he must have had rickets as a child, because in my mind I picture him as crooked—his bones crooked, his head crooked, his mouth crooked, his shoulders crooked. He even sat a little crooked, with his head slightly tilted to one side. But other times I remember him as having perfect posture, and wonder if I ever saw his shoulders stoop. Then, again, I think he had weak muscles in the back of his neck and he might have been a little self-conscious about it and made a special effort to keep himself erect all the time. Woodrow Wyatt, the former English M.P., once told me that he remembered Bapu as looking rather like a polished nut, all bright and shiny, with no spare flesh —a brown nut, carefully cherished. He gleamed, you know. His chocolate-colored skin was smooth, healthy, and young-looking, and shone all over.

"As a rule, he went about completely naked except for his bright white dhoti, neatly tied around his loins and thighs, and his spectacles, with their cheap wire frames. His dhoti was always white, because he thought dye concealed dirt, and it was always of khadi [homespun cotton cloth]. He wanted to wear or use only what was within the means of any peasant, however poor. He mostly went barefoot or wore wooden clogs. When he went on long walks, he wore a pair of leather sandals, and sometimes also a white cheesecloth shawl around his shoulders and a white kerchief on his head, tied under his chin. The sandals were made from the hide of a cow that had died a natural death. As a good Hindu, Bapu believed that the cow was sacred; moreover, he didn't believe in killing anything.

"Though he was old when I knew him, he had such fine muscles and strong bones that, as I remember him most often, he appeared well built. He had a short, thin neck, a noble chest, a narrow waist, big, expressive hands with well-formed fingers, and long, thin, firm legs with knobby knees. His head was large, and his ears stood out abruptly. Because he had high blood pressure, the veins in his temples protruded a little. His nose was fat and pointed downward. His lower lip was sensitive and somehow conveyed suffering. Whenever he smiled, he revealed naked gums. He had lost most of his teeth by the time he reached his mid-fifties. He was actually a very ugly man, and took pride in being ugly. I saw him once on his day of silence—he observed silence every Monday, as a religious duty—and I told him, 'Bapu, I think I saw the ugliest man in the whole world yesterday.' He frowned. Then I remembered, and said, 'No, the second-ugliest.' That made him smile. He liked to be teased. In repose, his face certainly was ugly, but it was seldom in repose. His eyes were soft and gentle, yet compelling and challenging. You felt naked and exposed before them, but more often than not they were twinkling in affectionate amusement. On his day of silence, they seemed sad and a little blank.

"He spoke in a low singsong. His tone was always conversational, even when he was addressing millions of people. Whatever he said was to the point, and he used mostly simple words to say simple things. He never resorted to histrionics, or any rhetorical device, although he was fond of using parables and proverbs, and quotations from the Bhagavad Gita and other sacred books.

"I stayed with him several times at Sevagram Ashram [Sevagram means "village of service." Ashram means "hermitage" or "sanctuary"], which was in Central India, and which was his home from the mid-thirties to the mid-forties. He used to say that at Sevagram he felt as insignificant as a frog at the bottom of a well but that for him this well was India—was, in fact, the whole universe.

"From a distance, Sevagram Ashram looked like a stockade in the

4

middle of nowhere. Only a dirt road connected it to Wardha, the nearest town, and so to the outside world. The land was flat and arid, baked dry much of the year by the burning sun. The summers were interminable. Frequent whirlwinds coated everything with dust and sand, the temperature never seemed to budge from a hundred and twenty degrees, and the grass seemed to die as soon as it sprouted. Often, the monsoon was late and then came in a deluge. In no time at all, the land was waterlogged, mosquitoes were everywhere, and scorpions and poisonous snakes boldly slithered all over the place. They seemed to know they were safe in Bapu's country, where reverence for all life was an unquestioned law and the worst that could happen to them was a few minutes' discomfort in the teeth of a pair of tongs as they were carried away from the ashram and set loose in the nearby fields.

"The ashram was on the edge of the village of Segaon, which was just a few mud-and-bamboo huts with a primitive communal well. There were no shops worthy of the name, and no amenities of any kind. Most of the villagers were untouchables, and every last one was a victim of chronic malaria, chronic dysentery, or chronic malnutrition. Not even the children had enough energy to brush away the flies that settled on them. Who but Bapu would have thought of trying to teach these villagers anything? One of my earliest memories of Bapu is seeing him trudge along the tracks sweeping up the excrement that the villagers had left around like dogs, even by the well. That was his way of setting an example, of teaching the villagers the most elementary lesson of all the lessons he wanted to teach—that human and animal filth was the main cause of disease throughout the land. The whole ashram was really a lesson in what a village could be. We had well-kept communal latrines, from which all the excrement was carried first to trenches outside the ashram, to make compost, and then to the fields, for fertilizer. These fields we carefully planted with sugarcane and vegetables—the staples of our diet. Although, like Segaon, the ashram was not much more than mud-and-bamboo huts, the main buildings were neatly ranged around a central courtyard covered with gravel.

"More than anything else, though, the ashram was a community of men and women dedicated to Bapu's ideals of truth and nonviolence, industry and humility. Who can say which, if any, of us there, with our very dissimilar temperaments and capacities, ever came near to realizing those ideals? Of course, when we were living with Bapu we felt we could do anything, and yet we also felt we needed him to solve all our problems. We became so dependent on him that we couldn't make any decision without consulting him: 'Bapu, how much hair oil should I use?' 'Bapu, should I get my head shaved?' 'Bapu, should I have one or two spoonfuls of soybean paste?' 'Bapu, won't you bless our marriage?' Bapu's prescripts were based on his particular religious and moral principles, and some of them were a little hard to accept at first. He once gave a couple his blessing after their wedding ceremony and said, 'Now you should live like brother and sister.' He believed in celibacy for spiritual growth, even in marriage.

"Some outsiders said we were a pitiful bunch of broken reeds, all dependent in some way on Bapu for support. Some said that Bapu had gathered us up from here and there just to gratify his own ego, or to use us as guinea pigs in his experiments with truth and nonviolence. Some said that all of us—including Bapu—were mental cases, and that healthy people, like Jawaharlal Nehru, had no need of ashrams. Bapu himself once wrote, 'I am physically and even mentally an invalid and I have collected about myself a crowd of invalids.' Invalids, my foot! We were very hardworking and devout, and Bapu more than any of us. Have you ever heard of Jai Krishna Bhansali? He used to teach Sanskrit in the city of Ahmedabad. Then for years he wandered naked in the Himalayas with just an iron belt around his loins, searching for God. One night, someone stepped on him while he was asleep. He had taken a vow of silence unto death, but he cried out involuntarily, 'Look out! What are you doing?' He was so dismayed at his lack of self-discipline that he sewed up his lips with copper wire. He supposedly threw himself on a large cactus and rolled around until he had thorns in every pore of his body. He wouldn't allow anyone to pick them out, and in a few days he was covered with septic sores. Somehow, he found his way to the ashram and to Bapu, who convinced him that the way to spiritual enlightenment lay in the world of action rather than in silence and mortification of the flesh. Bapu persuaded Brother Bhansali to unstitch his lips, but they were scarred for the rest of his life.

"Brother Bhansali didn't need to sleep much, and often worked through the night at the grinding stone in the communal dining hall, grinding wheat. It became his duty to wake up the ashram. The clock in the dining hall was synchronized every evening with Bapu's pocket watch. Everything had to be done at a set time in the ashram, because Bapu believed in absolute regularity in daily life. At exactly four in the morning, Brother Bhansali strode across the courtyard with a bamboo stick and struck a heavy piece of iron hanging outside Bapu's hut as a makeshift going.

"The gong had scarcely stopped ringing before Abha Chatterjee, a pretty, young Bengali sister, who later married Bapu's grandnephew Kanu, was at Bapu's bedside with a lighted lantern and with an iron bowl, a tumbler of water, a twig of neem, and a fine powder made from charcoal and the shells of almonds and walnuts. She had prepared the powder and beaten one end of the twig into a splayed brush with a stone the night before. Bapu sat up in his bed, which was just a hard board raised a little above the ground, with a thin khadi pallet and a khadi sheet, a couple of pillows at the head, and a couple of woollen shawls at the foot. His wife, Kasturbai—or Ba [Mother], as we all called her—lived and slept in her own hut, next to Bapu's. None of their children—four sons—stayed at the ashram for long. It was Sister Abha's duty to attend to Bapu's personal needs. Bapu took the iron bowl in his lap and, with obvious pleasure, set about brushing his gums and cleaning his tongue with the twig of neem and the powder. A lot of us didn't like the bitter taste of neem and objected to its strong smell, but Bapu liked the taste and he had practically no sense of smell. Sister Abha meanwhile took away a brass spittoon that was kept at Bapu's bedside through the night—he suffered from catarrh—and emptied it in the adjoining bathroom.

"After Bapu finished washing his mouth, he changed out of the dhoti he'd slept in into a clean one, and put on his spectacles. He picked up the lantern, crossed the room, slipped his feet into his wooden clogs, which had been left at the door, and went out into the shadowy morning light, with Sister Abha at his heels carrying his backrest—a plain board with a prop—and his cushion. He walked over to the pipal tree at the far end of the courtyard, where we had all gathered for morning prayers; Bapu believed that praying and constantly repeating the name of God were the best ways to purify the mind of evil thoughts. The prayers had been held under the tree ever since he founded the ashram, in 1936, at the advanced age of sixty-six. Sister Abha set up his backrest and cushion under the tree. Bapu took off his clogs and sat down cross-legged on the cushion, and the rest of us, including Ba, sat in front of him in a semicircle on the bare ground, the sisters on one side and the brothers on the other. One of the ashram children put around Bapu's neck a string of prayer beads and a garland of marigolds or some other flowers that had been freshly picked and strung together. It was four-twenty—time to begin the morning prayers.

"Lord Krishna says in the Bhagavad Gita, 'He whose mind is not troubled in sorrow, and has no desire in pleasure, his passion, fear, and anger departed, he is called a steady-minded sage,' and 'He who moves among the objects of sense with the senses under control, and is free from desire and aversion, he who is thus self-controlled, attains serenity of mind.' What better place to search for that serenity than under the pipal tree with Bapu, who was our steady-minded sage? Prayer meetings had been a ritual with Bapu for almost forty years. The prayers were drawn from many religions, and generally followed an established order. In fact, when I was there we had our own prayer book, the 'Ashram Bhajanavali,' which was revised every now and again to include a new prayer or a new hymn that we'd learned from a visitor and adopted as our own. If Bapu heard someone make a mistake or mispronounce a word—after all, there were Bengalis struggling with Marathi, and Gujaratis with Urdu—he would call out 'Stop!' and correct the mistake.

"We usually began with a Buddhist chant that a Japanese monk had taught us. Someone beat a little drum and said in Japanese, 'I bow to all the Buddhas, I bow to all the Buddhas, I bow to all the Buddhas, I bow to all the Buddhas.' After that, we meditated for two minutes and then recited together, in Hindi, our Hindu morning prayer: 'O God with a curved mouth, a big body, refulgent like ten million suns, keep me ever free from harm whilst doing beneficent acts. . . . I bow to Vishnu, who is peace incarnate, who lies on a snaky bed, from whose navel grows the lotus.' Then Brother Kanu read a few Arabic verses from the Koran in praise of Allah:

For those that fear the majesty of their Lord there are two gardens . . . planted with shady trees. Which of your Lord's blessings would you deny? . . .

Each bears every kind of fruit in pairs. Which of your Lord's blessings would you deny?

8

They shall recline on couches lined with thick brocade, and within their reach will hang the fruits of both gardens. Which of your Lord's blessings would you deny? . . .

Virgins as fair as corals and rubies. Which of your Lord's blessings would you deny? . . .

And beside these there shall be two other gardens . . . of darkest green. Which of your Lord's blessings would you deny? . . .

In each there shall be virgins chaste and fair. Which of your Lord's blessings would you deny?

Dark-eyed virgins sheltered in their tents . . . whom neither man nor jinni will have touched before. Which of your Lord's blessings would you deny?

They shall recline on green cushions and rich carpets. Which of your Lord's blessings would you deny?

Blessed be the name of your Lord, the Lord of majesty and glory!

"There were no Muslim priests living with us at the time, but Brother Kanu had been trained to read the Koran in their special guttural, singsong way. After that, we reaffirmed our dedication to Bapu's principles with these resolutions: 'We will be nonviolent; we will be truthful; we will not steal; we will be continent; we will not hoard; we will all wear khadi clothes; we will work with our hands; we will eat simple foods; we will be fearless; we will treat people of all religions equally; and we will work for the eradication of untouchability.' Then came a Pahlavi verse from the common Zoroastrian prayer of the Parsis. We seldom had a Parsi among us, but it was an easy prayer to say, and we took turns reading it: 'O Ahura Mazda, reveal unto me the Word and Actions of the highest religion, so that, keeping to the path of righteousness, I sing thy praises. Lead my path as you desire. Grant freshness to my life and the bliss of paradise.'

"Then we sang a lot of hymns, keeping time with tiny metal finger cymbals or by clapping our hands. Bapu had a thin, uncertain singing voice, which was never quite in tune with the others. One of his favorite hymns was the Christian hymn 'Lead, Kindly Light,' but neither he nor anyone else ever mastered the tune. We all had our favorite hymns. I think I liked best the Urdu hymns in praise of Allah—they are so poetic. But I also especially liked the Hindi hymn with the line 'Learn good sense from a tree, O mind,' and the Bengali hymn that says, 'Make my heart fixed on Thy holy lotus feet and make it full of joy, full of joy, full of joy.' A foreign visitor once remarked that our singing seemed to be one long wail, but we always enjoyed the sound of our own music.

"Then came the *dhuns,* the invocations of the Hindu God under His various names and incarnations. Every child knows Bapu's favorite *dhun,* in praise of Ram:

> *Raghupati Raghava Raja Ram,*
> *Patita pavana Sita Ram.*
> *Ishwara Allah Tere nam,*
> *Sabko Sanmati de Bhagavan.*

[This can be translated as "O King of Raghu clan, Ram, you and Sita are the purifiers of sinners. Ishwar and Allah both are your names. Give us good sense, O Lord." Sita is Ram's wife, Ishwar is the God of the Hindus, and Allah, of course, is the God of the Muslims.]

"But we said so many others. We said one for Krishna:

> *Jai Krishna, Hare Krishna,*
> *Jai Govind, Hare Govind,*
> *Jai Gopal, Radha Gopal.*

["Hail Krishna, God Krishna, Hail Govind, God Govind, Hail Gopal, Radha's Gopal." Govind and Gopal are two of Krishna's names, and Radha is his consort.]

"We said one for Shiva:

> *Samb Sadashiv Samb Sadashiv*
> *Samb Sadashiv Samb Shiva;*
> *Har Har Har Har Samb Sadashiv*
> *Samb Sadashiv Samb Shiva.*

[These are all names of the god Shiva, Har being another form of Hare, signifying God.]

"We said another one for Ram:

> *Hare Ram, Hare Ram, Hare Ram, Hare;*
> *Bhaj Man Nishidini Pyare.*

["O God Ram, God Ram, God Ram, God; O mind, think of the beloved day and night."]

"We chanted innumerable rounds of *dhuns,* clapping out the

10

rhythm faster and faster and louder and louder. Nothing thrilled Bapu more. He was in ecstasy as the names of God rolled over us.

"The prayer meeting finished with someone reading from the Bhagavad Gita in Sanskrit. The Bhagavad Gita was the most important book in Bapu's life—over the years he must have read it thousands of times—and it was read through from beginning to end every week at morning and evening prayers in the ashram. Bapu didn't mind who did the reading, of course—a Brahman or an untouchable—but Ba, who remained somewhat orthodox despite Bapu's efforts to reeducate her, preferred to hear it from a Brahman's lips.

"At five, the prayer meeting was over. Bapu returned to his hut and sat down cross-legged on his bed. Sister Abha brought him his special drink—bicarbonate of soda, honey, and lemon juice in a glass of hot water—which he sipped slowly from a wooden spoon. After that, he got down to his paperwork. A Lifebuoy-soap crate turned upside down and spread with a khadi cloth served as his desk. On it were a makeshift clipboard and a pad of paper, a handmade wooden penholder with three or four old pens in it, a few loose nibs, an ink bottle, and three or four shiny, polished stones, which he used for paperweights. On a little shelf at his elbow were a few books—the Bhagavad Gita, the Koran, the Bible, an English dictionary—and a red khadi satchel of manila files containing papers. He balanced the clipboard and pad on one knee and propped up on the desk his pocket watch, a fat, cheap, old Ingersoll. Turnip watches, I think they're called—the kind that Englishmen in Victorian novels wear at the end of chains in their waistcoat pockets. He adjusted his spectacles and started writing. His writing was rather sprawly, but he filled every corner of whatever he was writing on, until it looked as though ants had trailed ink all over it. When the pad ran out, he wrote on the backs of letters he'd received, or even on the envelopes. What a Banya he was! [A Banya belongs to the caste of shopkeepers.] He didn't believe in wasting anything; he once scolded his son Devadas for losing a pencil stub! Now and again, when he didn't like what he'd written and the paper he was writing on was completely used up, he dropped it into an embroidered woollen wastepaper basket—a present someone had brought him from Kashmir, and probably the most expensive thing in the ashram. His secretaries often fished out the day's discards and saved them.

"Whenever he did any paperwork, he was attended by several

secretaries. There was Mahadev Desai, Bapu's chief secretary. He was a tall, good-looking Gujarati with a neat mustache and thinning hair on an intellectual head. He was the only person who had a complete grasp of the complicated details of Bapu's work, and he was, so to speak, Bapu's alter ego. There was Pyarelal Nayar, Brother Mahadev's chief assistant, who was as absentminded and dreamy as Brother Mahadev was attentive and precise. Brother Pyarelal was the kind of man who would stand stirring a kettle of goat's milk with one hand while he held a book of Shelley's poems in the other—and the milk would evaporate and all but burn up the kettle while he was puzzling over his favorite poet. There was Brother Pyarelal's sister, Dr. Sushila Nayar. She was a doctor trained in Western medicine, who could keep a check on Bapu's blood pressure, and who also, incidentally, happened to be good at taking Hindi dictation. And there were numerous others. At one time, there was Rajkumari Amrit Kaur, who sat elegantly poised for English dictation. She was a princess and a Christian. She wore well-stitched clothes made out of the finest khadi, and spoke fluent English with a real English accent. At another time, there was Madeleine Slade. After she became Bapu's disciple, he gave her the Hindu name Mirabehn, or Sister Mira. She was the daughter of an English admiral and liked to lord it over everybody.

"Bapu worked continuously for an hour and a half with one five-minute break for a glass of orange juice flavored with lime, or a glass of pineapple juice when we could get it. He was constantly in touch with his lieutenants in the field, especially those working for his Constructive Programme: Dattatreya Balkrishna Kalelkar—or Kaka-Saheb [Honored Uncle], as we called him—who devoted himself to the campaigns for basic education and for Hindi as a national language; Satishchandra Das Gupta, who did so much to promote the cause of khadi and to help eradicate the slur of untouchability from the Calcutta tanners; and Abdul Ghaffar Khan, a Pathan, who was so successful at teaching nonviolence to his notoriously warlike tribesmen in the Northwest Frontier Province that he was called the Frontier Gandhi. Bapu wrote or dictated letters, telegrams, speeches, or articles for his weeklies in English, Hindi, and Gujarati. He checked the translations. He planned his national campaigns for independence and for khadi and against untouchability. Bapu knew how to make the best use of his various secretaries, whether it was for drafting a defiant cable to the

Viceroy or merely for carrying it to the nearby office hut to be typed. He could concentrate on his work regardless of the comings and goings —and people were constantly coming and going, like birds.

"I remember once Ba rushed in. 'There's a madman in the kitchen!' she cried. 'I've never seen him before. He was trying to set fire to my sari.' Everyone ran to the kitchen. The madman was waving a burning log. Bapu caught hold of his wrist and took the log away from him. The madman was so frightened that he passed his stool in his dhoti. Ba and Bapu tussled over who was going to wash the dirty dhoti. Bapu, of course, won. He never missed an opportunity to show us what an elevated and holy office it was to clean up someone else's excrement.

"At six-thirty, he always fastened his pocket watch to the waist of his dhoti with a safety pin, slipped his feet into his leather sandals, took up a tall bamboo staff, and set out for his morning walk, along the dirt road toward Wardha. Most of the time, the sun was already quite hot, the air was dry, and the earth smelled of stale manure. Many of us rushed after him, clamoring for his attention. A number were less nimble-footed than he and almost had to run to keep up with him— he took such long, quick strides. The children of the ashram danced around him, pestering him with their questions. They had little opportunity to spend time with him otherwise, so they made the most of his walks. I remember that one of them said, 'Bapu, in the Bhagavad Gita the hero Arjuna asks short questions and Lord Krishna gives long answers. But when we ask you questions, you always give us short answers.' Bapu laughed, and said, 'Lord Krishna had only one Arjuna to contend with. I have dozens of you.'

"Along the way, Bapu greeted pilgrims who had come great distances for their darshana, and peasants who had left off their work in the fields to watch him go by. Sometimes, when he got a little tired, he gave his staff to the first person who reached for it, and put his hands on the shoulders of the sisters walking beside him. These 'walking sticks,' as he affectionately called them, were then usually Sister Abha and Sister Sushila. Sister Sushila was about ten years older than Sister Abha and was as domineering and pushy as Sister Abha was quiet and retiring. Bapu invariably asked them, 'Did you have a good bowel movement this morning, sisters?' Constipation was the commonest complaint in the ashram, and no one thought anything of talking about it. Bapu taught us to be open about everything—with him and with each other. His standard prescription for constipation was more vegetables, and, if that didn't work, an enema, which he taught us to administer to each other without any embarrassment.

"We often met Ba on our way back. She didn't go on Bapu's long walks. Instead, she bathed, read a little of the Ramayana, and then took a stroll through the ashram with some of the other older women. She was about the same age as Bapu, and, like him, she was toothless. Her face was quite sunken, but she always looked contented. By the time Bapu returned to his hut, it was about seven-thirty. Sister Abha took off Bapu's sandals, which were covered with dust and caked with mud, cleaned them with a rag, and put them out in the sun to air.

"Bapu then spent at least twenty minutes squatting on the commode in his bathroom; he had chronic amebiasis and always had trouble with his bowels. He was completely unself-conscious about urinating and defecating, rather like a child. He believed that these bodily functions were as natural and sacred as eating, and used to say, 'The bathroom is a temple. It should be so clean and inviting that anyone would enjoy eating there.' If any of us wanted to talk to him, we could go in and out as we pleased. There was no such thing as privacy in the bathroom or anywhere else in the ashram.

"Next, Bapu washed himself with water that Sister Abha had left in a mug near the commode, and then she helped him wash his hands with ashes or mud. We seldom used soap—it dried out the skin. Abha removed the chamber pot from the commode and took it out to a trench where all the pots were emptied. She rinsed it with water and mud and set it in the sun to dry.

"Bapu, meanwhile, went off to an alcove next to the bathroom for his daily massage. He liked to keep his body—his 'machine,' he called it—in tip-top working order. He used to say that in this harsh environment everything was so quickly eaten up by heat, disease, and dust that it was of the first importance to stay healthy. Sister Sushila helped him onto a high bamboo table and, as he lay back, slipped his dhoti off and put a khadi napkin across his loins. She mixed mustard oil and lime juice in an old Hazeline Snow cold-cream jar, poured some of the mixture into the palms of her hands, and started rubbing it into Bapu's scalp. She had a doctor's touch and was especially good at massaging. Sister Abha joined them and started massaging Bapu's feet. The two women worked their way up and down Bapu's body, back and front, kneading and rolling, slapping and patting, pinching and twisting, and filling the air with the heavy smell of oil. All this massaging was meant to keep the skin clean, young, and supple in our hot, dry climate, and was part of the ancient Hindu nature-cure regimen in which Bapu placed his faith. Except for a few emergencies, such as when he was obliged to have his appendix out, he would have nothing to do with modern, Western medicine, because he believed that any sickness could be cured by God-given, natural means. During his massage, Bapu dozed intermittently or read a book on the nature cure. Ba looked in occasionally, and silently fanned him or swatted a few flies or dusted away the sand that was always blowing in through the open doors and windows. I don't remember ever seeing her without a duster in her hand or tucked into the waist of her sari.

"After forty-five minutes or so, Bapu returned to his bathroom, this time for a bath and a shave. He sat in a small tin tub that had been filled with lukewarm water, and washed off the excess oil while Brother Pyarelal shaved him with a straight razor, using water from the tub. Bapu never used a safety razor, because new blades were expensive. The straight razor was usually dull and sometimes drew blood, nicking his skin or cutting open a wart—no matter what Bapu did for his skin, now and again a blemish appeared—but generally Brother Pyarelal could shave him without any trouble, because Bapu had a soft, downy growth that came off with a few experienced strokes. Bapu ran his hand over his face, and if there was a rough spot, he attended to it himself. He always cleaned his feet himself, with a pumice stone, and trimmed his nails when it was necessary. He then moved over into another small tin tub, filled with cold water, for a quick rinse. He stood on a wooden rack and dried himself with a couple of khadi towels while Sister Abha used the warm bathwater to wash his dhoti. Nothing was wasted in the ashram. He put on a clean dhoti, slipped his feet into his clogs, and strode into his room gleaming from head to toe.

"Sister Sushila had a glass of fresh orange or pineapple juice ready for him, or sometimes a coconut. When she gave him a coconut, he drank the milk from a hole bored in the top, and cracked the coconut open with a stone to get at the meat. Then he settled down to another hour's paperwork. After that, Bapu made his daily visit to the sick members of the ashram. He stopped in the hut of the leper Parchure Shastri and gave him his daily massage. Brother Parchure's body was wasting away, yet he remained cheerful and kept himself busy studying Sanskrit. It was a joy to see Bapu give him a massage. Bapu's touch was firm yet delicate. Visitors who saw him tending the sick—massaging, lancing boils, applying unguents, giving enemas—remarked in wonder on his nursing skill.

"At eleven, Bapu went for the first of the ashram's two meals of the day. We all ate together, sitting on the floor in the dining hall. Ba had spent most of the morning in the kitchen supervising and cooking. The water had to be carried from the ashram well, the cow's milk and goat's milk brought from the shed and boiled, the fire under the large clay stove fanned almost continuously by hand, the fruit and vegetables picked, washed, peeled, cut, and steamed, the dough kneaded and fried for *khakhras*, a Gujarati bread we ate. The brothers and sisters who took turns helping in the kitchen were constantly complaining about having a fever, a headache, or stomach trouble, but Ba found time to comfort them in the middle of everything, just like a mother.

"There was quite a lot of confusion in the dining hall at mealtimes, because there were more than a hundred of us to be fed. The brothers and sisters who were waiting on us moved in and out putting down brass plates, brass bowls, and brass tumblers, and the big pots of food. Some people needed help in serving themselves. Children clamored to be served more of this or that. Bapu took his place on a small cushion and served himself and those near him. When everybody was served, Brother Bhansali struck the gong, and one of the brothers in charge of bringing in the food stopped where he was, closed his eyes, and started chanting a prayer, in which everyone joined.

"After the prayer, Bapu fished his dentures out of a brass bowl of water that Ba had brought him, and, holding them up, said, 'See, children, I have an adjustable set of teeth.' He had an abhorrence of anything artificial, but he needed false teeth to eat. The *khakhras* were wafer-thin, crisp, and hot. They were made with wheat flour and baking soda, and fried in ghi on a griddle. The vegetables were all steamed without salt, sugar, or oil. The only relishes that Bapu ate were ground neem leaves and crushed garlic. According to the nature-cure principles, neem leaves were good for boils and skin eruptions, and garlic aided digestion and kept the blood pressure down. Bapu always had a big bowl of crushed garlic by his plate. He ate a lot of it and dished some out to anyone who he had decided needed it. In accordance with the Bhagavad Gita, Bapu believed we had to discipline the palate before we could discipline the whole of our bodies and, ultimately, our minds. He also believed we should eat a simple, cheap, and nutritious diet that even the poorest of our countrymen could afford. But he didn't lay down the law on every aspect of what we ate or how we ate. People were free to sprinkle lots of salt on their vegetables, put big dabs of ghi on their *khakhras,* and add as much sugar as they liked to their milk, which they could drink to their heart's content.

"Like a good host, Bapu knew the smallest habits and preferences of each of his guests. He never forgot who liked cream, who liked curds, and who liked milk. He even arranged to have meat served to meat eaters. I remember once Padmajani, whose mother was the Night-ingale of India, the poet Sarojini Naidu, came to spend a day at the ashram. Because of her poise, wit, and charm, she was known as the glamour girl of India, and Bapu had a soft spot for her. He used to begin his letters to her, 'My dear Lotus-Born'—that was the English translation of her name—and close with 'Your loving playmate and comrade the slave driver.' When she sat down to her meal, she was astonished to see a lovely pink bone-china bowl full of slices of orange and melon in cream—her favorite dish—and a matching jug full of hot cow's milk. The two Kumarappa brothers, Bharatan and Joseph—great organizers of village industries in Bapu's Constructive Programme—happened to be sitting next to Padmajani. They had been served huge quantities of soybean paste on two of our plain brass plates. Around this time, Bapu, who was always experimenting with diets, had fixed on soybeans as the best staple diet. The brothers eyed Padmajani's feast with envy, and one of them said, 'Bapu, may the downtrodden speak?' 'I didn't know there were any downtrodden in my ashram,' Bapu said. 'Where are they and what have they to say?' 'Must we eat soybean paste, and must we eat it off these drab plates?' 'It's good for you,' Bapu said, 'and the plates aren't so drab. You shouldn't be envious of our dear Lotus-Born. She's a guest and has to be fussed over a little.' Ba never tired of telling this story. She was self-effacing and abstemious, but she must have been a little pampered as a child, because she always kept peppermints, dried fruits, and other goodies for the ashram chil-dren, and even secretly served guests coffee and tea, although Bapu said they were bad for you.

"When Bapu was eating, he didn't talk much. He chewed his food thoroughly, taking about an hour over his meal, which he finished off with a glass of goat's milk. Sister Abha cleared away Bapu's utensils. Sister Mira once tried to do that. She kept hovering over him, saying, 'Bapu, have you finished? Bapu, have you finished?' Bapu spoke sharply to her. 'How often have I told you not to bother about these things? Abha will see to them. That's her job.' Bapu wanted everyone to stick to what he or she did best. Sister Mira was best at editing Bapu's English and at treating people's cuts, sores, and fevers, but she aspired to do everything. We all ate with our fingers and afterward gathered, laughing and chatting, outside the kitchen at a tap to wash our hands and utensils, and clean our teeth with neem twigs. Then we went off to continue working—carding, spinning, studying. The ashram was immediately filled with the clatter of kitchen pots and pans, the buzz of carding bows, the hum of spinning wheels, and a jumble of voices reciting Sanskrit verses.

"Bapu returned to his hut and napped for half an hour. He had developed such control over his mind and body that he could sleep anywhere, under any circumstances. Sister Abha put a mud poultice on his forehead and over his eyes and another on his stomach. She had boiled the mud to destroy the bacteria, cooled it in the open air, and made two poultices by wrapping it in soft khadi cloths. The poultices gave Bapu a little respite from the afternoon heat and helped his digestion. At one time or another, we all used this mud treatment to ward off sunstroke, prickly heat, headaches, stomach aches, and other aches and pains. It was a standard part of the nature cure. When the day was especially hot, Ba laid a damp kerchief on his bare chest, and kept the kerchief cool by frequently dipping it in water. She also rubbed ghi into his skin, particularly on his feet. He had poor circulation, and no matter how much ghi or oil was rubbed into his feet, the skin there was always cracking. I once rubbed ghi into his feet, but I didn't manage to wipe off all the excess between his toes, because I did not want to wake him. He felt it as soon as he woke up, and told me not to worry about disturbing him in the future.

"When he got up, Sister Abha handed him his second glass of bicarbonate of soda, honey, and lemon juice in hot water, and Bapu gave Ba a lesson. She had very little education, and it was hard for her to study, but she wanted to please Bapu. She read out loud from a Gujarati primer, which she labored over as best she could. She painstakingly copied out a few sentences in order to improve her handwriting. Bapu used an orange to represent the world and told her about longitude and latitude. But what she learned one day she forgot the next. I think she was happiest when she was cooking or cleaning, sewing or spinning, and looking after everyone. No one quite realized how much we all depended on her. After she died, I once heard Bapu say, 'I now feel really alone—Ba was the warp and woof of my life.'

"After the lesson, and another twenty minutes on the commode, Bapu settled down on the cushion in his hut for an hour or two of spinning. Any of us could go and sit with him then. His thin, slightly nervous hands worked rapidly, the spinning wheel made a soft, warm, comforting buzz, and his lap was soon filled with fluffy cotton fibre. He could spin half a hank of thread, or four hundred and twenty yards, at one sitting. This thread ordinarily went into the common pool, but sometimes it was woven into cloth for Ba. I once heard Bapu say to Ba, 'When I married you, I promised to supply you with food and raiment. I cannot claim to have supplied you with food—we both have to thank our benefactors for that—but I can at least supply you with raiment.' At the time, Bapu was using a very compact spinning wheel, which opened and closed like a box. Maurice Frydman had invented it for him. Mr. Frydman was a Polish engineer who became Bapu's disciple, and he spent his time in the ashram dreaming up new types of spinning wheels. Bapu was always interested in Mr. Frydman's inventions, because he was eager to find the most efficient and economical spinning wheel for our country. Through spinning, Bapu hoped to instill in us something of his own reverence for manual labor. He wanted us all to do some physical labor, so that we could identify with the workers who earn their bread by the sweat of their brow. He wanted to teach us the dignity of 'bread' labor, as he called it, and restore to us the self-respect we had lost through slavery to the British, so that we would have the inner strength to stand up to the British lords and Indian sahibs who propped up the raj. Sometimes Bapu lectured us on politics over his spinning wheel, and that would make us cry out, *'Bapu ki jai!* ["All hail to Father!"] Bapu has fired another missile from his spinning wheel! Bapu has scored another hit on Whitehall!'

"Sometimes Bapu received visitors while he was spinning. Magistrates, police superintendents, Congress Party workers, cultivators, Constructive Programme workers all flocked to the ashram by train, by bullock cart, on foot—most of them without letting us know first. Important guests, if we knew about their coming, were met at the station at Wardha by our Ox-Ford—that's what Bapu called the ashram's only means of transport. It was an old Ford that had to have a team of oxen hitched to it before it would go anywhere. Like the land on which the ashram stood, it was a gift of our great benefactor the cotton merchant Jamnalal Bajaj. The visitors left their footgear outside Bapu's hut and sat down wherever they could, in and around the hut, on thick, colorful khadi-and-bamboo mats. When it came to things like mats, Bapu liked a lot of color. An encouraging nod or a quick yes from Bapu, who remained sitting on his little cushion, was usually enough to start the visitors talking.

"I remember that once a boy came to Bapu and said that his father had forbidden him to marry the girl he loved. He begged Bapu to write to his father and plead his case. 'Can you support yourself and a wife?' Bapu asked. 'No,' said the boy. 'I live with my father.' 'As long as you live with your father, you must obey him in all matters,' Bapu said. 'Before you think of marriage, you must become independent. Go and work as a laborer for two years. If at the end of that time you still want to marry the young woman, and you can support her, you will have my blessing.' Afterward, we asked Bapu why he didn't recruit the boy for the freedom struggle. He said, 'He is caught up in his little sorrow. He's like a man who has got a thorn in his foot or has lost his way in the woods of life. Until he can conquer his little sorrow, he will not be a good soldier in the struggle for freedom.' Another time, a man came and told Bapu that he suffered from heavy nosebleeds. He said he had tried all kinds of medicines but nothing helped. Bapu gave him a tin of brown powder and told him to take it like snuff. 'What is it?' the man asked. 'Don't you bother about that,' Bapu said. 'Just do as I say.' The man went away, and came back some time later to say that he was cured. 'What was that miraculous powder?' he asked. 'I'm not sure I should tell you,' Bapu said. 'But I might need it again,' the man protested. 'Well, if you must know, it was an ancient nature-cure formula—powdered cow dung,' Bapu said.

"Such conversations were usually conducted in public, and a secretary took notes on them. If Bapu thought that any of them were of general interest, they would be published in a subsequent issue of one of his weeklies.

"When Bapu had finished his spinning, and his visitors had gone, he lay down for another nap. In fact, the rest of Bapu's day was a sort of repetition of the morning routine. He did more reading and writing till five, when everyone gathered for the evening meal, and after that he went out for another long walk. The lanterns were filled with kerosene, and their wicks raised, trimmed, and lit, for the evening prayer meeting under the pipal tree. This time, Bapu gave a discourse on celibacy, sanitation, or some other subject, and we each called out how much thread we had spun during the day. Then Bapu retired to his hut to do more reading and writing, and we sat with Ba on charpoys put out in the courtyard for those who liked to sleep in the open, and rubbed each other's feet and backs and chatted and gossiped. Before going to bed, Bapu had a cleansing enema. By nine or nine-thirty, all the lanterns were out and the entire ashram was fast asleep—except, perhaps, for Brother Bhansali, who went on grinding wheat and murmuring verses from the Ramayana: 'Listen, my friend, there is another kind of chariot, which brings certain victory. Its wheels are made of strength of mind and patience. Truth and dignity are its firm flagstaff and its flag. Strength and discretion are its two horses. Forgiveness and benevolence are its two reins. Faith in God is its wise charioteer. Absolute contentment is its dagger. Charity is its axe. Knowledge is its bow. Steadfastness is the quiver and self-discipline its arrows. Respect for the learned is its impregnable armor. . . . Listen patiently, O friend, the brave man who has this chariot shall be victorious over the greatest invincible enemy—which is life in this world.' "

Relics and Monuments

THE ROAD LEADING TO WARDHA AND SEVAGRAM ASHRAM IS barely wide enough for two cars. It is jammed with numerous cars, trucks, buses, and herds of cows and goats. For many miles, the land is flat and uncultivated, broken up only with scrub and small trees, but as I get closer—I've hired a driver and a car for the trip—the monotony of the landscape is relieved by a series of low cultivated plateaus. Wardha consists of white buildings with red tile roofs neatly clustered around a statue of Gandhi with his right hand raised and the palm turned outward, to signify peace. The ashram is six miles southeast of the town, and as we drive along, the road—now macadamized—is lined by bright-green fields and shaded by neem trees. It is crowded with a succession of wooden carts drawn by bullocks, their necks hung with brass bells that ring in the still air. Then, suddenly, we come upon a row of low, boxlike modern buildings of red brick and gray concrete standing incongruously alongside some charming old mud huts. This is Sevagram, more than a quarter of a century after Gandhi left it.

Waiting in front of one of the new buildings is the man who is to be my guide through Sevagram, which by now includes, in addition to the ashram itself, many institutions that grew up here around Gandhi and in memory of him. "All these modern buildings are part of the medical college and the hospital," my guide says, getting into the car. He is the director of the medical college—a friendly man with wavy black hair, who wears black-rimmed spectacles, a green-and-white plaid shirt, brown-and-white checked khadi trousers, and sandals. "The college is named after Mahatma Gandhi and the hospital after his wife, Kasturbai. Both institutions were founded by our government in 1969, with help from the United States Agency for International Development, during the centenary celebration of Bapuji's birth." (The suffix "-ji" is an honorific.) The first stop is at a small, unremarkable building, of which the director says, "In Bapuji's time, this building used to be the headquarters of the All India Spinners' Association, but now it's a Gandhi museum."

The museum consists of several rooms filled helter-skelter with models, photographs, framed quotations, and prints. The place has a certain spontaneity and exuberance. Above an altarlike platform in the main room is a large photograph bearing the inscription "From Mohan to Mahatma" (as a boy Gandhi was often called Mohan) and showing within a flame various stages of Gandhi's life. On the platform itself are a couch, with a white cover and pillow, and a vase of fresh flowers. Nearby is a glass case containing three large dolls dressed in white khadi kurtas and miming the three monkeys in one of Gandhi's favorite mottoes: "Hear no evil. See no evil. Speak no evil."

We drive on, and pass some fields and then a small brick-and-mud building, from which some teen-age boys are emerging, each carrying a spade over his shoulder. "That is Bapuji's Basic Education Centre," the director says. "As in Bapuji's time, the boys get some elementary education, but most of their training is in practical work, because Bapuji believed that that was the best education for our impoverished people, whose main concern is to have a cloth over their bodies and at least one square meal a day in their stomachs."

We drive past the village of Segaon, which is a collection of mud huts connected by muddy lanes that are choked with manure, refuse, sickly, aimless cattle, and bullock carts. It seems never to have been touched by Gandhi's residence in the ashram.

Everywhere, the air is thick with flies. "The ashram has its own dairy farm, and it breeds flies like anything," the director says as he tries, in vain, to brush them away.

"Who lives at the ashram now?" I ask.

"Some of the old ashramites are still around, and the medical college makes use of the empty space. But Bapuji's hut is, of course, kept as a shrine."

The ashram proper is a series of low buildings with light-brownish-gray mud walls and dark-red tile roofs grouped around a gravelled courtyard about thirty feet square. By the main entrance to the court-yard is a rusting tin latrine shed with its door open, showing a platform of bamboo poles above a small pile of cut grass. In the courtyard, some girls in plain khadi saris and some boys in textured shirts of white khadi and pajama trousers of brownish-gray khadi are busy spreading straw mats near a big pipal tree, at the base of which are a white cushion and a weather-beaten slab of wood. A sign on the slab identifies it as "Backrest for Bapu at Prayer Time." "Those are students from the college," the director says. "We have our daily prayers under the pipal tree, facing Bapuji's old cushion, just as the ashramites did when he was alive."

"All of us are staying at the ashram for a one-month orientation in Bapuji's ideas," says a talkative student. "When we are admitted to the medical college, we all give a pledge to spend three years working in the villages after we finish our training."

The students sit down cross-legged on the mats and start their prayers, and the director and I go into one of the bigger buildings. I find myself in a large hall painted with primitive murals of Buddha, Jesus, and various Hindu gods and goddesses. "This is the oldest building in the ashram," the director says. "This is where they ate in Bapuji's time. We still use the building for meals."

In an adjacent kitchen, by a wood-burning clay stove, several people are sitting on the floor eating. All around are brass kitchen utensils, screened cupboards, and burlap bags of onions and squashes.

As we enter a smaller building, the director says, "We call this the Last Residence. Bapuji was unwell toward the end of his stay and moved here from his own hut to catch more of the sun. He left the ashram from here in 1946 and never returned." The Last Residence is crowded with a variety of objects: paper streamers with Gandhi quotations on them dangling from pegs, foodstuffs hanging from the rafters, bundles of papers on the tops of cupboards, and piles of books and khadi clothes. There is also a spinning wheel, a little pair of prayer cymbals, and a spade, recalling some of Gandhi's favorite occupations. A half-naked, rather emaciated man—his arms gnarled, his ribs protruding—lies on a wooden charpoy with his knees bent, looking at a newspaper. He has large, deep-set eyes and thin, short-cropped dark-gray hair. "This is Mr. Chimanlal Shah," the director says. "From his student days, he was with Bapuji, and he was manager of the ashram in Bapuji's time. Now he makes his home here." Chimanlal Shah scarcely looks up from his paper.

24

We leave the building by a back veranda, and go across to Gandhi's hut, which is marked off by a bamboo fence. "This is a very solid structure," the director says of the hut. "It was built to Bapuji's specifications, by covering a bamboo frame first with cow dung, then with mud."

The windows of the hut have palm fronds fastened around them to keep out the monsoon rain, and the door is a simple one of bamboo and wood. Just inside the door is a glass case containing Gandhi's tall bamboo staff and his special wooden clogs, with single capped pegs to keep the clogs on the feet. In the main room are the makeshift bed covered with a white sheet, a pillow propped against the wall next to a square prayer rug, a low brown wooden bench with a lantern on it, a wooden footstool, and, on a small shelf, a sewing kit, a first-aid kit, an inkstand, some polished stones, a water bottle, a Bible, a Koran, and a Ramayana. Against a wall is another glass case, displaying two bowls, a fork, a spoon, a statuette of the three monkeys, a pen, a spittoon, a boxlike spinning wheel, a letter opener, a pair of spectacles, a pocket watch, a string of holy beads, a Bhagavad Gita, a pair of leather sandals, and a second pair of wooden clogs. Up near the ceiling is a shelf where a wooden stool is stored, and on the walls are a picture of Jesus, with the caption "He Is Our Peace," and little handwritten signs reproducing Gandhi's favorite quotations from the Bible, the Bhagavad Gita, and Ruskin's "Unto This Last." On one of the walls is a small molded relief of two palm trees with the sacred word "Om" between them. "Everything in the hut had a special association for Bapuji," the director tells me. "That relief was done by Madeleine Slade. The picture of Jesus was given to Bapuji by Rajkumari Amrit Kaur. The stool on the shelf was kept at the ready for Sarojini Naidu. The Nightingale of India was fat and had difficulty sitting on the floor."

Passing an alcove that served as a bedroom for Gandhi's secretaries, we come to Gandhi's bathroom, containing a toilet, two tin tubs, a bucket, a stool, a jug, and a scrub brush. A sign over the toilet, which is made of stone and has a wooden cover, reads, "This septic tank was built for Bapu as an experimental model by Shri [Mr.] E. G. Williams of Ushagram." "This is where Bapuji kept books and clippings to read when he was on the comfort seat," the director says, tapping a wooden box fixed to the wall near the toilet. By the box is a black slate bearing the message "He used to think of this bathroom as a temple."

A door leads from the bathroom to the room where Gandhi had his daily massage, and here a benchlike cot, a high trestle table, and portable steps are set up. A man is taking down clothes from a line and folding them. He has tufts of gray hair, a stubbly beard and mustache, and a deeply lined forehead. "This is Haribhai, one of Bapuji's attendants," the director says.

"I have been in the ashram for thirty-five years," Haribhai says, adjusting his dhoti, which is tucked up above his knees. "I served Bapuji all the time he was here, and go on taking care of his things just as I used to."

"Nothing was more important to Bapuji than sanitation," the director says outside, as we come upon what look like several sentry boxes made of sheets of tin but turn out to be latrines. All have their doors open, and inside are planks over holes in the ground. "In Bapuji's time, these sheds were made just of bamboo matting, but we've modernized them."

As I leave the ashram, a woman resident stares at me through a window of one of the huts. She is dressed in a pink choli and an orange-and-red sari, and looks curiously out of place. She leans indolently toward me and shouts, "The next thing you know, there'll be a Gandhi cigarette! It's about the only thing left that hasn't been used to commemorate him!" She spits out an orange seed. (According to "Gandhi: 1915–1948: A Detailed Chronology," by C. B. Dalal, around the end of December, 1946, someone actually did start the "manufacture and sale of country cigarettes with 'Mahatma' as a trademark.")

In India today, there is scarcely a town or village that does not try to perpetuate in one way or another the memory of Gandhi, who was assassinated on January 30, 1948. In Delhi, there are numerous Gandhi shrines, museums, and other monuments, many of which are clustered around the place where Gandhi was cremated. The Gandhi Samadhi, or Cremation Ground, is a large enclosed area on the west bank of the sacred river Jumna. As I approach the entrance gate, a snake charmer strikes up a tune and a toothless old lady hawking flowers redoubles her cries, but the sentry—a sullen fellow with bloodshot eyes, dressed in a dirty white shirt and trousers—hardly gives me a glance. I pass a notice that reads, in part, "This sacred place should be free from smoking, domestic animals, or any other undesirable activities," and make my way among well-trimmed but dusty lawns and flower beds, past half-empty lakes and ponds, and up a little hill. I come upon an archway cut into the hillside, where I am asked to remove my shoes. I walk barefoot through the archway into a large, walled-in open square. On all sides are arched alcoves containing stone slabs on which are carved quotations from Gandhi in various languages. A flagstone path covered with wooden racks—to keep the feet cool—leads to the center of the square, the actual site of Gandhi's cremation, which is marked by four upright blocks of white marble set around a polished black slab lying flat on the ground and bearing the inscription *"He Ram,"* or "O God." Eyewitnesses have said that Gandhi died instantly, but the myth has grown up that as he was struck down he called out, *"He Ram! He Ram!"* Incongruously, on two of the white marble blocks are tin boxes with slots in them to receive alms for the upkeep of the shrine.

The Gandhi Darshan, or Exhibition, is next to the Gandhi Samadhi. It was opened in 1969 to celebrate the centenary of his birth and has become another permanent memorial. The exhibition, which is spread over forty acres and is housed in several red-brick-and-dark-wood pavilions, is somewhat reminiscent of Disneyland. In the entryway is a cactus garden with a large concrete bust of Gandhi and signs pointing to the pavilions, which are identified as "India of My Dreams," "Evolution of the Philosophy of Satyagraha," "Gandhi and Man in Evolution," "Constructive Programme," "The World Is My Family," and "My Life Is My Message." A different hymn is coming from each pavilion, and is relayed over loudspeakers at full volume.

The exhibition pavilions turn out to be a maze of dimly lit, windowless rooms and corridors, which are suffocatingly hot and are crammed with people and relics. I pass photographs of Indian village life; murals of starving people; an abstract sculpture inlaid with bits of glass; a large circle on a ceiling which contains a quotation from Gandhi about ever-widening circles; a map of India showing the places where he lived and worked; a painting of his mentors, including Jesus, Buddha, Socrates, and his own mother, who is shown worshipping the sun; a bench on which he supposedly sat during a protest demonstration; photographs of the 1963 civil-rights march on Washington; murals portraying the goals of the Constructive Programme (village industries, equality of religions, women's rights); one of Gandhi's spinning wheels; a huge mural entitled "Cow Also in the Centre of National Economy;" live demonstrations of village crafts; actual pages from *The Vegetarian,* the journal of the London Vegetarian Society, to which Gandhi belonged; an array of centenary postage stamps from various countries; photographs of Gandhi's school reports, his London clothes, his barrister's certificate, and his favorite spiritual books; a full-sized model of a jail cell in which he was once imprisoned, with one wall cut out to show its interior. Outside one of the pavilions is a large green jeep with the words "Mahatma Gandhi" and the inscription "This gun carriage carried Gandhi's body to the funeral pyre" on the front license plate. On a wooden board in the back of the jeep is printed, "Shoes should be discarded when working on this vehicle."

I pay a brief call on Anil Sengupta, the curator, who is sitting in a small, untidy office crowded with visitors. "Gandhi Darshan is very popular," he tells me. He is a large man in his early forties, with gray-flecked black hair, a heavy face, and a mouth stained red by betel juice. He has on a shirt of ivory-colored raw silk, and around his right wrist is the sacred red thread of an orthodox Brahman. "We get three or four hundred visitors each day, and during the holidays as many as five to ten thousand," he continues. "We stage song, drama, and dance performances—just now we are doing a ballet on untouchability. Our people need mass activating and awakening." He tells me that the centenary symbol is a large hand with the palm outward and with a diamond shape in the middle. "The diamond indicates the greatness or potential greatness of a humanitarian. In the years I've been working here, I myself have developed a diamond on my palm." He proudly displays some threadlike creases in his palm.

"But I thought Gandhi didn't believe in such superstitions," I say.

"It's not a superstition. It's a fact," says Sengupta.

The Gandhi National Memorial Museum, which is also near the Gandhi Samadhi, is a large gray building trimmed with the Moghul pinkish-red sandstone often used on public buildings here. One of Gandhi's favorite sayings, "Truth Is God," is written in white letters on each side of the entrance. Just inside, next to a bookcase overflowing with materials containing his pronouncements in favor of prohibition, is a life-size bronze bust of Gandhi with his eyes cast down. Through the museum's public-address system hymn-singing blares away. Upstairs is a life-size wax-museum set of Gandhi, a contemporary biographer, C. F. Andrews, and the poet Rabindranath Tagore seated in rattan chairs on a veranda, among potted plants and apparently deep in conversation. In addition to the usual gigantic photographs bearing captions like "With Malaviyaji admiring a cow, Mysore," and models of Gandhi's various dwellings, complete with drainpipes and with windows that actually open and shut, are some grimmer exhibits: a bullet lies on some clothes with reddish stains, in a glass case labelled "One of the three bullets that took Bapu from us" and *"He Ram,* these bloodstained clothes were worn by Bapu on his last day;" and standing on a pedestal is the sacred urn in which his ashes were first placed.

I walk into the museum's wood-panelled library, which houses a valuable collection of Gandhiana, and talk with the librarian, Mrs. S. K. De. She is a plump, black-haired lady in her forties, wearing a white khadi sari with a border of multicolored stripes. "My job is facilitating research," she says. "We have in this library five to six thousand photographs and thirty-seven thousand photostat copies of letters written by Gandhiji. But there are many other museums where Gandhi scholars can research. There is a major museum in Patna, one in Barrackpur, one in Madurai, and one in Bombay, and hundreds of minor museums throughout the country."

"How are all the museums financed?" I ask.

"By the government and various charitable Gandhi trusts," Mrs. De replies.

The first of the numerous charitable trusts set up after Gandhi's assassination to promote his work is also the most important. It is called the Gandhi National Memorial Fund, and is housed in a small two-story building a few hundred feet from the Gandhi National Memorial Museum. A young woman seated behind an old-fashioned wooden switchboard tells me that Lele will show me around. She bangs an office bell furiously for the office peon, but no one appears, and she calls out, "Mr. Lele, you have a visitor!"

In response, an elderly man with white hair, a large head, and a heavy face, wearing a short-sleeved white khadi shirt and thick glasses with black rims, comes out of a nearby room. He is Lele—Indians often have only one name. "After Bapuji's assassination, the Gandhi National Memorial Fund collected about a hundred and ten million rupees," Lele tells me. There are about seven rupees to the dollar, so this sum amounts to something like fifteen million dollars. "Most of the money was handed over to the states for local Gandhian activities, but part of it was reserved for national activities. The Fund financed the Gandhi Peace Foundation, among other major Gandhian institutions. We also have a few practical programs of our own, like experimenting with latrines of various models. As you know, Bapuji devoted his life to helping the untouchables, who did the society's menial dirty work. He felt that sweepers with pails of human excrement on their heads should not be necessary in modern India. Even though our villages have no plumbing of any kind, Bapuji thought we could still have hygienic latrines. There are over one hundred million untouchables in India today, and despite Bapuji's efforts, their lot has actually deteriorated. We're trying to do something about it. Just outside here, we have mounted an exhibition of latrines suited to the various regions and local conditions of our country."

Lele takes me out to what looks like a small golf course, except that among the lawns and flower beds stand simple latrines, some of concrete, some of brick, and some of wood. There are at least fifteen types, which are variations of septic tanks, mere holes, or primitive flush systems, and all of which are designed to make use of the waste directly as fertilizer or indirectly as cooking gas. The exhibit is completely deserted, and the latrines are beginning to be overrun with weeds.

Perhaps the most influential of the institutions engaged in Gandhi's practical work is the Gandhi Peace Foundation. Its headquarters, in another part of Delhi, occupy a new three-story red brick building with narrow cantilevered balconies. On either side of the building are dusty rosebushes and, near them, signs saying "Enjoy but do not pluck the flowers." Inside, the place looks something like an Indian version of a Holiday Inn. In the front hall, a hemp wall hanging partly covers the windows, and on another wall is a hanging that depicts an orange sun. There is a bulletin board announcing special events of the India International Centre, the weekly meeting of the Sufi Centre, and a lecture, "The Role of Khadi and Cottage Industries for Economic Growth and Social Justice." Signs point to the back garden, the general office, the library, and the auditorium, and to upstairs guest rooms, which are for rent. The reception desk, covered with Gandhian literature, is attended by earnest-looking young women.

I go past the general office, where perhaps twenty clerks are working at two long rows of desks, and into a rather bare room, the office of the secretary of the Foundation, Radhakrishnan. He is a middle-aged man with a big head, big eyes, and a soft, full face, and he is dressed in a simple white khadi kurta and dhoti—the Gandhian uniform. On his desk are a dusty appointment book and, under glass, an Indian Airlines schedule so old that it is almost certainly out of date; there are more paperweights than papers.

"We now have more than ten million rupees in capital and use the interest on it for operating expenses," he tells me. "We carry out researches into peace activities, and publish the *Gandhi Peace Foundation Newsletter* and a magazine called *Gandhi Marg.* [*Marg* means "path."] We have about forty-five branch offices throughout the country, which provide information on Gandhian ideals, and we sponsor lectures, seminars, and workshops. Sometimes the workers in the branch offices are even called upon to arbitrate community disputes. We are in the mainstream of Gandhian work, and our more recent heroes are Martin Luther King and Danilo Dolci." He suggests that I go with him to the auditorium next door, where a six-hour film on Gandhi produced by the Fund is about to be shown. "It is the longest film ever made on the greatest man who ever lived," he says.

The film opens with shots of the sun breaking through clouds, of snow-capped mountains, and of ocean waves, and continues with still photographs of Gandhi's life interspersed with captions like "Told mostly in Gandhi's own words," and visual tricks like moving handwriting. The narration, done by a droning, somnolent voice, lacks the power of Gandhi's unedited utterances. It soon becomes apparent that the photographs and sets are identical to some I encountered in a pavilion in Gandhi Darshan.

Sabarmati Ashram, which is in Ahmedabad, in the state of Gujarat, and is where Gandhi lived most of the time from 1917 to 1930, is much like many of the other Gandhian shrines. Combining the brashness of the new with the simplicity of the old, it is part museum, part library, part school, part hostel, part ashram, but mainly a rather chaotic exhibit, in which the occasional genuine relic is lost among endless replicas of replicas. When I arrive, the director, Krishnan Trivedi, a kindly, worried-looking man, is seated behind a Brobdingnagian modern Western desk lecturing about Gandhi to tourists seated on Lilliputian Indian stools. I join them.

"In Bapu's time here, the ashramites bathed and washed their clothes in the Sabarmati River," Trivedi is saying. "On the riverbank nowadays, we have a *son-et-lumière* production about Bapu and the ashram. It is put on by the government during the tourist season and is a great success. So we are now constructing a spectators' gallery for it."

He guides us on a tour of the whole complex. Here and there, old people—apparently residents—are reading newspapers or dozing, indifferent to us and to some scrawny, barefoot children who trail after us and also seem to live here. On the veranda of Gandhi's hut, we come upon a remarkable-looking man, with unruly long white hair and a long beard, sitting hunched in a chair. He is thin, and, except for white khadi trunks and brown-rimmed spectacles, he is naked. His skin is pale and is ravaged by patchy-looking sores. He is apparently half blind, one eye being almost completely closed. By his chair is an old radio blasting out simple scales at full volume. "This is Mama Saheb Phadke," Trivedi says. "He came to Bapu in this ashram in 1917, and he's been here ever since. He has his own hut, but he likes to spend his day on the veranda here. He is at least eighty-seven."

Trivedi tries to rouse the old man to say something about Gandhi. After a lot of prompting, the old man shouts out, "Truth and nonviolence are as old as the hills! But nobody listens!"

Editors,

Biographers, and Bibliographers

IN 1956, THE GOVERNMENT OF INDIA ESTABLISHED A SPECIAL department of the Information and Broadcasting Ministry called The Collected Works of Mahatma Gandhi, with a view to compiling, and publishing both in Hindi and in English, all Gandhi's surviving writings and utterances, from the earliest known, written in 1884. The department has published fifty-nine large-format volumes of the English edition so far, each with an average of five hundred and fifty pages. The completed English edition will run to some eighty volumes. The general preface states, "This series proposes to bring together all that Gandhiji said and wrote, day after day, year after year. . . . Those who knew him in the body as he trod this earth, striving every moment to practice what he believed, owe it to those who cannot have the privilege of learning by his presence and example, that they should hand over to the coming generations the rich heritage of his teachings in its purity and, as far as possible, in its entirety."

The copyright on everything Gandhi wrote and said in the contemporary record is held by the Navajivan Trust, which Gandhi himself established, and which has its own publishing house, in Ahmedabad. "The Collected Works" is printed here—the city, in fact, is the center of the whole industry of books about Gandhi—and most of the editorial work is done here, by the deputy editor of the project, C. N. Patel. Patel has had a hand in drafting prefaces for most of the volumes and probably knows more about the contents of "The Collected Works" than anyone else.

The Navajivan Press is housed in a large gray concrete building in a somewhat neglected garden—the topiary work on the hedges sprouting whiskers, and the flower beds threatened by weeds. In the lobby, several Gandhians, all dressed in khadi, are reading newspapers while the presses thunder in the background. The corridor leading to Patel's office is littered with heaps of wood shavings, scraps of paper, and big burlap bundles. In the office itself, wooden shelves are piled high with papers, and so is Patel's desk. A small Nehru jacket of gray khadi and a white Gandhi cap hang on a hook behind a desk. (A Gandhi cap is a simple cloth cap—shaped something like a rowboat—that Gandhi's followers wear as a symbol of their adherence to his principles.)

Patel is a tiny, frail, emaciated man with a square head, bulging eyes, a large nose, and pronounced cheekbones. He has thinning black hair parted slightly to the right, a long, fuzzy gray beard, and a full gray mustache. He wears black-rimmed spectacles, a short-sleeved white khadi kurta, white trousers, and leather sandals, and clutches a handkerchief nervously in one hand.

"What do you think is the value of 'The Collected Works'?" I ask.

"The only people who will have any use for it will be researchers," he says. "I remember that someone attacked our second entry in the first volume as gratuitous. It is only one sentence. It appeared in an obscure little newspaper and is a quotation from a speech Gandhiji made to his high-school classmates at Rajkot just before leaving for his studies in England: 'I hope that some of you will follow in my footsteps, and after you return from England you will work wholeheartedly for big reforms in India.' To me it is significant that he should be telling his classmates this at the age of eighteen."

"Is there a danger of not being able to see the forest for the trees?"

"Yes, there is. But I get a very clear impression of Gandhiji's life from 'The Collected Works.' There was a marked discrepancy between Gandhiji the politician and social reformer and Gandhiji the man searching for God. He was drawn into political life by the force of historical circumstances, but his natural bent was that of a holy man. Although he imparted to his countrymen, humiliated by their British enslavement, a certain self-confidence and energy, he felt toward the end of his life that he had failed in everything, and, in a sense, he had, whether it was in his struggle for Hindu-Muslim harmony or in his struggle for the uplift of the untouchables or in his efforts to introduce true economic and social democracy. Yet at the same time he went a long way toward attaining knowledge of God."

"Has Gandhi affected your life in any way?"

"I never knew him, but I've learned from him how to discipline my body, how to be patient with it. Like Gandhi and most of our countrymen, I've had quite a lot of trouble with my stomach. Some years ago, I started trying all kinds of drugs, I went on a liquid diet of milk, but nothing helped. My doctor began to suspect a cancer of the stomach, so he did exploratory surgery. His diagnosis was that I didn't have cancer, but he came to the conclusion that by this time, because of the milk diet, my intestines had shrunk and atrophied and I'd lost the ability to digest solid food. Nothing he recommended to restore my digestion worked. So now I'm trying some of Gandhiji's nature-cure techniques. I eat only two pounds of curds and five ounces of raisins a day—though I don't actually eat the raisins, just suck their juice."

The offices of the department of The Collected Works of Mahatma Gandhi take up about thirty rooms in a large government building on the outskirts of Delhi. Here I call on K. Swaminathan, who became chief editor in 1960 and has been supervising the publication since then. (The first chief editor, Bharatan Kumarappa, died in 1957; the second, Jairamdas Doulatram, resigned in 1959.) He works out of an austerely furnished room—a few pictures of Gandhi, Kasturbai, and Nehru hang on the walls, and a single bookshelf holds a Roget's Thesaurus, a Bhagavad Gita, and a few standard books on Gandhi. Swaminathan is a friendly man in his sixties, with a professorial air. He is lean and dark, has a square face, bushy eyebrows, and long fingers, and is dressed in a white bush shirt with short sleeves, gray-and-white plaid slacks, and sandals.

"How is the project coming along?" I ask.

"We've had problems with cost overruns," he says. "That's because we've had some very unexpected expenses, like providing Pyarelal, the custodian of important Gandhi papers, with an assistant for two years in return for his cooperation. When it comes to his material on Gandhi, he's like Othello guarding Desdemona. There's such a mountain of material. People knew very early that Gandhi was a great man, and everything he said or did was recorded and preserved. Sometimes each person near him would record his conversations with visitors. Gandhiji would then go over their records, choose the one he liked best, correct it, and send it off for publication in one of his weeklies— *Indian Opinion, Young India, Navajivan,* and *Harijan.* One of his little jokes was 'You know how the gospels of Matthew, Mark, Luke, and John differ. I want only one gospel of my life.' Our task is not only to bring all the material together but also to translate it into Hindi or into English, or both—Gandhiji spoke and wrote in Gujarati, Hindi, and English—and to arrange it in chronological order whenever possible, with the necessary footnotes, appendices, and indexes. We do our best to authenticate the documents. A letter has to be signed by Gandhiji, a speech must have been reported in the press within a day or two of its delivery. Whenever we are in doubt about an item—say, whether or not a resolution was drafted by him—we include a note giving our reason for thinking that it came from his pen. After we publish a volume, new material often turns up, and this we hope to publish in supplementary volumes."

"What about the letters signed by Gandhi but drafted by his secretaries and assistants?"

"They all have to pass our tests for authenticity."

"Do you ever feel that there's a danger of drowning Gandhi in a sea of documentation?"

"Maybe you mean to say a sea of words," he says. "The Hindi title for 'The Collected Works' is 'Sampurna Gandhi Vangmaya,' which means, more or less, 'The Complete Wordiness of Gandhi.' People can fish out what they like from the wordy sea."

"There must be a lot of repetition," I remark.

"Most certainly. He said the same thing over and over again—but with different emphasis. Gandhi scholars actually use the amount of his repetition as a measure of his faith in a particular concept or course of action. When we first started, we had no idea of the scale of the project, the amount of the extant material. We thought that Gandhi's South African period could be covered in one volume. It actually took twelve."

"And yet Gandhi himself never wrote a single full-length book," I remark. Although Gandhi was a prolific writer of articles and filled his weeklies with them, he published only two books as such—"Indian Home Rule" and "Satyagraha in South Africa"—and they were actually no more than pamphlets. Even his well-known autobiography, "The Story of My Experiments with Truth," was a collection of articles.

"That's so," Swaminathan says equably.

"What would Gandhi have thought of your project?"

"He wouldn't have liked it at all. He said repeatedly, 'It's not what I say but what I do that matters.' In fact, his main disciple, Vinoba Bhave, told me that we were doing a disservice to Gandhiji by publishing his every word and thus showing up all his inconsistencies and contradictions. But my answer is that Gandhiji didn't mind being inconsistent. He is one of the few men in history who were never ashamed of anything they thought or said, however contradictory it might be."

"What do you regard as Gandhi's most memorable sayings?"

"Many years ago, I used to think that Gandhiji's saying 'There can be no happiness for any of us until happiness has been won for all' was the best. Now I've seen so many of his sayings that I can't choose."

"Do you find that some parts of 'The Collected Works' read better than others?"

"I'm so busy supervising the whole project that I'm not able to read very much that goes into it. I have to look after fifty researchers and editors and thirty clerks just here in Delhi, and there are many others in Ahmedabad working on our great project."

In 1948, a few months after Gandhi's assassination, a number of prominent Gandhians and national leaders, including Nehru, invited Pyarelal (he no longer uses his surname) to undertake the official biography of Gandhi, which was to be written in English. Pyarelal had served Gandhi since 1920, first as assistant to Mahadev Desai, and then, after Desai's death, in 1942, as Gandhi's chief secretary. He has been at work on Gandhi's biography for the last twenty-eight years—a project subsidized by the Gandhi National Memorial Trust, the Collected Works department, and the Navajivan Trust, among others. Like everything to do with Gandhi, it has assumed monumental proportions. The first installment of the biography, entitled "The Last Phase," appeared in two hefty volumes in 1956 and 1958; it covers only the last four years of Gandhi's life. The next installment, entitled "The Early Phase," appeared in 1965, as another vast tome; it covers Gandhi's first twenty-seven years. Since the material for this early period is very sketchy, the condensation is more apparent than real. And since Pyarelal has now spent eighteen years of his own life recording thirty-one of his subject's, no one, least of all Pyarelal, can be confident that he will live to complete the biography: he is in his seventies, and forty-seven years of his subject's life remain to be chronicled. He often dwells on the overwhelming nature of the enterprise. In the Preface to "The Last Phase," he writes:

I must confess that I was hardly aware of the colossal nature of the task and the tremendous difficulties, abysses and pitfalls in the way when I launched on this venture. . . . To interpret the record correctly and fully . . . to make disjointed bits of information fall in their proper places and yield a clear, coherent meaning, and unravel the tangled skein of the story with the help of clues hunted up from collateral sources of evidence called for Job's patience, a faculty of divination (to which I could lay no claim) and some deft sleuth-work—very interesting but extremely time-consuming. It was only by a reckless expenditure of time coupled with some providential chance contacts and the pointers provided by Gandhiji's letters to me during the period under review and what he had shared with me during the last two months of his earthy sojourn when a merciful Providence again enabled me to be near him that the work could be completed.

Soon I discovered, too, that there was hardly a comment of importance on men and events in this crucial period or a conclusion based thereupon that I could record but provoked a challenge. . . .

In preparing these pages, I have drawn upon, in the first instance . . . Gandhiji's office records, his own writings in *Young India* and *Harijan,* and statements and interviews to the Press, and his personal correspondence including jottings, instructions and scribblings . . . on odd bits of paper which I had carefully preserved. . . . Knowing my passion for collection and preservation of scraps of paper having a bearing on his life and activities, and knowing that others might be free from that addiction, he sometimes used to pick out choice morsels and send them to me as "love tokens." . . . I had, besides, my own notebooks and diaries . . . notebooks and diaries of some other members of his party and my own firsthand information either from him or from others to go by. Last but not least, I have relied on his own journal [May, 1946, through July, 1947] which he began specially to keep for me to make up for my absence from him.

In the Introduction to "The Early Phase," Pyarelal says that this time his trials were, if anything, even greater:

> Luckily Gandhiji had brought with him from South Africa a boxful of correspondence and other documents relating to his work there. . . . He had also maintained a systematic and fairly exhaustive record of clippings from contemporary newspapers for the period 1889–1900 in thirteen scrapbooks. He had spoken to me about them. . . . They were pretty often in a bad shape—sometimes mutilated or jumbled into a pie, or obscured by the growth of black fungus. At other times the source and date line were clipped out, or obliterated, or were otherwise missing. The portions, that were mildewed or were covered with gummed strips of butter paper for repairs, became altogether undecipherable in the photostats, though in the original record—which had in the meantime been returned to the owners—the writing could still sometimes with effort be made out. All this resulted in . . . no end of agonizing eye-strain in spite of the use of higher-power magnifying glasses and other devices on my part and on the part of my colleagues, in order to decipher them.
>
> I had likewise to get quite a lot of old records, source books, and even reference books from various institutions laminated for safe handling, and as an inducement to the custodians to let me have them photostated for my use. . . .
>
> Absence of reference facilities in India added to the difficulty. To verify the date or source of an important clipping . . . or for a "Who's Who" of the *dramatis personae* one had to seek the assistance of friends in South Africa, or of the editors of newspapers there, with varying success.

From what Pyarelal has published so far, it is clear that he is not a biographer but, rather, a hagiographer, who celebrates the miraculous deeds of his hero under such chapter headings as "The Sentinel on the Watch-Tower," "Zero Hour," "The Greater the Sinner the Greater the Saint," "Bitter Brew," "Dragon's Teeth," "Turn Poison Into Nectar," "Search for the Panacea," "Crumbling Heavens," "The Titan at Work," and "The Hinge of Fate." Pyarelal is in the tradition of Gandhian hagiology, which is noted for its ornate redundancy, its petrified Victorian Indian-English, its grandiloquent claims, and its reverent lore. He has this to say about the intention of his undertaking:

> This book is not a verdict on men and events—though men and events are discussed in it—but only an attempt to understand and explain certain events and the actions of the men who made those events and in the process were themselves made by those events, in the context of Gandhiji's great experiment to discover the Law of Love and how it could be applied to solve the problems that face the present-day world.
>
> A word to the Indian reader. . . . We invoke the name of the Father of the Nation on all important occasions. . . . It is vital for us to know the road on which he set us and that by which we arrived and where the two bifurcated. . . . Almost the first thing a foreign visitor does on arrival in India is to visit Rajghat [another name for the Cremation Ground]—if he happens to be an official guest or otherwise an important personage, he is escorted there—to pay homage to the Father of the Nation. Before he leaves India, he invariably ends up by asking: Where is Gandhi in India of to-day? . . . This book is an attempt to help us turn the searchlight inward and find the answer.

Pyarelal's office is in a decrepit building in Shankar Market, a garish, rather shabby bazaar in the center of New Delhi, known for cheap ready-made clothes and for black marketeering. A flight of dark, dirty stairs leads up to a door with Pyarelal's name on it. The door opens onto a long balcony that is piled high with innumerable steel trunks and boxes, all crammed with papers, and at the far end is a very large room, glaringly lit and, if anything, even more chaotic. Filing cabinets and cupboards of all descriptions—of metal, of wood, of wood with glass doors—and a variety of tables, shelves, desks, and typewriters have somehow been crowded in, leaving little space in which to move about.

A short, plump, sallow man shuffles toward me as best he can through the chaos, and greets me warmly. He has large ears and rather thick lips, and wears bifocals; he is dressed in a white kurta with a collar that seems too tight and sleeves so long that they have to be turned back at the wrists. He is Pyarelal. "Bapu the philosopher, the statesman, the moralist was a very serious-minded man, and the world knows about

his grave thoughts, but there was also a humorous side to him," Pyarelal says. "I'll tell you a story that only I know, because I was the only
witness. Bapu and I were aboard ship on our way to the Second Round
Table Conference in London in 1931. A man appeared in Bapu's cabin.
He said, 'Mr. Gandhi, I am a member of the Billy Goats, a club of virile,
hard-drinking passengers here on board. I have been asked by my
fellow Billy Goats to present you with today's edition of *Scandal Times*.
We would be glad to have your opinion of it.' He handed Bapu a
couple of sheets held together with a straight pin. Bapu glanced at the
sheets, removed the pin, and returned them to the waiting Mr. Billy
Goat. 'If you don't mind, I'll keep the pin,' he said. 'That's the most
valuable part of your publication.' " Pyarelal laughs heartily, and ab-
sentmindedly wanders off in the direction of a desk in the back of the
room, followed closely by a tall, burly, fearsome-looking man, who
turns out to be his secretary, Dewan Vasudev. Pyarelal brushes past
glass-fronted cupboards that contain book after book on Gandhi and
look as though they were seldom opened, and pauses before some
cabinets displaying massive bound volumes of *Indian Opinion* and
Young India.

"These are the only sets in private hands," he says proudly. "Each
volume is so heavy that Vasudev and I between us can hardly lift it."

"The pages are laminated," Vasudev puts in. "We are going to
rebind them in smaller volumes to reduce their weight."

"So much of my time is taken up with the problems of laminating
and rebinding, preserving and guarding Gandhiana," Pyarelal says.

Farther along are open shelves holding notebooks, scrapbooks,
government reports, and pamphlets strung together and labelled "Official Files."

"Everything on these shelves relates to Gandhi," Pyarelal says.
"Each piece of this material is being numbered. I'm up to twenty-two
thousand one hundred and eighty-three so far, and that takes me only
to 1932." He waves a hand toward other shelves, overflowing with yet
more files and papers. "That's original source material, which I collected myself when I was with Bapu—my own diaries, drafts of articles
with Bapu's handwriting on them, newspaper clippings cut under
Bapu's own supervision by his fellow prison inmates . . ." His words
trail off.

"Up there are photostat copies of Bapu's original handwritten letters, along with my typed transcripts of them," Vasudev puts in, indicating some brown-paper bundles on the highest shelves.

"What will eventually become of all these papers and books?" I ask Pyarelal.

"I'm still negotiating. Whether they'll be left to the National Archives, the Gandhi Peace Foundation, or a center to be established in my memory is still to be decided," he says, adding portentously, "However, there are some materials I have decided to suppress."

"Such as what?" I ask.

"Gandhi's views on Israel, for a start," he says, with a mysterious air. "I am able to suppress them from history, since by God's grace I am the only one who knows about them. Because of His good will toward me, although I frequently went to prison, my papers miraculously survived."

Pyarelal sits down at his desk, which is strewn with fountain pens and paperweights. Vasudev sits down beside him, and prompts him when he loses the thread of what he is saying, as he often does.

"My father was a petty official in the Punjab," Pyarelal tells me. "He was so clever his British superiors never realized that he didn't read or write English. He used to get telegrams and communiqués in English all the time, and he would get them translated on the sly, and would always look knowledgeable when he talked to his superiors, even when he wasn't following a word they said. After my father died, in 1915, my uncle, who was a man of stern character and strong moral principles, brought us all up. We were two brothers and three sisters."

"Pyarelalji and Sushilaji are the only surviving members of the family," Vasudev puts in.

"How did you happen to meet Gandhi?" I ask.

"I was studying in Lahore and heard Bapu speak at the railway station there," Pyarelal says. "There was something in the flat, level tone of his voice that electrified me. It was like the depth of the ocean—something indescribably simple and vast. After speaking, he nimbly prevented anyone from touching his feet and so paying him the homage due the great and holy. In that way, he put himself on the level of the common man like me. I managed to see him alone on his next visit to Lahore. He had just come out of his bath, and his bare arms and legs glistened with oil. He was wrapped in a white cashmere shawl, and there was a glow on his face. I told him, 'I feel very dissatisfied with the prospects for young people like me in India. I want to give up my studies and become your follower.' He said, 'Don't get involved unless you feel a call, but when you do, see it through.' I took his wise text to heart and returned to my studies. After my graduation, I felt the call, and in the fall of 1920 I took the train for Ahmedabad. I felt I was Columbus going in search of the New World. I arrived at Sabarmati Ashram with my bedroll on my back and a bundle of clothes on my head. Bapu was away on tour, and when he came back he asked me to write him a little essay on a subject of my choice. I happened to light upon one of Bapu's weeklies, which contained his review of Tolstoy's 'The Kingdom of God Is Within You.' I wrote something modelled on his review. Bapu liked it, and he made me an assistant to Mahadev Desai. In time, of course, I succeeded Mahadev as chief secretary.''

"I'm Pyarelalji's chief secretary," Vasudev puts in.

"What did it involve—being Gandhi's chief secretary?" I ask.

"The job of everyone around Bapu was to be a soldier ready for anything," Pyarelal says. "One day you might be asked to take dictation, another day to edit newspaper copy, and the day after that to arrange for a broadcast. You might also be asked to clean the latrines, grind wheat, wash pots, sweep floors, and go on tours with Bapu. When he was unwell, or was fasting for his own purification or for causes dear to his heart, I nursed him. I gave him enemas, and kept a clinical chart, noting down the pallor of his skin, the color of his urine, the appearance of his stool, how much water he drank, whether he complained of nausea. I turned him on his side, brought him a urine bottle or a bedpan, and gave him sponge baths.''

"Were you ever reluctant to do any of these tasks?"

"Not at all. No one was. It was all very natural. And as a matter of course we all did such things for one another in the ashram.''

I try to draw Pyarelal out on one of the most controversial and central aspects of Gandhi's life—his brahmacharya experiments. "Brahmacharya" literally means "the realization of Brahma," and one of the prerequisites for realizing Brahma is celibacy. Gandhi had been a brahmachari, or celibate, since he was thirty-six, but toward the end of his life he engaged in experiments to test his mastery of celibacy by taking young women to bed with him. In "The Last Phase," Pyarelal tries to justify these experiments on historical, philosophical, and spiritual grounds. Some Gandhians claim that he glorifies the experiments, others that he obfuscates the whole issue. To a non-Gandhian reader, Pyarelal's account of Gandhi's brahmacharya, as of many other things, seems extraordinarily incomplete, despite its length, and, as always, he is uncritically accepting—this despite the fact that Gandhi himself took on his critics in public debates about every aspect of his life, including the brahmacharya experiments.

"Bapu often used to say, 'Truth was inborn in me, nonviolence came to me with great effort, brahmacharya I'm still striving for,'" Pyarelal tells me. "Still, he was a great brahmachari. He had only one seminal emission in his middle and late years—it was in his sleep in 1936, when he was sixty-six, and it dismayed him a lot—but that is a matter of public record. I saw with my own eyes that even when he was asleep his hands were moving as if he were saying his beads—he was so far along in his realization of Brahma."

"But, whatever Gandhi's own spiritual attainments, don't you think that the effect of the brahmacharya experiments on at least some of the women involved might have been psychologically damaging?" I ask.

"How could it be?" he asks rhetorically. "Let me tell you a story to illustrate what I mean. Once, in the ashram, I heard a woman screaming. I rushed into her room and saw that her sari was on fire. I ripped it off. She felt no embarrassment, because she knew I was a brahmachari and so almost like a sister to her."

"But surely any woman would have been relieved to be rescued, whether by a brahmachari or not?"

"Oh, no! If I had not been a brahmachari, her scruples, not to mention my scruples, would have prevented me from doing what was clearly my duty, and she would have burned to death."

There are two standard bibliographies of Gandhian literature: "Mahatma Gandhi: A Descriptive Bibliography," by Jagdish Sharma, which was first published in 1955 and was brought out in a second edition in 1968, and "Gandhi Bibliography," by Dharma Vir, which was published in 1967. Both editors try to catalogue all well-known and some not so well-known remarks by or about Gandhi, with the result that both volumes, in addition to being formidable in size, are rather clumsy specimens of their genre. Vir's bibliography, which serves as a sort of stepping stone to Sharma's monolith, has three thousand four hundred and eighty-five numbered entries either by or about Gandhi. Listed are biographical studies of Gandhi ("Mahatma Gandhi: The Man Who Became One with the Universal Being," "Romantic Gandhi: A Search for Mahatma's Originality"); poems about Gandhi ("Gandhi: An Epic Fragment"); plays about Gandhi ("Gandhiji in South Africa: An Historical Drama in Five Acts," "Gandhi: The Man of Destiny: A Passion Play"); novels about Gandhi ("Waiting for the Mahatma," "Nine Hours to Rama"); collections of essays on Gandhi's influence upon literature ("Impact of Gandhism on Marathi Literature," "Gandhi in Kannada Literature"); albums of paintings, drawings, and photographs of Gandhi ("Mahatma Gandhi: Pictorial History of a Great Life," "A Glimpse Into Gandhiji's Soul"); compilations of Gandhi's thoughts and sayings ("My God," "My Non-Violence," "My Philosophy of Life," "My Picture of Free India," "My Religion," "My Socialism," "My Soul's Agony," "Precious Pearls: Glittering Galaxy of Gandhian Gems, Teachings of Mahatma Gandhi on More Than Five Hundred Topics"); periodicals devoted to Gandhi's ideas; other bibliographies of Gandhian literature; sections on science, technology, agriculture, animal husbandry, medicine, art, philosophy, religion, psychology, education, and economics, each from a Gandhian point of view; and so on. Vir goes to the length of listing in a separate section two hundred and fifty-three books that Gandhi is known definitely to have read ("Constipation and Our Civilization," "How Green Was My Valley," "Trips to the Moon," "The Strange Case of Dr. Jekyll and Mr. Hyde," "The Greatest Thing in the World"). For Kasturbai, however, there are only eleven entries, three of them mentions by Western writers. Gandhi's wife was neglected in life and seems to have been all but overlooked after death.

Now and again, a title or an annotation brings Gandhi to life and one can almost hear him inveighing against industrialism, atheism, cities, sex, drink, drugs, or even the use of English in India, or commending handicrafts, godliness, the village and the soil, or self-discipline and abstinence, but most of the time, as one leafs through Vir and Sharma, one's mind boggles at the benumbing crisscrossing of sometimes nearly identical titles and at the vast extent of Gandhiana. One gets the impression that practically everyone who ever spoke to Gandhi and could put pen to paper has written something about him, and that by now his every thought and action has been worked over and pre-served by his editors, biographers, and bibliographers.

How strange, I think, that, of all people, Gandhi, who lived in such starkly simple circumstances, should be so encumbered after death. Perhaps part of the explanation lies in the fact that the recording and preserving of data are still something of a novelty for Hindus, who have in the past traditionally neglected history in favor of speculation, and whose written records, in any event, have rarely survived the ravages of conquerors and climate. Albert Einstein once said about Gandhi, "Generations to come, it may be, will scarce believe that such a one as this ever in flesh and blood walked upon this earth." Gandhi's contem-poraries could themselves scarcely believe in the man of flesh and blood, so what hope is there of ever rediscovering him behind the myths, the legends, the apotheoses?

Family

GANDHI WAS EXCEPTIONAL AMONG HOLY MEN IN BEING A husband and father and in keeping his wife and children around him, even in the ashrams. All his children are now dead, but many of his relatives, including two daughters-in-law, the father of one of them, and at least forty-seven direct descendants, are alive today. At the last known count, twenty-seven of the descendants lived in India, ten in South Africa, six in the United States, three in Italy, and one in Switzerland. The adults among them do everything from selling life insurance to working in space engineering; one is a Moral Re-Armament evangelist.

Many of Gandhi's surviving relatives knew him intimately, and I visit a few of them in India, my first call being on Chakravarti Rajagopalachari, the father-in-law of Gandhi's youngest son, Devadas, who was born in 1900. With Nehru, Rajagopalachari was Gandhi's leading political associate, and from 1948 to 1950 he was Governor-General of independent India. When I visit Rajagopalachari, or Rajaji, in Madras, he is ninety-three years old, and spends most of his time in a bare room that has the antiseptic smell and look of a hospital room: trays of medicine and neat piles of books are lined up next to a high bed, which is almost covered with white pillows of various shapes and sizes.

Rajaji sits in a wheelchair near a long bench with a white cloth over it, apparently meant for visitors. He has little hair; small, lively eyes behind brown-rimmed spectacles; no teeth; a cleft chin; and strong, smooth hands. He is wearing a beige khadi shirt and vest, and has a brown robe thrown over his knees. "I have more ailments than I can count," he tells me. "And whenever the medical men come up with a treatment, I turn out to be allergic to it. On top of all that, look at the state the country's in—it's enough to turn me into a mental case."

As the founder and guiding spirit of the conservative Swatantra Party, Rajaji is famous for relentless diatribes against India's more recent rulers, who in his view have been leading the country to perdition. I quickly turn the conversation to Gandhi, and ask him what it was like to be Gandhi's fellow father-in-law.

"It is commonly said that the reason I was against my daughter Lakshmi's marrying Devadas was that we were born top Brahmans and the Gandhis were lower-caste Banyas," Rajaji says. "The truth is that Gandhiji and I both felt that our political association should not be cemented by a marriage alliance. We made the children wait for five years—or however many years it was—and then, since they still wanted to marry, we gave them our blessing. There are so many stories going around about Gandhiji. The tellers all claim them to be firsthand recollections, but they're mostly romanticized versions of reality."

"What do you have in mind?"

"It is now said that he was born so holy that he had a natural bent for fasting. In reality, he was one of the hungriest men I have ever known. That's why he thought of fasting as a penance. Vegetarians eat a greater bulk of food than non-vegetarians, but even for a vegetarian he had a huge appetite. He once told me that when he was a student his landlady in London was astonished by the amount of bread he consumed. Similarly, it is now said that he was born so holy that he had a natural bent for brahmacharya, but actually he was highly sexed. He tried to control his sexual desires, because he was convinced—and rightly so—that sex fritters away human energy, which is best conserved and directed into other channels. Will that do? That will do, I think. Everything he achieved was achieved through extraordinary self-discipline and renunciation. As I'm always saying to my Swatantra Party colleagues, character is the foundation of civilization. And nobody had more character than Gandhi. If we'd paid him enough heed, we would now have a whole new civilization, based on the principle of service."

"Have you ever looked at any of the books about Gandhi?"

"I don't care to. I knew him better than any of the authors, and that includes his so-called secretaries. They waited on him, they nursed him, but they didn't share in his intellectual life, as I did. As I never tire of

48

saying to my Swatantra Party colleagues, everybody likes a successful man. Gandhi was strong and successful, so all kinds of people latched on to him. Nonetheless, he was starved for good conversation. That's one reason he especially appreciated me. I often made him laugh, but I can't remember how anymore. I think he mostly laughed at small things, and we joked a lot about the British. Now I would like to drop the subject. If I go on any longer, I will be writing a book myself."

Although talking seems to be a strain on Rajaji and he is often on the point of putting an end to the conversation, I still get the impression that he is enjoying himself.

"What do you think is Gandhi's future in India?"

"I have to give you a depressing answer, much as I don't like to. The glamour of modern technology, money, and power is so seductive that no one—I mean no one—can resist it. And it may be that because of Gandhi we got our freedom before we were ready, before we had developed our character to match the responsibility. The handful of Gandhians who still believe in his philosophy of a simple life in a simple society are mostly cranks."

Of Gandhi's four daughters-in-law, Nirmala, who was the wife of his son Ramdas—born in 1897—was closest to him. She continues to live in the Gandhian way, staying in an old hut in the Sevagram Ashram, and I call on her there one morning. She is a short woman in her early sixties, with a generous mouth, large, weak eyes, and gray hair pulled back in a rather untidy long braid. She wears a white khadi sari with a simple hand-stitched purple border, and glasses with brown frames. Her manner is warm, energetic, and matronly. We sit on the veranda, on a small wooden bench with a turquoise khadi cloth over it. The sound of ashram residents praying can be heard in the background.

"I try to follow Bapu's example as best I can, though I do permit myself the luxury of electric lights," she tells me. "Bapu used to say that we shouldn't have electricity until every village in the country had it." She goes into the hut and returns with a cup of coffee for me. "Because coffee and tea were against Bapu's dietary rules, I don't drink either, but I serve them to my guests, as Ba did."

"Did you know Gandhi before you married?"

"My father died when I was nine," she says. Many of Gandhi's disciples grew up fatherless or orphaned. "I went to stay with my aunt, who lived in Sabarmati Ashram. I read the Bhagavad Gita every day for hours and secretly decided to become a brahmachari. But I was a favorite of Bapu's, and when I was sixteen he chose me to marry Ramdasji, who insisted on getting married, even though many people didn't in those days, because they didn't want to produce more slaves for the British. Bapu's wishes were law to me. When the details of my marriage were being discussed, my aunt told Bapu that, although I was perfectly healthy in every way, I was somewhat constipated. Bapu said, 'I know how to put that right.' He asked me, 'Will you do as I tell you to?' I said, 'I am a member of your family now, Bapu—I want you to teach me all your ways and look after me.' He put me on a diet of prune and orange juice, and told Ba to give me an enema. I felt very shy about taking an enema from my future mother-in-law, but Ba was gentle and motherly. After a couple of days, I learned to give myself an enema, and after a few days of juice I was also allowed to eat boiled vegetables and *khakhras.*"

"Did you get married right away?" I ask.

"No," she replies. "Although Ramdas lived in the ashram, at that time he was in the nearby county of Bardoli. Poor peasants there were in revolt against heavy taxes, and he had told Bapu that he wanted to go just for a visit. But Bapu had said, 'You don't go to a fire just to look at it—you take a pitcher of water and try to put it out.' That's how Ramdasji came to take up his work in Bardoli. He turned out to be a very good organizer. I didn't like being left behind, but Bapu wanted us to wait until I was eighteen before we got married, so that I would be more mature."

"How did you occupy yourself in the ashram?"

"I cut up fruit for Bapu, brought milk for Ba, washed clothes in the river, and fetched water from the well. I was very busy in the kitchen, too. We prepared meals for at least a hundred people every day, and making nice light *khakhras* for everybody took hours. Then, there was spinning and weaving, and teaching hymns and patriotic songs to the ashram children. In January, 1928, Ramdasji and I were married, at the ashram, and we went to live in Bardoli. I discovered that he was slightly constipated. I would make him eat boiled vegetables and *khakhras* for a few days—Bapu's plain diet—but then he would go back to his old eating habits. He liked rich, hot, spicy foods."

"What was it like living in Bardoli?"

"Ramdasji took a large house for us and filled it with expensive English things—spoons, china, clocks—and was always giving me beautiful khadi clothes. He was earning only forty rupees a month as a volunteer worker. I would say, 'We should live within our means. Anyway, what is the point of all this finery and good living? You may be sent to jail at any time.' And he would say, 'This home may be our last home, so let's be jolly, eat well, and be carefree. Let tomorrow take care of itself.' He was happy-go-lucky. He had a generous, extravagant nature. The simple, restrained ways of Bapu were not for him. I fell in step with him and kept our house in great style, giving frequent dinner parties for as many as twenty people. I worshipped Ramdasji and could never do enough for him, but there was no hiding our differences. He liked the cinema; I thought it corrupting. Right after we were married, he found me reading one of Bapu's tracts on celibacy. He said, 'What are you doing, reading that stuff?' One morning, I started vomiting. We were both frightened, not knowing what caused it, but the women neighbors laughed and said, 'You're not sick—you're expecting.' A doctor confirmed that I was. Ramdasji took very good care of me. He would sit with me all day long, rubbing my head and massaging my feet. Imagine, a man ministering to a woman! It made me very shy, especially since he wouldn't stop even when we had visitors. Our daughter Sumitra was born in October, 1929, but our carefree days were short-lived. In April, 1930, Bapu marched to Dandi, on the seacoast, in order to defy the oppressive salt laws, which, among other things, required every Indian to buy salt from the British and pay a tax on it. Bapu made his own salt, and tens of thousands of people, including Ramdasji, followed his example. They were all sent to jail for their civil-disobedience campaign. I, too, would have marched to defy the laws, but Bapu directed some of us women to stay home and take care of the children, the old, and the sick. For the next three years, Ramdasji was in and out of jail, and by the time he was out of jail for good he was a physical wreck—even an orange would upset his stomach. He couldn't find a job, and we had two daughters and a son by then. Poor Ramdasji! He always blamed Bapu for not giving him any formal Western education to speak of—Bapu didn't believe in it. He thought all types of work, big or small, equally worthwhile. In fact, he thought that running a good kitchen was more important than teaching at a university, since the universities supported British rule. Poor, poor Ramdasji! His happy moments were really few and far between. He had been born and brought up in South Africa, with its bracing climate, good food, and domestic comforts. He was seventeen when he came back to India, and was quite Anglicized. He never really adjusted to our hot climate and Bapu's decision to live like a poor man. Moreover, just at that time Bapu was experimenting with diet, and all that anyone in the ashram ate was groundnuts, dates, gur, and *khakhras*. The diet did not agree with Ramdasji at all. Later on, Bapu sent him back to South Africa, where he really belonged. But he died in Bombay, in 1969."

"Did you go to South Africa with him?"

"No, I went back with the children to live with Bapu."

One of Gandhi's granddaughters—Sumitra, the eldest daughter of Ramdas and Nirmala Gandhi—is a Member of Parliament. She is married to Gajanand Kulkarni, a college teacher. They have three children and live in a pleasant, modest house in Delhi.

A servant shows me into a dining room furnished in middle-class fashion, with several electrical appliances on display, and a blue batik of Ganesh, the elephant god, on the wall. Mr. Kulkarni is supervising the children at lunch—nine-year-old twin boys and a seven-year-old girl. There is a lot of laughing and talking.

"I'm Shrikrishna Kulkarni," one of the boys announces self-importantly. "My brother's name is Ramchandra Kulkarni. My sister's name is Sonali Kulkarni."

"I'm seven and a half," Sonali says.

"You're eight and a half," the boys say in unison.

The children's lunch is over, and the boys get down on the floor and start drawing rockets and bombers on sheets of paper.

"This is Soni and that's Mumtaz," Sonali says, pointing to a black Pomeranian puppy and a Siamese cat.

"Who named the cat Mumtaz?" I ask, struck by the fact that Gandhi's great-grandchildren should have a cat with the name of the Moghul empress extravagantly immortalized in the Taj Mahal by her bereaved husband, the Emperor Shah Jahan.

"The emperor did," Sonali says, chasing Mumtaz around the room.

"We have a house in Ahmedabad, where I teach at the Indian Institute of Management," Mr. Kulkarni tells me, "but since my wife's election to the Parliament we must also keep a house here. I'm constantly flying back and forth." He is a mild-mannered man with a round face and a broad, flat nose, and is dressed in a beige-and-brown plaid bush shirt, light khaki pants, and leather sandals.

I ask him how his wife happened to go into politics.

"Mrs. Gandhi spotted her at a political rally and offered her the chance to run on the New Congress Party ticket for Gujarat." The reference is to Prime Minister Indira Gandhi, who is not related to Mahatma Gandhi. "Sumitra hesitated, because for seventeen years she'd been an officer in the Indian Administrative Service, with a good salary and life tenure, and she didn't want to give all that up, but eventually she accepted. The election was a hard fight, for even though Gandhiji came from the Gujarat area, people said that she was not really a Gujarati. Still, she won."

Mrs. Kulkarni arrives in a great flurry. Moving with a good deal of energy and speaking rapidly in a somewhat high voice, she greets everybody, including Mumtaz and Soni. She is a short, plump woman in her forties, with black hair pulled back into a large bun at her nape. Like her mother, she has a generous mouth and large, weak eyes. She is dressed in a light-gray sari with green embroidery, and black patent-leather sandals, and wears tortoise-shell glasses, a *bindi* (the beauty mark that a Hindu woman often puts on her forehead), a pair of diamond earrings, a two-strand necklace of black beads, a gold bangle wristwatch, a gold bracelet, and, on her left hand, a large gold ring with a red stone. Her toenails are painted red and her fingernails pink.

"At least have some rice pudding," she says to me. "I had it made specially for you, because we believe that it brings a guest good luck."

After lunch, she and I retire to the living room, which is sparsely and rather haphazardly furnished. A small photograph of Gandhi, smiling, sits on the mantel over the fireplace, and on one wall are pictures of Kasturbai and Ramdas.

The telephone rings, and she says demurely into the mouthpiece, "What news? . . . I'm expecting no news. . . . News about being appointed Minister? . . . No, I don't believe . . ." She gesticulates a lot at the mouthpiece—shakes a finger for emphasis, and spreads out her palm eloquently. Suddenly, her voice becomes excited and eager.

"You've heard something? . . . What? . . . Oh, you think the Council of Ministers is meeting this afternoon? . . . The moment you hear something, ring me."

She hangs up, and says to me, "If I have ended up with some power, it's because I'm a very determined woman. You see, I was an ungainly child with an acute squint in my left eye. In fact, I was going blind. Gandhiji, whom we called Grandfather, used to say, 'What will happen to this child with a squint? Who will marry her?' Everyone felt sorry for me. I resented it but bore it silently. My squint was finally corrected—or ninety-eight per cent corrected, anyway—at the Massachusetts General Hospital. I happened to be in the United States doing my postgraduate education. If it hadn't been for the squint, however, I would never have broken out of Grandfather's self-contained little world, worked so hard and with such determination, and got so far. But you probably don't want to hear all this." I say I do, and she continues, "My earliest memories are of Sevagram. It was like Peyton Place." Her whole face wrinkles with laughter. She has a hearty, happy chuckle.

The telephone rings again, and there is more speculation on whether she will or will not be invited to join the Council of Ministers.

"I didn't like Sevagram," she says afterward, "and insisted on a formal, Western type of education with degrees—something that I knew my father always resented having been denied by Grandfather. It led to a lot of dissension between Grandfather and me. He wanted all his grandchildren to go to his Basic Education Centre at Sevagram. I refused to have anything to do with it. He was very angry, but when I was ten he let me go to a school that was something between his school and an English-type boarding school. After I graduated, Grandfather said, 'Where is the need for further formal education? Come and be my secretary—I will train you.' I said, 'I don't want to be one of your inferior secretaries, who wash your clothes and utensils, organize your meals, make appointments, usher people in and out, and are filled with self-importance.' The really superior people, like Nehru, were never Grandfather's secretaries. They had been educated in England and were so independent they didn't feel the need to live with him at all. I wanted to be like them."

"What did Gandhi say?"

"He said I was a very obstinate girl. But he let me go to the Hindu University, at Benares. All the time I was there, though, he kept saying,

'Come and work as my secretary. What sense is there in degrees?' I was working for my M.A. when he died." She takes off her sandals, rubs her feet together, and tucks them under her. "Everyone under the sun wanted to be known as a secretary to the Mahatma. The moment he died, they were all suddenly brought face to face with reality—without him they were nothing."

Benefactors

ALTHOUGH GANDHI LIVED LIKE A POOR MAN, HIS ASHRAM WAS the headquarters of a vast social and political movement, reaching into every corner of the country, and it required considerable financial support. Ironically, it was not easy, either, to maintain Gandhi in his exacting, simple style of life, especially when he and his entourage were travelling from village to village or from continent to continent. The poet Sarojini Naidu, who has been described as "the licensed jester of the Mahatma's little court," once quipped, "It costs a great deal of money to keep Gandhiji living in poverty." Most of the money for the support of both Gandhi and his movement was donated by three merchant princes—Ambalal Sarabhai, Jamnalal Bajaj, and Ghanshyam Das Birla—who were among his followers. In fact, practically all the members of the Sarabhai and Bajaj families became devotees of Gandhi.

Ambalal Sarabhai, a great calico merchant and patron of the arts, is survived by his wife, Saraladevi, who lives, as she and her husband did for many years, in a huge family compound called the Retreat, in Ahmedabad. A guard at the gate waves my car through, and I am driven along a curving dirt road through junglelike luxuriance, alive with chipmunks and peacocks. Magnificent lily ponds, exquisite old statues, and Moghul-inspired decorative pavilions appear one after another, providing a fairyland setting for a half-dozen large, modern houses, in which various members of the Sarabhai family live. How it contrasts with Gandhi's ashrams, not to mention the hellish stench, clash, and clatter of the Sarabhai Calico Mills, on which the family's fortunes rest! I visited the mills, which are just a few miles away, earlier in the day, and was overwhelmed by the mixture of primitive and modern industrial working conditions: armies of women carrying loaded baskets on their heads, men with skin diseases pushing low carts, and everything and everyone covered in a blizzard of cotton lint flying off sleek, high-powered machines. After losing my way several times in the Retreat, I eventually arrive at Mrs. Sarabhai's house—an elegant two-story beige stucco structure, which was probably built around the time of the First World War—and am received in a drawing room.

Mrs. Sarabhai turns out to be a small, self-contained, aristocratic woman, possibly in her sixties, with graying black hair. She is dressed in a white khadi sari and is carrying a small white cloth bag and a prayer book.

She telephones for a servant to bring us tea—servants, all dressed in white khadi kurtas, pajamas, and Gandhi caps, are constantly passing to and fro—and I try to get her to talk about her husband and Gandhi and their business relationship, but she is not very forthcoming. I gather that for her both men have become such sacred memories that even talking about them would be a profanation. At one point, however, she tells me, "There was something in Bapuji that was irresistible. Because of him, my husband did all he could for his workers and their families—medically, educationally, and in whatever way he could. In his own way, he became imbued with the spirit of Bapuji and became what you might call a benevolent paternalist. He used to say that Gandhiism alone had the power to defeat Communism. I myself started wearing khadi about 1928, not because it was in vogue at the time but because I really believed in its message—decentralization of industry and work. Most of us think in one way and speak in another way and act in yet another way. Not so with Bapuji. He said what he believed and put into practice what he said, so his mind, spirit, and body were in harmony."

Jamnalal Bajaj was born into a poor family but at the age of four was adopted by a wealthy man. When he was seventeen, he inherited a fortune from his foster grandfather, and he used it to become one of the leading financiers and cotton merchants in India. He and his wife, Janakidevi, sometimes lived with Gandhi in his ashrams, and, in fact, it was Bajaj who gave Gandhi the land for Sevagram Ashram. When Bajaj died, in 1942, his wife gave away most of their wealth to the particular Gandhian cause in which her husband, an orthodox Hindu, had been most interested: the breeding and tending of cows, which

Hindus worship as a symbol of motherhood—in part, no doubt, because they provide milk for nourishment, dung for fuel and fertilizer, and bullocks for plowing the fields and drawing water from the wells.

Mrs. Bajaj is at present staying with her married daughter in Old Delhi, and she and her daughter receive me in a drawing room typical of the modestly well-to-do. It has a semicircular gold couch, a multicolored rug, and numerous ivory, wood, and terra-cotta curios. Mrs. Bajaj is a gray-haired woman with a girlish air. She has a strong, wrinkled face with small features, brown eyes (one slightly larger than the other), and smooth, young-looking hands. She is wearing a white khadi sari, the loose end of which covers her dark-gray hair, and she has a green shawl over her shoulders. She is carrying a green drawstring bag embroidered with white camels. On her left arm are white bracelets, and on her right are wooden holy beads, which she casually fingers, murmuring "*Hare Ram, Hare Ram.*"

"I got married when I was nine, *Hare Ram, Hare Ram,*" she tells me. "My husband was thirteen, and we were both from orthodox Banya families. I had been brought up hearing that our women ancestors in Rajasthan used to commit suttee and afterward were worshipped as goddesses. As soon as I got married, I thought of committing suttee, so that I, too, would be worshipped, *Hare Ram, Hare Ram.* I didn't know you had to be a widow before you could commit suttee. I found out just in time, *Hare Ram, Hare Ram.*" She spits out a bit of something she is chewing.

"How did your husband become Gandhi's benefactor?" I ask.

"My husband had read a lot about Bapuji's activities in South Africa, and he was overwhelmed by the thought that any Indian could be so famous abroad. When Bapuji returned to India, my husband went to see him. The moment my husband—he was twenty-six at the time —set eyes on Bapuji, he recognized a new father in him. He asked Bapuji, 'What are the expenses of your ashram?' Bapuji named a figure, and my husband immediately wrote out a check." She makes a small, delicate gesture with her right hand, without disturbing the holy beads on her arm. "It was fifteen thousand rupees, *Hare Ram, Hare Ram.*"

"That would be fifteen hundred thousand rupees at today's value," her daughter says, in a strident voice, giving what is actually an exorbitant figure. She is a prosperous-looking black-haired woman wearing large glasses with black half frames and a white sari printed with small red flowers, and she has clearly been waiting for a chance to break into the conversation.

"They used to say that Bapuji was a storm that blew my husband hither and thither," Mrs. Bajaj continues. "Bapuji said, 'Boycott British goods, they are sinful,' and in 1921 we made a bonfire of everything we had that was British, *Hare Ram, Hare Ram*—the carpets, the upholstered furniture, the silk saris. What we burned was worth three hundred thousand rupees."

"That would be thirty million rupees today," the daughter puts in.

"Didn't Gandhi disapprove of such ostentatious waste?" I ask.

"If he had known of our intention, he would have made us give all those things to an institution," Mrs. Bajaj replies. "But my husband said, 'Since it's sinful for us to enjoy these things, it must be sinful for other people to enjoy them. Why should we pass on our sin?' *Hare Ram, Hare Ram.*" She spits out another bit of whatever it is she's chewing. "After the bonfire, we covered everything—our bodies, our beds, our floors, our sofas—with coarse khadi, dyed in turmeric from my own kitchen."

"After Bapuji's death, Mother accepted Vinoba Bhave as her guru," the daughter says.

"I walked with Vinobaji for years," Mrs. Bajaj says. "Ten or fifteen miles a day, begging land for the poor. It was very hard, changing camp every day, because I never eat anything I haven't prepared with my own hands. Everyone knows that Muslims and Harijans have dirty habits." ("Harijans," or "children of God," was Gandhi's term for untouchables.) She spits.

"How did you manage in Gandhi's ashrams, where you had to eat food communally prepared by Muslims, Harijans, and all sorts of other people, whatever their caste or religion?" I ask.

"In the ashrams, everyone was very clean," she replies. "We all ate out of each other's hands. But everyone knew that Muslims and Harijans outside the ashram had dirty habits, *Hare Ram, Hare Ram.*"

Ghanshyam Das Birla, benefactor and follower of Gandhi for thirty-two years, gave him more money for his causes than anyone else. The Birlas and their rivals the Tatas are business dynasties that have been responsible for most of the major privately owned industry in India, the

Birlas having an interest in practically everything—metal, coal, chemicals, plastics, textiles, jute, paper, automobiles, bicycles, foodstuffs, sugar, real estate, banking, insurance, newspapers. In a book that Birla wrote about Gandhi in 1953, entitled "In the Shadow of the Mahatma," he is quite vague about how his family accumulated its wealth, except to say that his grandfather, at the age of eighteen, with scarcely a paisa to his name, set out from his village in Rajasthan to make his fortune in Bombay, and that by the time he himself was born, in 1894, the family was well established. He says that he entered the family business when he was twelve, and eventually became managing director. In the book, he never addresses himself to vague allegations, made by some detractors, that in the years following Gandhi's death he exploited his connection with Gandhi to get favored treatment from the government, enabling him to consolidate and expand his monopolies. He does print an abundance of letters and telegrams that he and Gandhi exchanged, which show that they enjoyed a close relationship. Once, when Birla came down with a cough, Gandhi, ever ready with nature cures and home remedies, sent him the following letter:

SEVAGRAM, 20–3–45

MY DEAR GHANSHYAM DAS,

. . . What are you taking, how much and when, what vegetables are you taking, and are you taking them raw, or boiled? I hope the water is not thrown away. Bread prepared from bran will not be a better substitute for toast. The flour is not separated from the chaff, I hope. If you are taking milk, then how much? Whatever else you may take, you must take one-half ounce of butter well spread over the toast or bread prepared from bran, together with salad. If you develop indigestion, then you can discontinue other things, but not butter. Take a deep breath; it is very necessary. Close one nostril and breathe deeply with the other—by increasing it gradually you can do it for half an hour at a stretch. Utter the word Ram with every breath you take. When doing breathing exercises, you should have air on all sides; open air is preferable. This has to be done in the morning as a matter of course; and thereafter when the food has been digested. This exercise must be taken at least four times a day. After taking a deep breath, it should be discharged. This practice should be observed from the beginning. This moves the bowels and induces sleep. If you will do this exercise wisely you will get rid of the cough soon enough.

With Bapu's blessings.

Though Birla is in his eighties now, he continues to play an active part in his business empire, flying from city to city, often in his private plane, and staying at one or another of numerous houses he or his businesses own. He is probably the most inaccessible public figure in India, but I eventually track him down at Vihar House, on a large estate thirteen miles outside Bangalore, in South India.

A long, winding drive bordered by beds of flowers of all kinds leads up to a rather substantial suburban-looking house, which stands next to a gleaming, white-domed temple. The living room is large and airy. Its floor, of stone, is mostly covered by a plain beige carpet, and on the carpet are two opulent Oriental rugs. There are a couch and armchairs upholstered in rich orange brocade. One wall is lined with books—mostly Western best-sellers, and volume upon volume of the *Reader's Digest* Condensed Books. French windows framed by lavender-pink draperies look out onto a terrace, and at the far end of the room, partly concealed by a carved wooden screen, is a long, polished dining table, near which a servant hovers. The clink of china and rattle of silver come from somewhere nearby.

A tall, slightly potbellied elderly man enters and sits down in an armchair next to a bright-red modern telephone. He is handsome and well preserved, with straight white hair neatly trimmed at the back of his head. There are vertical wrinkles in his forehead between small, watchful eyes, and he has a large, straight nose and thin lips. His mouth is slightly askew with age, but he seems to have all his teeth. He wears a gold polo shirt made of a crinkly material, light-beige linen trousers, sporty brown suède shoes, avocado-green socks, and a gold wristwatch. He is Birla.

I compliment him on his garden.

"I'm not responsible for it," he says offhandedly. "It's the beautiful Bangalore climate that does it."

It is said that, unlike J. R. D. Tata, the head of the Tata empire, who is a modern, Westernized business executive, Birla is a money-lender and merchant of the old school, an Indian-style tycoon, secretive about his wealth and power. I ask him about the two methods now.

"The difference is that I am religious and Tata is not," he says. "He's therefore frustrated, and I am content. I don't know about his business methods, but my business runs on autopilot—I'm only called in to make the big, momentous decisions."

"Mr. Birla has no equal in business," says a man who has come in and is standing like a bearer behind Birla's chair. He is in his forties and has thick, wavy black hair and a square, heavy face—slightly pitted —and he wears a green-and-white striped shirt and gray trousers.

Birla introduces him perfunctorily as the director of the Mysore Cements, Limited, of which he himself is the chairman, and goes on, "I can't speak for Tata, but I am a simple man, with simple habits. I live simply and eat simple food. I was left a widower when I was thirty-two, and I have never remarried. I have always gone it alone."

"What did you think of Gandhi's business acumen?" I ask.

"He was certainly a Banya," Birla says. "He sent me detailed accounts of everything that he spent or that was spent for him, down to the last paisa, even though I told him he could spend the money I gave him in any way he liked. But he had no business sense in the real meaning of the term. His greatness lay in other fields."

Birla, who seems to have a slight catarrh, clears his throat frequently. At every cough, the director starts, as though expecting a command. Receiving none, he continues to listen with devout attention from behind Birla's chair.

"How much money would you say you contributed to Gandhi's causes over the years?"

Birla bites his lip and picks at the arm of his chair. "I could refuse him nothing—I financed all his spiritual activities in the Sevagram period—but I never kept account of what I sent him. I could probably come up with a rough estimate, but I'd just as soon not."

"Did your connection with Gandhi ever prove useful to you in a business way?"

"Gandhiji was certainly not of any use to me in a business way. He did, however, influence my character. No one could be close to him without being transformed. He knew he had this effect on people. He told me once, as a joke, 'I would not mind living even with Satan, but I don't think Satan would live with me for long.' "

"Did you ever live with him?"

He continues to bite his lip and pick at the arm of his chair. "I once lived in Sevagram Ashram for a whole month. It was an awkward business. Gandhiji had instructed his secretary Mahadev Desai to clean my commode. When I found out, I told Gandhiji that my servant would clean my commode in the ashram, just as he did at home. Gandhiji said he wouldn't countenance this, and I said, 'In that case, I won't stay in your ashram. I certainly won't allow Mahadev Desai to do something I wouldn't do myself, and it would be hypocritical for me to do something in the ashram that I would never do at home.' Ultimately, I won out. The servant did it."

"I get the impression from your book that Gandhi was practically your family doctor."

"He was a great doctor of the nature cure. I used to get lots of colds, and, as with most of our countrymen, my digestion has always been poor. He helped me by supervising my diet, and doing other things like that. But he helped everybody. When Sir Stafford Cripps was in Delhi, he developed some stomach trouble, and Gandhiji even helped him. He used to send Cripps a pot of curds every day."

"Did he ever encourage you to give away any part of your wealth?"

"Gandhiji had no particular animosity toward businessmen. He never tried to persuade them to renounce their wealth, because he believed that businessmen held their wealth in trust for the benefit of all. As the Bhagavad Gita says, every man must do his duty—which means that if you're a wealthy man you must do your duty by your wealth. A businessman's karma is to amass wealth, and his dharma is to provide for the general welfare—always cultivating detachment from his wealth, however."

"But Gandhi did not approve of big industries for India. Your own big, assembly-line factories surely run counter to his ideas of village handicrafts."

"I never agreed with his notions on economics, and he never tried to urge them on me. Gandhiji believed in a medieval economic system. He would say, 'My inner voice tells me such-and-such'—about economics or whatever—but he was hallucinating."

"Do you really think Indians are better off working in your factories than in village industries?"

"I think housing and education are better in the cities, but the factory workers become victims of other evils—alcoholism and worse —yet that's their own fault. People aren't satisfied living in the villages anymore. The simple life might have done for the Middle Ages, but it simply won't do for modern times. People want more and more."

"Are you implying that you are more modern in your outlook than Gandhi was?"

"No, he was more modern than I. When he was a student in England, he learned ballroom dancing and was a regular dandy. He knew the ways of the modern world. But he made a conscious decision to go back to the Middle Ages."

"You wouldn't deny that you and Gandhi are very different in your approaches to the poor. He tried to identify with them."

"His way of identifying with the poor was to wear khadi. And to please him even I sometimes used to put on khadi."

"It wasn't just khadi, was it? I thought he tried to set an example of how one could live simply, do everything with one's own hands. Anyway, how does it feel to be such a rich man in such a poor country?"

"Why should I feel guilty? I live for the poor people. When I ride through the Bombay streets in my car, I see a little vacant lot and I say to myself, 'This is a good site for a school for the poor,' and I am able to build it."

"So what you mean by living for the poor is that you espouse good causes."

"Yes. But, as it happens, I've also renounced all my wealth. For instance, I'm only a guest in this big house; it doesn't belong to me— it belongs to the Mysore Cements, Limited. Whatever wealth I had I've passed on to my sons or to other people. As I told the BBC the other day, I'm not a rich man—I don't even qualify for the supertax."

"Paying taxes is hardly a test of wealth. Plenty of the rich don't. Anyway, you are the managing director of the Birla group of industries."

"I don't know what you mean by the Birla group," he says. "I'm aware of no such animal."

"Do you mean you are denying the existence of the Birla group?"

"It's all shareholders' money, public money. We only manage it for them."

"Would you describe yourself as a capitalist?"

"No. 'Capitalist' to me means someone who keeps a certain

64

amount of capital for himself. I don't do that."

"But 'capitalist' usually means something quite different. It's usually applied to big industrialists who make money from other people's labor."

"All I'm prepared to say is that I am for importing the American capitalist system into India and Indianizing it."

"I remember reading a letter from Gandhi in your book counselling you to go around on foot, so that you could get to know the common people. And yet you are the most inaccessible person in India."

"The difficulty with Gandhiji's counsel is that you can't define who the common people are."

"It's hard to imagine two people more different than you and Gandhi. What drew you to him?"

"I went to him when I was in my twenties. He gave me lots of his time, and afterward, when I wrote to him, he replied immediately. Both of these things were very unusual things for a great man to do, and they made me his devotee for life."

"Do you have any other heroes besides Gandhi?"

"Yes—one. General Dwight D. Eisenhower."

11

In the Steps of
the Autobiographer and
His Biographers

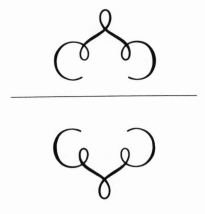

Banya Origins

GANDHI WAS NOT ENDOWED WITH ANY UNUSUAL ARTISTIC, scholarly, or scientific talents. He never earned a degree or received any special academic honors. He was never a candidate in an election or a holder of public office. Yet when he died, in 1948, at the age of seventy-eight, practically the whole world mourned him. Albert Einstein said in his tribute, "Gandhi . . . demonstrated that a powerful human following can be assembled not only through the cunning game of the usual political maneuvers and trickeries but through the cogent example of a morally superior conduct of life." Other tributes compared Gandhi to Socrates, to Buddha, to Jesus, to Saint Francis of Assisi. Gandhi, who once said, "Action is my domain," himself strove to follow their examples, but at the same time he thought of his whole life as just a series of experiments in humility—in the practice of the Hindu law of ahimsa, which teaches reverence for all living things. In his autobiography, entitled "The Story of My Experiments with Truth," he writes:

> To see the universal and all-pervading Spirit of Truth face to face one must be able to love the meanest of creation as oneself. And a man who aspires after that cannot afford to keep out of any field of life. That is why my devotion to Truth has drawn me into the field of politics; and I can say without the slightest hesitation, and yet in all humility, that those who say that religion has nothing to do with politics do not know what religion means.
>
> Identification with everything that lives is impossible without self-purification. . . . To attain to perfect purity one has to become absolutely passion-free in thought, speech, and action; to rise above the opposing currents of love and hatred, attachment and repulsion. . . . To conquer the subtle passions seems to me to be harder far than

the physical conquest of the world by the force of arms. . . . I must reduce myself to zero. So long as a man does not of his own free will put himself last among his fellow creatures, there is no salvation for him. Ahimsa is the farthest limit of humility.

Gandhi was born on October 2, 1869, in the town of Porbandar, in the princely state of Porbandar, in the Political Agency of Kathiawar, in Gujarat, a region in the Presidency of Bombay. He was the third son and fourth child of Karamchand and Putlibai Gandhi. At the time, Karamchand was about forty-seven years old, and Putlibai, who was his fourth wife, was about twenty-five. Everyone remarked on the baby's sweet, cheerful face, lively eyes, and big ears.

Gujarat is in western India, and Kathiawar is a peninsula that juts into the Arabian Sea. The peninsula, because it is connected to the mainland only by a salt plain, which is sometimes underwater, has been isolated from the major events of Indian history. It used to be divided into numerous small, feudal princely states, notorious for palace intrigues and local wars. A princely state was sometimes no more than a village—and in at least one instance it was not much more than a well. The British left the princely states, in Kathiawar and elsewhere, more or less intact, even after the Mutiny of 1857 was suppressed and direct British sovereignty established in India. In fact, they created many new ones, which they felt would act as buffers against any further general uprisings like the Mutiny, and, in addition, would lend pomp and circumstance to the British raj. In the late years of the nineteenth century, all the princely states became, if anything, more deeply entrenched in their feudal ways, and, for the most part, remained untouched by such benefits of the British raj as macadamized roads, railway tracks, a uniform legal system, and a centralized administration. But their princes ruled only at the pleasure of the British. They owed allegiance to the British Crown, and were called to account by its local agents. One agent often had authority over many princely states; and on the Kathiawar peninsula an agent exercised authority over some two hundred princely states, grouped together in what was called the Kathiawar Political Agency. The life of the Gandhis centered on three of these princely states—Junagadh, Rajkot, and, of course, Porbandar. The three were adjacent, forming a sort of rough triangle; the capital of each princely state was a town of the same name; and none of the towns was much more than a hundred miles from either of the others. Nor was there much to distinguish the three states. Each had its Hindu rana or Muslim nawab—the prince—who, in turn, had his dewan, or prime minister. The dewan was a sort of majordomo, who helped his prince administer affairs of state and deal with the British political agent. The inhabitants of the Kathiawar Political Agency were mostly Hindus and Muslims, and, as Gujaratis, were known for tenacious, frugal, and hardworking ways.

In the census of 1872, the state of Porbandar had a population of seventy-two thousand and the town of Porbandar a population of fifteen thousand. The town stood on the coast, with the wooded Barda Hills in the background, and was surrounded by high, thick walls. When the tide was in, the sea swept right up to the walls. The houses were all built of soft white limestone, which gave the town the nick-name of the White City. There were scarcely any trees or other green-ery on the streets, but nearly all the Hindu inhabitants kept pots or tubs of the tulsi, or basil, plant in their homes and temples. They prayed in front of the plants, and wore strings of the seeds around their necks and arms as good-luck charms. The Hindus rarely ventured to put out to sea, because any Hindu who crosses the "black waters" loses his caste. Instead, working in their homes, they made silks and cottons, which their Muslim neighbors loaded onto ships and traded in Aden, Zanzi-bar, Cape Town, and other ports of Arabia and Africa.

Little is known of Gandhi's ancestors before the nineteenth cen-tury. According to legend, he may have been descended from a man called Lal who lived in the village of Kutiyana, in the state of Junagadh, in the seventeenth century. Lal had a son Ram, who had a son Rahidas, who may have been the father of Harjivan, Gandhi's great-grandfather and the earliest ancestor of whom we have a record—though no dates. (Actually, most facts relating to Gandhi's ancestry—indeed, to Gan-dhi's own early years—are in doubt; many of them are gathered from his autobiography, which was written when he was nearly sixty years old.) It seems that Harjivan bought a house in the town of Porbandar and set himself up as a tradesman—probably a grocer—sometime late in the eighteenth century. Harjivan had a son Uttamchand. We don't know when he was born, but we do know that he somehow managed to become dewan to the rana of Porbandar, whose name was Khimoji.

Khimoji died in 1831, when his son and heir, Vikmatji, was only eight years old. Uttamchand soon fell out with the queen regent, Vikmatji's mother, known as Rupali Ba, by taking the opposite side in a domestic dispute involving her maids. Rupali Ba had Uttamchand's house—the house that Harjivan had bought—surrounded by palace guards, who fired a number of shots at it from a cannon, the biggest gun in Porbandar. Uttamchand somehow escaped to the state of Junagadh, where he established himself in Kutiyana as a grocer. When he went to pay his respects to the nawab, he saluted the prince with his left hand, which Hindus use only for unclean activity. He excused himself by saying, "The right hand is already pledged to Porbandar." The nawab meted out a token punishment to Uttamchand for his insolence—he was made to stand in the sun barefoot for ten minutes—but rewarded him for his loyalty, even though it was to another state, by exempting him from the customs duties levied on nonresident merchants. In 1841, Rupali Ba died, and Vikmatji succeeded to the throne of Porbandar. He invited Uttamchand to return, which he did, and to become the dewan, which he didn't. Instead, Uttamchand recommended the fifth, and most gifted, of his six sons, Karamchand, for the post, and in 1847, at the age of twenty-five, Karamchand became dewan of Porbandar—an office he held for some twenty-eight years.

Karamchand married for the first time when he was about fourteen, and for the second time when he was about twenty-five. He had two daughters by the first two wives, but both wives died without bearing any sons, and nothing is known about either of the daughters. There is no record of when he married for the third time, but it is believed that that marriage was childless and that he got permission from his third wife—as a matter of courtesy—to marry again while he was still married to her. (It was not unusual for a man who could afford it to have two or more wives at a time, especially if one wife after another failed to bear a son—for the principal function of an Indian woman was to produce breadwinning sons.) In any event, in about 1860, when he was over forty, he married Putlibai, who was then just in her teens. She bore him four children: a daughter, Raliat, in 1862; a son, Lakshmidas, in 1863; a second son, Karsandas, in 1867; and a third son, Mohandas Karamchand Gandhi (Gandhi's full name), in 1869. We don't know exactly when or how Karamchand started using the surname Gandhi—or, for that matter, when Gandhi himself started using his father's name as a middle name. On rare occasions when Indians were away from home—say, on a pilgrimage—they might identify themselves by mentioning the names of their fathers, their villages, their towns, or, most often, their castes or subcastes, but, by and large, until the time of the British raj Indians did not use surnames. The British, however, decided that a second name was necessary, for their modern system of record-keeping, so the Indians themselves—especially those connected in some way with British officialdom—began to use surnames. This was probably how Karamchand became Karamchand Gandhi. The Gandhis belong to the subcaste of grocers—*gandhi* is actually a Gujarati word for "grocer"—and grocers belong to a larger subcaste of shopkeepers and moneylenders, called Banyas. The Banyas belong to the Vaisya caste of farmers and traders, which is the third of the four castes into which Hindu society, with innumerable local minor variations, is irrevocably divided—the Brahman caste, of priests and scholars, being the first, the Kshatriya caste, of warriors and nobles, the second, and the Sudra caste, of manual laborers, the fourth. (The untouchables are casteless.) Each caste and subcaste is so closely identified with its own hereditary occupation and function that, for example, Banya is in India a term of opprobrium for a shrewd, grasping merchant.

Karamchand, Putlibai, and their children lived in the old family house in Porbandar, which had expanded in the three generations since Harjivan's time from a modest one-story affair to a three-story structure. The house was wedged between two temples. It had thick stone outer walls, which concealed a honeycomb of dark, mean rooms built around a small courtyard, their dinginess accentuated by the flickering light of kerosene-burning mud lamps. Karamchand and his family occupied two ground-floor rooms opening onto a veranda, and the rest of the house was given over to Karamchand's five brothers and their wives and children. Although they all had their own kitchens, they pooled their incomes to meet expenses, in the traditional manner of the Hindu "joint family."

Karamchand was a stocky, broad-shouldered man. In old photographs he is shown wearing pajama trousers, a shawl, soft leather slippers, and a full turban in the Kathiawari style, and has a gold chain around his neck. He was brought up as a Vaishnavi—a member of one of the principal Hindu sects. Vaishnavis worship Vishnu, or his incarnation Krishna, the voluptuary deity who is often portrayed as a cowherd playing the flute and making merry with milkmaids. Karamchand had only three or four years of schooling, and could read and write only Gujarati. Though he was naturally tactful, he seems to have had some difficulty in kowtowing to the British. Pyarelal reports in "The Early Phase" that Gandhi once told him, "Our household was turned upside down when my father had to attend the Durbar during a Governor's visit. . . . If I [were] a painter, I could paint my father's disgust and the torture on his face as he was putting his legs into his stockings and feet into ill-fitting and uncomfortable boots."

Putlibai was born in the village of Datrana, in the state of Junagadh. She was brought up as a Pranami—a member of a local ascetic, orthodox offshoot of the Vaishnava sect, which was, however, strongly influenced by Islam in that it emphasized direct communion with God. Putlibai was a simple woman who never learned to read or write. She was small and frail, with buckteeth and a sweet expression, and she smiled often. She had a graceful walk. She usually wore a coarse cotton sari and a Kathiawari-style blouse, which barely covered her midriff and was open at the back. She wore little jewelry by Indian standards—a gold nose ring, heavy silver anklets, ivory bangles, and a necklace of tulsi beads. On special occasions, she would don gold-plated bracelets. She liked to spin. Although she had no particular religious training, she devoutly followed the religious vows and fasts prescribed for self-discipline and self-purification. She took no pleasure in eating. One of Gandhi's more fanciful biographers, Ranjee Shahani, describes how she felt about food: "It was a pity that one could not dispense with it altogether, for, she reflected, and once or twice confided to a friend, its end was terrible. It entered the mouth fresh and fragrant, and left the body as waste. As a result of this attitude, she developed chronic constipation." During the four months of the monsoon season, she would fast, as her religion dictated, often for two or three days at a time, not breaking the fast until she had seen the sun. "We children on those days would stand, staring at the sky, waiting to announce the appearance of the sun to our mother," Gandhi writes. "I remember days when, at his [the sun's] sudden appearance, we would rush and announce it to her. She would run out to see with her own eyes, but by that time the fugitive sun would be gone, thus depriving her of her meal. 'That does not matter,' she would say cheerfully. 'God did not want me to eat today.'"

Kathiawari Boy

UNTIL GANDHI—OR MONIYA, OR MOHAN, AS HE WAS VARIOUSLY called as a boy—was seven, he lived in the family house in Porbandar, and he probably attended the local Dhooli Shala, or Dust School, so called because in such schools the schoolmaster taught the children to read and write by drawing letters with a stick on the dusty floor. Some of what we know about Gandhi at this time is based on a few perhaps apocryphal stories, the details of which vary from one telling to another. It is said that he once climbed a guava tree in the family courtyard and meticulously wound a piece of cloth around each fruit. When his father asked him what he was doing, he said that he was protecting the guavas from the preying birds. Another story has it that one summer Raliat took him on a day's outing to the Festival of the Full Moon. He gave her the slip and attached himself to a group of young girls dancing in the streets with flowers in their hair. He spent the day in their company, and arrived home in the evening with a sore throat and a stomach ache. A doctor was called to diagnose the trouble, and discovered that Gandhi had spent the day eating flowers that fell from the girls' hair. His father immediately hired a nursemaid for him, who was given strict orders never to let him out of her sight. One afternoon, Gandhi nevertheless succeeded in slipping away from her, and stole into a temple with some of his cousins while the priest was napping. They removed bronze statues of gods and goddesses from the sanctuary and tried to make off with them. They wanted real gods and goddesses to play with, for a change from the mud versions they usually played with. As they were running out of the temple, a couple of the statues banged together. The ringing clang aroused the priest, who gave chase. The plunderers dropped the booty and got home without being caught;

however, the priest reported them to one of Gandhi's uncles, who was a harsh disciplinarian, and he confronted them with their misdeed. They all denied it except Gandhi, who not only confessed but also pointed out the cousin who had put them up to it. Another time, it is said, Gandhi went into the prayer room at home, took a statue of a god off its pedestal, and climbed up in its place.

In 1876, Gandhi's father was appointed dewan to the rana of Rajkot, and he moved, with his wife and children, about a hundred and twenty miles northeast, to the town of Rajkot—a five-day trek from Porbandar in bullock carts over dirt roads. Rajkot was a gloomy contrast to the White City. It was inland, and was less outward-looking in every sense. It was, however, the headquarters of the Political Agency of Kathiawar, and therefore the dewan of Rajkot had slightly more standing than the dewan of Porbandar. Rajkot had grown up in the manner of other Indian towns where the British maintained a token establishment. There was the native city, consisting of crowded, dirty slums with high, squalid tenements topped by peaked tile roofs; and the British section, consisting of clean, low, spacious bungalows with flat roofs, each set in its own well-tended compound. The Gandhis moved into a tenement on the outskirts of the native city.

In Rajkot, Gandhi and his brothers attended first a local primary school, which was probably not very different from the Dhooli Shala, and then Alfred High School, the only secondary school in the area, which prepared its students for college. Gandhi was an indifferent student and found schoolwork hard—especially in upper high school, because there all subjects were taught in English, which he had trouble learning. At one point, he took up Sanskrit, but that proved difficult, too. He was tempted to drop it and one day sat in on the Persian class, which was supposed to be easier. Gandhi later recalled that the Sanskrit teacher stopped him afterward and asked, "How can you forget that you are the son of a Vaishnavi father? Won't you learn the language of your own religion?" Gandhi didn't like his father's praying, or his mother's fasting and temple-going, but still, for some reason, he went back to his struggle with Sanskrit. He was a puny boy, and was self-conscious about his frail constitution. He was forced to do gymnastics and play cricket, but he had no aptitude for either. He preferred going on solitary walks or playing a simple Indian street game called *gulli-danda,* which required only a wooden peg and a stick to hit it with.

One day, a British education inspector came to Alfred High School. He asked the boys in Gandhi's class to write down five English words, then went around the class checking their spelling. No one made a mistake except Gandhi, who misspelled "kettle." (We don't know how he spelled it.) The schoolmaster tried surreptitiously to get Gandhi to copy the correct spelling from his neighbor's slate, so that the inspector would give the class a perfect score. Gandhi wouldn't do it. The schoolmaster later chided him for stupidity, but Gandhi felt sure he had done the right thing.

At home, Gandhi and a cousin would watch one of their uncles smoke cigarettes. The uncle would puff out smoke through his nostrils and blow smoke rings. The two boys secretly tried smoking the stubs of his cigarettes but could not get many puffs out of them. They also tried smoking cheap cigarettes, which they bought with coppers stolen from the servants, but didn't know where to hide them. Then they tried the stems of a local weed that was reputed to be smokable, but found them hard to keep lighted. They despaired of ever becoming grown-ups, and decided that death was preferable to remaining children. They made a suicide pact, and foraged in the woods for belladonna seeds, which they had heard were poisonous. When they found some, they went to the temple to carry out their pact. But their courage failed them. "I realized that it was not as easy to commit suicide as to contemplate it," Gandhi writes. "And since then, whenever I have heard of someone threatening to commit suicide, it has had little or no effect on me."

When Gandhi was about twelve, he was considered old enough to marry, and his father made the arrangements. His bride, Kasturbai Makanji, was the daughter of a Banya merchant of Porbandar. She was a pretty, strong-willed girl with an oval face, large, widely spaced dark eyes, a sensuous mouth, and a firm chin. She and Gandhi were the same age and had probably played together as children. They had been betrothed since they were seven. Gandhi had earlier been betrothed, successively, to two other girls, both of whom had died. Child betrothals and child marriages were the rule in India, but there was a special urgency in Gandhi's case. His father was about sixty—an age that few Indians achieved—and he wanted all his sons married before he retired or died. Lakshmidas had already married, and it was now the turn of Karsandas and Mohandas. The father arranged a joint wedding not only for them but also for a nephew, who lived in Porbandar. He took his two sons out of school several months ahead of the event and sent them, with their mother, to Porbandar, where the wedding would take place. Preparations were made for a week of festivities.

Just before the wedding, Gandhi's father set out from Rajkot and, using relays of bullock carts and horse-drawn carriages, made the journey to Porbandar in the remarkably short time of three days. When he was almost there, however, his carriage overturned, and he was severely injured. (He had to spend the remaining three years of his life in bed.) But he refused to countenance a delay in the festivities and insisted on discharging his duties as a father from his sickbed.

What with the hymns and prayers, the feasts and processions, the pledges and presents, and, above all, the anticipation of having "a strange girl to play with," Gandhi forgot about his father's accident. At the culmination of the festivities, Gandhi went to the Makanjis' house. There he and Kasturbai sat on a dais and prayed. They then took the traditional seven steps around a sacred fire, reciting the Hindu marriage vows:

"Take one step, that we may have strength of will," Gandhi said.

"In every worthy wish of yours, I shall be your helpmate," Kasturbai said.

"Take the second step, that we may be filled with vigor."

"In every worthy wish of yours, I shall be your helpmate."

"Take the third step, that we may live in ever-increasing prosperity."

"Your joys and sorrows I will share."

"Take the fourth step, that we may be ever full of joy."

"I will ever live devoted to you, speaking words of love and praying for your happiness."

"Take the fifth step, that we may serve the people."

"I will follow close behind you always and help you to keep your vow of serving the people."

"Take the sixth step, that we may follow our religious vows in life."

"I will follow you in observing our religious vows and duties."

"Take the seventh step, that we may ever live as friends."

"It is the fruit of my good deeds that I have you as my husband.

You are my best friend, my highest guru, and my sovereign lord."

Gandhi put a sweetened wheat cake in Kasturbai's mouth, Kasturbai put a sweetened wheat cake in Gandhi's mouth, and they were pronounced husband and wife. It was 1882.

The pernicious effects of child marriages were often mitigated by having the bride return to her family house after a symbolic visit to the groom's family house; then it was only after a year or so, when the bride went to live with her husband, that the marriage was consummated. This was not the case with Gandhi and Kasturbai. After some initial nervousness, their marriage was consummated on their wedding night. Gandhi writes that Lakshmidas' wife coached him before the wedding on how to conduct himself in the conjugal bed, but that he already knew instinctively what to do, from his experiences in previous incarnations.

Gandhi seems to have been a jealous and imperious young husband. Although Kasturbai gave him no cause for suspicion, he lectured her on the virtues of fidelity and submission. He forbade her to go anywhere, even to the temple, without first obtaining his leave. He tried to instruct her in reading and writing, for she could do neither. But the more he tried to order her around, the more she resisted him, and the crosser he became. "Refusal to speak to one another thus became the order of the day with us, married children," he writes.

Gandhi had always been afraid of snakes, thieves, and ghosts—creatures that came out at night—and even after his marriage he would not sleep without a lamp burning at his bedside. When he finally returned to school after the wedding (he had missed almost a year), he became fast friends with Sheikh Mehtab, who boasted, in Gandhi's words, that "he could hold in his hand live serpents, could defy thieves, and did not believe in ghosts." Mehtab was a couple of years older than Gandhi and had originally been Karsandas's friend. He lived across the street from the Gandhis, and had a reputation in the neighborhood as something of a wastrel. He prided himself on his physical prowess on the sports field and in the brothels of Rajkot. Gandhi's mother had not considered Mehtab fit company for Karsandas, and both she and Kasturbai warned Gandhi against falling under Mehtab's bad influence. But Gandhi found Mehtab irresistible. One day, Mehtab made an appointment for Gandhi in a brothel. He paid in advance, arranged for a room, and told Gandhi that all he had to do was to amuse himself. Gandhi went in and sat down next to the woman on the bed. He couldn't do or say anything. The woman abused him roundly and pushed him out of the room. "I . . . felt as though my manhood had been injured, and wished to sink into the ground for shame," he writes.

At school, Gandhi had often heard his fellow-students recite this doggerel:

> Behold the mighty Englishman.
> He rules the Indian small,
> Because, being a meat eater,
> He is five cubits tall.

Mehtab was a Muslim, and therefore he, too, was a meat eater. Gandhi, an orthodox Hindu, was a vegetarian. Mehtab told Gandhi that he had induced Karsandas to eat meat secretly many times; that many of their schoolteachers and fellow-students ate meat; that they were stronger and hardier because of it; and that if, like them, all Indians ate meat, they would be rid of the enfeebling boils from which they suffered, and would also be able to throw out the Englishmen who ruled them. At length, Mehtab took Gandhi to a lonely spot on the outskirts of Rajkot, on the bank of the River Aji. He had brought along with him some goat's meat and a loaf of bakery bread—the leavened kind that Englishmen ate. Mehtab gave Gandhi a slice of bread and meat. The meat was as tough as leather, but Gandhi persevered with it, and it made him sick. That night, he got little rest. "A horrible nightmare haunted me," he writes. "Every time I dropped off to sleep, it would seem as though a live goat were bleating inside me, and I would jump up full of remorse." In the Gandhi household, eating meat not only was forbidden but was also considered tantamount to eating human flesh, because of the strength among Kathiawari Hindus of Jainism, which had started out as a heretical reform movement against sacerdotal Hinduism in the fifth and sixth centuries B.C. but over the succeeding centuries had become more rigid and conservative than Hinduism. Jains believe, for instance, that not only men and animals but also insects, plants, earth, fire, water, and wind—every particle and every atom—have souls. In order to attain nirvana, a Jain must take care as best he humanly can not to injure any living creature; a man who believes he can be reincarnated as a goat or an insect must try to abstain from killing anything. Jain priests therefore wear white masks over their mouths to avoid breathing in insects, and do not go out in the dark for fear of stepping on insects. Some do not clean their teeth or wash their clothes for fear of destroying germs; others, still more austere, do not wear clothes. All Jain priests are very fastidious about where they eat, since a non-Jain household may be contaminated by meat, but Jain priests freely accepted food at the Gandhi house, because Vaishnavi Gujaratis were famous for their Jainlike horror of meat eating. Moreover, it was well known that Gandhi's mother would not allow insects to be killed in her home.

Still, Rajkot, in part because of the introduction of formal schooling, was opening up to new ideas, and Gandhi, under Mehtab's tutelage, eventually learned to enjoy eating meat. For about a year after first tasting meat at the River Aji, Gandhi would meet Mehtab and his meat-eating friends in the Rajkot State House, the local assembly rooms. They would order elaborate dishes in which the meat was disguised and made more palatable with familiar delicacies, and would eat them with their fingers, but sitting in chairs at tables, like Englishmen. When Gandhi got home after such feasts, he would have to dissimulate to his ingenuous parents. "My mother would naturally ask me to come and take my food," he writes, "and want to know the reason why I did not wish to eat. I would say to her, 'I have no appetite today; there is something wrong with my digestion.'" He knew how shocked she would be if she knew she harbored a meat eater. His guilt at the deception in time got the better of him, and he decided that out of respect for his parents he would postpone meat eating until they were dead and he was free to do what he liked.

Karsandas, however, continued to eat meat at Mehtab's feasts, and, as a result, ran up a twenty-five-rupee debt. He and Gandhi conspired to settle the debt by clipping a piece from a gold armlet that Karsandas wore. When their parents noticed that a piece was missing, both boys pretended that they knew nothing about it, and suggested that it must have been stolen in the night. But then Gandhi repented and decided to confess to the theft. He wrote out his confession and, trembling, handed it to his father. "He read it through," Gandhi writes, "and

pearl-drops trickled down his cheeks, wetting the paper. For a moment
he closed his eyes in thought and then tore up the note. . . . I also cried."

Gandhi's father, after his accident, had tried to carry on as dewan of
Rajkot from his bed, first in Porbandar and then back in Rajkot, but
after a year or so his deteriorating health forced him to resign his office.
He developed a fistula, and a local English surgeon advised an operation, but the sick man refused to have anything to do with such a
modern procedure. He became more and more helpless. He had to be
helped to the lavatory, and bathed and fed in bed. He became preoccupied with religion—and not just his own. From morning to night,
many priests—Vaishnavi, Jain, Muslim, Parsi—would sit by his bed,
and he would read their scriptures with them and discuss religion. A
friend named Ladha would chant the sixteenth-century version of the
Ramayana, composed by the Hindu poet Tulsi Das (1532–1623),
which, according to Sir Charles James Lyall, a Victorian student of
India, was perhaps better known at that time among the Hindus of
northern India than the Bible was among the rustic inhabitants of
England. It was said that Ladha had cured himself of leprosy by constantly reciting the Ramanama, or the name of Rama, the epic's hero.

By day, Gandhi often looked after his father and washed his feet,
and in the evening, while the priests chanted hymns and prayers, he
kneaded and massaged his father's feet and legs until the sick man
dropped off to sleep. It was Gandhi's religious duty as a Hindu to tend
his father in this manner. But he was also a young husband, impatient
for his wife's bed. One night, when he had just turned sixteen, he left
his father's side to make love to Kasturbai, who was pregnant with their
first child; then a servant knocked at the door and announced that his
father was dead. Gandhi seems never to have forgotten what he called
his "double shame"—leaving his father when he knew that his father
might die at any moment, and making love to his wife when he knew
that Hinduism forbade intercourse with a pregnant woman. The baby
died soon after it was born, and he felt that he was justly punished.

Rajkot Student in England

LATE IN 1887, WHEN GANDHI WAS SEVENTEEN, HE WENT BY train—a railway now connected Kathiawar with the outside world—to Ahmedabad, the capital of the province. There he sat for his matriculation examination, which was a prerequisite for admission to a college or university. He did poorly in all subjects, but his aggregate score, two hundred and forty-seven and a half points out of six hundred and twenty-five, was just enough to get him through. In January of 1888, therefore, he was able to enter a small, new, inexpensive college called Samaldas, in the town of Bhavnagar, in the princely state of Bhavnagar, which was near Rajkot. For the first time, he was living away from home—on his own, in a lodging, without even his wife. He didn't like college—his English was still very weak, and he did badly in his studies—and he was homesick. He began having headaches and frequent nosebleeds. In the spring of 1888, he went home to Rajkot. He never returned to Samaldas College; instead, he decided to go to England.

A Brahman lawyer named Mavji Dave, who was an old friend of his father's and a frequent visitor to the Gandhi home, told Gandhi's mother that British values were making such inroads into the life of the country that in the future formal qualifications would be required for all posts—that Gandhi could not hope to become a dewan, for instance, merely by the exercise of shrewdness, tact, and native intelligence, as his father and grandfather had done. Mavji Dave therefore counselled Gandhi to go to England and become a barrister-at-law—a title reserved for those who studied law in England. He said that his own son Kevalram had just returned from England as a barrister and was making a good living.

Gandhi was soon lost in what he describes as "madcap thoughts of

London." During his father's illness, he had considered becoming a doctor, but he knew how horrified his parents would be at the mere prospect of their son's cutting up cadavers, and so had rejected the idea. He knew that if he tried to become a lawyer in India he would first have to study for several years and pass difficult examinations in order to obtain a B.A. degree, and that would mean returning to Samaldas College. If, however, he went to England to become a barrister, he would not need a degree at all and could forget about Samaldas. So he went to talk to Kevalram, who warned him that he would need a lot of money, and that unless he was prepared to set aside his Kathiawari superstitions and his religion there was no point in his going to England. Gandhi said that he could probably get a government scholarship, since the family had claims on the governments of both Porbandar and Rajkot. But Kevalram seems to have been skeptical about whether Gandhi was cut out for England.

Undeterred, Gandhi went to Porbandar, where he made an appointment with F. S. P. Lely, the local British administrator, in the hope of presenting his family claims for a scholarship. Lely, however, didn't even let Gandhi inside his door. He dismissed him with a curt "Pass your B.A. first and then see me. No help can be given you now." It was Gandhi's first encounter with an Englishman. "I had made elaborate preparations to meet him," he writes. "I had carefully learnt up a few sentences and had bowed low and saluted him with both hands. But all to no purpose!" Gandhi never succeeded in getting a scholarship, but Lakshmidas apparently found the money to send Gandhi to England.

Gandhi next had to spend three days pleading with his Uncle Tulsidas, who, as his father's oldest surviving brother, was the head of the family, for permission to go to England. The uncle seems to have equivocated, saying, on the one hand, that he could not give his approval, because Gandhi would lose his caste and religion if he crossed the "black waters" and lived among heathen, and, on the other hand, that he would not stand in the way if Gandhi could get permission from his mother. His mother had always been opposed to the idea. She had heard that the heathen in England could not live without eating meat, drinking liquor, and going with women. But Gandhi made a vow to her in the presence of Becharji Swami, a Jain monk, that in England he would not go near meat, liquor, or women. In the end, his mother reluctantly gave her consent, and put a string of tulsi beads around his neck. (He wore the string for many years, and gave it up only when it broke.)

Gandhi bade farewell to the family—to a tearful Kasturbai, who had just given birth to a second child, a son, named Harilal—and set off for Bombay. There he was confronted with another hurdle. He was summoned before his Banya caste elders and given notice that if he persisted in going to England they would formally pronounce him to be a man without caste. He protested, citing his vow to his mother, and charging them with ignorance of conditions in England and—for reasons he doesn't explain—with malice toward him. The elders remained unmoved, and, since Gandhi would not heed them, pronounced him an outcaste.

In October of 1888, just after Gandhi turned nineteen, he disembarked from the S.S. Clyde at Southampton. A photograph taken about that time shows him to have thick hair parted slightly to the right of center, a big, pointed nose, full lips, and rather apprehensive eyes. Having got it into his head that English gentlemen in England always wore white, he had donned a white flannel suit, which friends had bought him in Bombay. But the Englishmen he now saw were almost all wearing dark colors.

During the voyage, Gandhi had successfully resisted adapting himself to new ways. He had at first scarcely stirred out of his cabin. Since he didn't know how to use a knife and fork, he had feared embarrassment if he took his meals in the public dining room, and had eaten in the privacy of his cabin, with his fingers, what little food he had brought along for the voyage. Later, when he did venture out, he and another Indian had arranged to have vegetarian meals cooked and served to them separately. But meat evangelists on the ship had made him fear that once he reached England he would have to eat meat in order to survive in the cold climate.

In London, he was taken in hand by some Indian acquaintances to whom he had introductions, and spent his first few days at the Victoria Hotel, a large, ornate, expensive establishment with lifts and liveried servants, on Northumberland Avenue, near Charing Cross. Afterward, he found digs first in Richmond and then in West Kensington. He shed his white flannel suit in favor of a black evening suit, which he bought in a shop on Bond Street. He bought a silk chimney-pot hat to go with it, and wrote home for a gold watch chain. He started spending ten minutes a day in front of the mirror combing and brushing his hair. He enrolled in a ballroom-dancing class and went to it twice a week, but he had trouble keeping in step with the music, and gave up after three weeks in order to learn something about Western music. He bought a violin and started taking private lessons, but he soon decided he could learn the violin just as well in India—anyway, he had no ear for music —so he gave that up and sold the violin. He cultivated the English habit of reading newspapers, looking every day at the *Daily News,* the *Daily Telegraph,* and the *Pall Mall Gazette,* and started taking elocution lessons to improve his diction. He struggled with Alexander Melville Bell's "Standard Elocutionist," beginning his study with a speech of William Pitt, Prime Minister of England at the time of the French Revolution. But he soon dropped that, too.

Gandhi's landlady in West Kensington was a widow with two daughters, and he ate all his meals with them. For breakfast he ate porridge; for lunch and dinner he had boiled vegetables and slices of bread (the kind he had first tasted with Mehtab) spread with jam. Occasionally, he even ate out with the family in a restaurant. Restaurants, like hotels, were practically unknown in Kathiawar. But he missed the spices and condiments of Indian cooking. Moreover, he found he was living beyond his means—he kept account of every farthing he spent—and so, after some time, he decided to move into less expensive digs where he could cook for himself. For the rest of his stay in England, he lived in various rooms, first in Holborn and then in Bayswater.

In his first few months in England, Gandhi neglected his studies; he got himself admitted to one of the Inns of Court—the Inner Temple—but did little else. After the move from West Kensington, however, he started giving them somewhat more thought. Studies at the Inns of Court at that time were mostly *pro forma.* A student had to exert himself only to read a handful of standard works and, at the end of three years, pass two simple examinations—one in common law and the other in Roman law. The examinations were so easy that practically no one failed. In addition, a student had to pay fees and "keep terms." To keep terms meant to have dinner six times a term at his inn. He didn't have to eat anything—just appear at the appointed time, dressed for dinner, and sit at table for an hour or so. He had to keep twelve terms altogether; there were four terms a year. After he had passed the examinations and kept his terms, he affirmed that he would uphold the gentlemanly code of the profession, and was called to the bar.

Gandhi decided that before he got down to the lawbooks he should strengthen his command of English and also study Latin, a smattering of which was necessary for the study of Roman law. He explored the possibility of getting formal instruction at Oxford or Cambridge— something he could easily combine with keeping terms at his inn—but that required more time and expense than he could afford. He therefore settled on a London University matriculation—a much more rigorous examination than the Ahmedabad one—and on a cram tutorial school to help him prepare for that. In January of 1890, he sat for the matriculation, writing three examination papers—one in Latin, one in French, and one in chemistry. He failed, and had to take the examination over again in June. The second time, he replaced chemistry with "heat and light," which he found easier, and passed.

"At first, Gandhi had thought he could become an 'Englishman,'" explains the late Louis Fischer, who has written perhaps the best general biography of Gandhi. "Hence the fervor with which he seized the instruments of conversion: clothes, dancing, elocution lessons, etc. Then he realized how high the barrier was. He understood he would remain Indian. Therefore he became more Indian." As a result of his friendship with Mehtab, Gandhi believed that it was all right for Indians to eat meat, and after the feasts in the Rajkot State House he had acquired a taste for it. But in London, as on board the S.S. Clyde, he persisted in keeping his vow and avoiding meat in any form, to the irritation of practically everyone, Indian or English, whom he came to know.

One evening, after Gandhi had been in England for several months, he was taken to dinner at the Holborn Restaurant by Dalpatram Shukla, a fellow-Kathiawari, who was also in England to study law. He had helped Gandhi find rooms in Richmond, and they had become good friends. But Shukla had been in England longer than Gandhi and had adopted some of the ways of an English gentleman. Now they sat across from each other at a small table in the middle of the restaurant, which was crowded with diners. A waiter served them soup. Gandhi hesitated, and then tried to get the waiter back. Shukla impatiently asked what the trouble was. Gandhi reluctantly confessed that he wanted to know if there was any meat in the soup. Friends had often argued with Gandhi about the necessity of eating meat in England, saying that a vow to an illiterate mother ignorant of English conditions could not be binding. One of them had read passages from Jeremy Bentham to Gandhi and had urged on him the utilitarian morality. Gandhi had not needed intellectual persuading, yet he had remained true to his vow. Shukla now told him angrily that he was not fit to eat in good restaurants, and that he'd better go and eat elsewhere and wait for him outside—they were going to the theatre. Gandhi cheerfully obeyed but the vegetarian restaurant nearby was closed and he had to go to the theatre hungry.

Gandhi spent many days walking the streets of London in search of a good vegetarian restaurant, and eventually came upon the Central Restaurant, on Farringdon Street, which was perhaps the city's best vegetarian restaurant, and there he had his first good meal since leaving home. The Central became his regular eating place, his club, his bookshop; through it he discovered the English —indeed, the worldwide—vegetarian movement, of whose existence he had had no idea. He was able to buy there and read Henry Salt's "A Plea for Vegetarianism," and was introduced to Howard Williams' "The Ethics of Diet" and Anna Kingsford's "The Perfect Way in Diet." He also met both Salt and Williams there (Anna Kingsford had just died), and other leaders of the movement as well, including Josiah Oldfield, a barrister and physician, who prescribed vegetarian and fruitarian diets and nature cures for diseases, and Dr. T. A. Allinson, another physician, of like mind. Here were people who, together with such poets and thinkers as Shelley, Thoreau, and Ruskin, believed that vegetarianism, far from being the enfeebling diet of Indians, was the only humane and morally defensible diet for everyone; that vegetarianism was in spiritual harmony with the rest of nature, because it insured that man didn't have to kill to eat; that the vegetarian diet was the health-iest, because it was free of the diseases transmitted through meat; that it was the most economical, because vegetables, grains, fruits, and nuts cost much less to produce than meat; that it made the most efficient use of land, because cultivable land that was used to grow vegetables and fruit could support more people than the same land used to raise cattle for meat; that it strengthened the national character, because a large farming population made for stability and prosperity; that it was a moral force, because it fostered humanitarian and nonviolent values. To prop-agate the vegetarian way of life, vegetarians had formed vegetarian societies in, among other countries, England, the United States, and Australia.

Gandhi moved in with Josiah Oldfield, in Bayswater, and founded the West London Food Reforms Society. Oldfield became its president, and the poet Sir Edwin Arnold its vice-president. Gandhi and other members went from house to house preaching vegetarianism and peace, and showing people how to prepare good vegetarian meals. Gandhi also became a figure in the London Vegetarian Society. He was made a member of its executive committee, and wrote both for its weekly, *The Vegetarian,* and for a sister publication, a Manchester jour-nal called *The Vegetarian Messenger.*

One of Gandhi's earliest attempts at public speaking was in the executive committee of the London Vegetarian Society, when he defended Dr. Allinson, who was also a member of the committee, against expulsion from the society. Mr. A. F. Hills, the proprietor of the Thames Iron Works and the society's president and benefac-tor, wanted Dr. Allinson expelled for advocating artificial methods of birth control. Hills believed that such methods not only violated the moral objectives of the society but also cut at the roots of all morality. Dr. Allinson, a Malthusian, believed that such methods were essential for controlling the increase in the numbers of the poor. Gandhi, like Hills, believed that Dr. Allinson's views were dangerous and should be publicly opposed, but, unlike Hills, he be-lieved that the objective of the society was merely to promote vegetarianism, not to advocate a system of morality, and that Dr. Allinson should therefore not be expelled. Gandhi was too nervous and tongue-tied to deliver his speech in the committee, but he had written it out, and someone else read it for him. Dr. Allinson was not expelled, and it seems that Gandhi's efforts were at least in part responsible for this outcome.

Vegetarians were by no means united on exactly what a vegetarian diet should consist of. Some, the moderates, merely avoided meat; others, more strict, would not eat fish, either; and still others, the strictest, also refused to eat eggs or drink milk, because they were animal products. Gandhi set about experimenting with his diet in order to find out for himself what the cheapest and most nourishing basic foods for a vegetarian were. At one time or another, he gave up tea, coffee, sweets, and condiments, on the ground that they were unnecessary stimulants. For a while, he made do with plain porridge and cocoa in the mornings, a mainly vegetable lunch, and bread and cocoa in the evenings. In this way, he succeeded in cutting his daily food bill almost in half, to one shilling and threepence. Once, he tried living on just milk, cheese, and eggs. Then he renounced eggs. Another time, he tried subsisting on only bread and fruit. Then he gave up bread, because he thought that starch was not essential, and ate only fruit, so becoming a fruitarian. He seems, however, never to have settled for long on any particular variation of the vegetarian diet.

Gandhi found it at least as easy to keep his vow against liquor as to keep his vow against meat. But keeping his vow against women was more difficult. He once went for a short vacation on the Isle of Wight. As was then the custom, the daughter of the boarding house in which he stayed took him for a walk. Gandhi noticed that she was a sprightly, spirited woman in her twenties. She skipped along and chattered away. Gandhi had trouble keeping up with her, and was ashamed of himself. He managed to follow her to the top of a steep hill, but, to his great distress, he had to stumble and crawl his way down while she watched in amusement from the bottom. It was his first encounter with an unchaperoned woman.

In London, for some time Gandhi went to lunch every Sunday with an elderly widow whom he had met in Brighton during another vacation. He passed himself off as a bachelor and allowed her to introduce him to marriageable young women. He and one particular woman were left alone on numerous Sundays, and things came to such a pass that the widow apparently expected Gandhi to propose marriage to his Sunday friend. Full of alarm, he wrote the widow a letter in which he said, in part, "I knew that Indian students in England dissembled the fact of their marriage and I followed suit. I now see that I should not have done so. I must also add that I was married while yet a boy, and am the father of a son." He offered to stop going to the widow's house, but she would not hear of it, and the Sunday lunches went on as before.

He seems to have almost succumbed to temptation in Portsmouth, a seaport with numerous brothels, and with even more numerous boarding houses run by lascivious landladies. Gandhi and an Indian friend were in Portsmouth for a meeting of the Vegetarian Federal Union, an organization of various vegetarian societies in England. They stayed in a boarding house, and in the evening their landlady, an attractive, vivacious woman, joined them and another lodger for a rubber of bridge. The four of them started making indecent jokes. "Just when I was about to go beyond the limit," Gandhi writes, "leaving the cards and the game to themselves, God . . . uttered the blessed warning, 'Whence this devil in you, my boy? Be off, quick!' . . . Remembering the vow I had taken before my mother, I fled from the scene. To my room I went quaking, trembling, and with beating heart, like a quarry escaped from its pursuer."

To be an Indian student in London in the late Victorian period was to move on the fringes of English society, not just among vegetarians and birth-control advocates but also among a variety of cranks, radicals, obscurantists, and romantics who subscribed to many ideologies born of the Darwinian and Marxist revolutions: anarchism, feminism, Fabianism, atheism. For instance, it is known that Gandhi came across people who, advocating a return to nature, built their own cottages, designed and made their own furniture, their own clothes, and even their own sandals, and organized their own utopian communities, willingly walking miles from one to another in order to discuss their ideas over a cup of tea.

Gandhi seems to have developed an early taste for eccentrics of all kinds—Indian as well as English. At the National Indian Association, he met a young man named Narayan Hemchandra, a small, short Gujarati with a round, pockmarked face and an unkempt beard, who wore just trousers and a shirt, and had virtually no command of English. It appears that he did not have much education of any kind, yet he aspired to translate the great books of the world into his native Gujarati, thinking he could do the work merely by means of good will and enthusiasm. Gandhi was captivated by his innocence and his exuberance. They started seeing each other regularly, and would often cook and eat meals together. Gandhi would teach him English and talk to him about Disraeli and Cardinal Manning. At Hemchandra's behest, Gandhi wrote to the Cardinal, saying that Hemchandra wanted to call on him in London and congratulate him on his humanitarian work, and that he, Gandhi, would act as interpreter. The Cardinal granted them an audience. Gandhi writes:

> We entered the Cardinal's mansion. As soon as we were seated, a thin, tall, old gentleman made his appearance, and shook hands with us. Narayan Hemchandra thus gave his greetings:
> "I do not want to take up your time. I had heard a lot about you. . . . It has been my custom to visit the sages of the world and that is why I have put you to this trouble. . . ."
> "I am glad you have come [the Cardinal said]. I hope your stay in London will agree with you and that you will get in touch with people here. God bless you."
>
> With no more ado, the Cardinal bade the two friends goodbye.

Many of the eccentrics with whom Gandhi came into closest contact were either Theosophists or devout Christians, who urged their own faiths on him. In 1875, Elena Petrovna Blavatsky, a Russian émigré, had founded the Theosophical Society to propagate her particular system of theosophy—a mixture of vegetarian, Hindu, and Buddhist thought, emphasizing the occult, the esoteric, and the mystical. The term "theosophy" had previously referred to various ancient and modern systems of philosophy positing direct knowledge of God. Mme. Blavatsky's system centered on what she called the Secret Doctrine— a single, underlying, ageless truth, of which, in her view, all religions and philosophies were but reflections. She proclaimed that through the ages the Secret Doctrine had been in the custody of a few "mahatmas;"

that she was now in communion with these mahatmas; and that they had vouchsafed to her the Secret Doctrine, making her its sole living custodian. She and her followers strove through secret initiation into and membership in the society to form the nucleus of a mystical universal brotherhood of man; studied all religions and philosophies to understand the ramifications of the Secret Doctrine; and sought contact with spirits to investigate the mystical forces of life and matter. Gandhi dipped into Mme. Blavatsky's "Key to Theosophy," her disciple Annie Besant's "How I Became a Theosophist," and the Bible. He went to a few meetings of the Theosophical Society, where he was introduced to Mme. Blavatsky and Annie Besant. He attended church services, where he heard such well-known Nonconformists as Charles Haddon Spurgeon and Dr. Joseph Parker preach. The humanitarian spirit of the Theosophists and the moral lessons of the Sermon on the Mount made a lasting impression on him. He was not tempted to become a convert to either Theosophy or Christianity, however, feeling that he could not embrace a new faith when he knew little of his own; and his friends did not press him, probably because the Theosophists held Hinduism in high regard and the Christians he came to know were mainly Nonconformists, and tolerant. It was actually thanks to his Theosophist friends that Gandhi started learning about his own religion, by reading the Bhagavad Gita, which he was ashamed of never having read, either in the original Sanskrit or in a Gujarati translation, and which he now tackled eagerly in Sir Edwin Arnold's popular English translation. In time, the Bhagavad Gita became the most important book in his life.

The Bhagavad Gita, written about twenty-five hundred years ago, is part of the Mahabharata, one of India's two great epics, the other being the Ramayana. The Mahabharata is a miscellaneous collection of fables, legends, stories, and poems woven around a quarrel over the succession to the kingdom of Bharata—an ancient name for India— between the Kauravas and the Pandavas. The Bhagavad Gita is a long philosophical dialogue between Arjuna, the chief warrior of the Pandavas, and his charioteer, Lord Krishna. The dialogue takes place on the plain of Kurukshetra, in the Punjab (now in the state of Haryana), where the armies of the Kauravas and the Pandavas are preparing to do battle for dominion over the kingdom. In Arnold's translation, Arjuna says:

Krishna! as I behold, come here to shed
Their common blood, yon concourse of our kin,
My members fail, my tongue dries in my mouth,
A shudder thrills my body, and my hair
Bristles with horror; from my weak hand slips
Gandiv, the goodly bow. . . .
Nothing do I foresee save woe and wail! . . . nought of good
Can spring from mutual slaughter! Lo, I hate
Triumph and domination, wealth and ease,
Thus sadly won! . . .
Govinda [another name for Krishna], what rich spoils
Could profit; what rule recompense; what span
Of life itself seem sweet, bought with such blood?
Seeing that these stand here, ready to die . . . grandsires, sires,
    and sons,
Brothers and fathers-in-law, and sons-in-law,
Elders and friends!

Krishna remonstrates that the wise in heart mourn neither the living nor the dead, because the atman, or soul, can neither slay nor be slain. He reminds Arjuna that the body is merely a suit of clothes, a station, an incarnation of the atman, and that in his present incarnation it is his karma to be a Kshatriya, or warrior, and his dharma to fight, to be the best warrior he can.

For a Hindu, karma is the hand dealt to him at birth from a celestial pack of cards—his fixed destiny. Dharma is his religious and moral duty to play the hand in the best possible way—his free will. The point of the card game is salvation—to free the atman from the bondage of the body, or matter, through a cycle of death and reincarnation, and to reunite it with God. Insofar as a man fails to fulfill his dharma, he prolongs his sufferings in the world and retards his journey toward God. Insofar as he fulfills it, he shortens the time of his suffering and hastens his journey. The Bhagavad Gita's essential teaching is that one should do one's duty irrespective of reward or punishment, pleasure or pain, gain or loss, victory or defeat, life or death; that the highest action is that which has the least regard for results or consequences; and that any action is better than no action.

"Even in 1888–89, when I first became acquainted with the Gita," Gandhi writes, "I felt that it was not a historical work, but that, under the guise of physical warfare, it described the duel that perpetually went on in the hearts of mankind, and that physical warfare was brought in merely to make the description of the internal duel more alluring." For Gandhi, the two armies were the forces of good and evil—the higher and baser impulses—and the battlefield of Kurukshetra was the atman. For him, the forces of good and evil were constantly at war in the atman, and every action, however insignificant or inconsequential, was a cause for battle.

In December, 1890, Gandhi took and passed his final bar examinations, but, because he had to keep two more terms before he could be called to the bar, he stayed on in England until the following June. In the interval, when he was not promoting vegetarianism he was worrying about his future. What had he really learned to equip him to be a barrister in Kathiawar—or, indeed, anywhere in India? Would he ever be able to stand up in court and argue a case? Did he really know enough to earn a living? He sought out Frederick Pincutt, a barrister-at-law and a Conservative Member of Parliament, who had a reputation for helping Indian students. Pincutt laughed at Gandhi's fears and told him that anyone with common sense who was honest, industrious, and, above all, a good judge of character could make a decent living at the law. He recommended a couple of books on the art of telling a man's character from his face, and wished Gandhi well.

Barrister

IN JULY, 1891, GANDHI ARRIVED BACK IN INDIA. HE WAS TWENTY-
one. He was met in Bombay by Lakshmidas, who told him that in his
absence their mother had died. Lakshmidas had kept back the news of
her death so as not to disturb Gandhi's studies in a foreign land. "My
grief was even greater than over my father's death," Gandhi writes.
"My cherished hopes were shattered. But I remember that I did not
give myself up to any wild expression of grief. I could even check the
tears, and took to life just as though nothing had happened." Lakshmidas told him that it had been their mother's last wish to have
Gandhi received back into his caste—to wipe away the stain of his
having crossed the "black waters." Gandhi asserts that he never believed he was an outcaste but that he wanted to honor his mother's last
wish, and so he went with Lakshmidas on a pilgrimage to Nasik, a holy
place about a hundred miles northeast of Bombay, where he had a ritual
cleansing bath in the holy waters of the Godavari River. From Nasik
they proceeded to Rajkot, where Lakshmidas informed the caste elders
of Gandhi's act of penance and invited them to dinner. Some of the
elders came, and accepted food from Gandhi, who waited on them as
a further act of penance. The more orthodox stayed away, thus making
it clear that in their view Gandhi would always be an outcaste. Among
them were the elders of the family into which his sister had married;
this meant that Gandhi was never able to take food at her house.

Gandhi, Kasturbai, and their son lived with Lakshmidas and Karsandas
and their families in the family house in Rajkot for about a year, during
which everyone fussed over Gandhi as an important barrister newly

96

returned from England, but during which he was unable to find any work. For a brief time, in his presence, the family sat on chairs, at a table, and ate—albeit with their fingers—from china plates (all new purchases), as the English did, instead of following the Indian custom of sitting on floors and beds and eating from brass plates and bowls. They ate porridge in the morning, and drank tea, coffee, or cocoa along with the usual buttermilk. The children even wore shoes and English-style coats and trousers instead of going barefoot and wearing loose Indian shirts and pajama trousers. Gandhi wanted Kasturbai to be a wife worthy of a barrister. Because she had remained illiterate, they had not corresponded while he was in England, and now he tried again to teach her to read and write, but neither of them could concentrate on the task, and soon they gave it up. Kasturbai's lack of sophistication and unregenerate Indian ways exasperated Gandhi, and though he continued to be jealously possessive, he found no pleasure in spending time with her.

Lakshmidas, who had been trained in India as a vakil, or lawyer, was practicing law in Rajkot and was supporting the entire family; Karsandas, who never finished school, seems also to have been without work. As a barrister, Gandhi was entitled to at least ten times the fee of a vakil, yet he was ignorant of Indian law and history, some knowledge of which was essential for practicing law in India. He was afraid of exposing his ignorance in Rajkot, so he went off to Bombay, with money from Lakshmidas, to do some studying on his own and to acquire practical experience. He rented a couple of rooms, engaged a servant to cook for him, and got hold of some books on Indian law and history. Every day for six months, he walked to the Bombay High Court, forty-five minutes away from his lodgings, to observe the proceedings, and walked home again. The court sessions were so boring that they put him to sleep. He was shocked to discover that not only the most humble vakils but also the most exalted barristers all obtained cases by paying touts, who hung about the court. Gandhi felt that the touts were a disgrace to the profession, and refused to have anything to do with them, so for several months he did not get a single case. He did finally land a petty case without a tout—not in the High Court but in the Small Causes Court. As counsel for the defense, he appeared for the first time in his barrister's wig and gown. When he rose to cross-examine a witness, he was so unnerved that he couldn't think of a single question, and sat down. He had to turn over the case, and the small fee he had received, to a mere vakil.

In the entire six months he lived in Bombay, he did not get another case. He thought of abandoning the legal profession and taking up teaching. He went as far as to apply for a job at a school, but was told that he was not qualified, because he did not have a university degree. Discouraged, he returned to Rajkot, where Lakshmidas found him a job in his own firm, filling out application forms and drafting petitions for poor clients—legal donkey work even for a vakil.

One day, when Gandhi had been back in India for almost two years, he heard of a job in South Africa with a Meman, or Muslim, merchant from Porbandar who was involved in a civil suit with a relative, another Meman merchant, also in South Africa. The local Indian lawyers working on the case there were all so deficient in English that they could not even carry on the necessary legal correspondence, and the merchant decided that he wanted someone trustworthy from Porbandar who had been to England to help them with their English for about a year. The merchant offered to pay for a single passage to and from South Africa, to pay all expenses in South Africa, and to pay a nominal fee of a hundred and five pounds. Gandhi felt that the job was more suitable for a clerk than for a barrister, but he did not like living in Rajkot. He felt uncomfortable working with Lakshmidas, who had persuaded him to use touts and had involved him in at least one humiliating attempt to pull strings to further Lakshmidas's own interests. Moreover, Gandhi was not adjusting to married life with Kasturbai, although she had given birth to a third child—a son, Manilal —in 1892, while Gandhi was away in Bombay. He was, in fact, so eager to leave India again that he decided to set aside his pride, and, as he puts it, "closed with the offer without any higgling."

In April, 1893, he once more said goodbye to his family, and, for the second time in five years, set off alone across the "black waters."

After a month at sea, Gandhi disembarked at Durban, the chief port of the British Crown Colony of Natal, wearing a starched white shirt, a black tie, a black frock coat, striped trousers, a black turban, and black patent-leather shoes. The harbor seemed to stretch for miles in both directions. The beaches, skirted by open, clean boulevards, looked wide, long, and white; the hills beyond the boulevards, precipitous; the trees along the boulevards, big and sturdy. The people appeared tall and healthy. The weather was chilly, for it was late fall in South Africa.

Gandhi was met by the merchant himself, Dada Abdulla Sheth, and for about a week stayed with him in his rooms, in Durban, which also served as his offices. Gandhi found that Dada Abdulla Sheth, an oldish man, was practically unlettered and had a very meagre knowledge of English, even though he was probably the richest Indian in Natal. Dada Abdulla Sheth, for his part, was struck by his employee's stiff appearance and thought him young, foolish, and inexperienced, but he had his clerk fill Gandhi in on the details of the case. It seemed that over a long period Dada Abdulla Sheth had lent his relative Sheth Tyeb Haji Khan Muhammad large sums of money in good faith but without proper records. His relative had defaulted on the loans, and Dada Abdulla Sheth was now suing him for forty thousand pounds.

The suit was actually being conducted in Pretoria, in the neighboring Boer territory of the Transvaal, where Sheth Tyeb Haji Khan Muhammad lived; South Africa was composed of two independent Boer territories, the Transvaal and the Orange Free State, and two British colonies, Natal and Cape Colony. But Dada Abdulla Sheth, before sending Gandhi off to Pretoria, took him to the Durban court one day, so that he could familiarize himself with the workings of a South African court. The English magistrate kept staring at Gandhi's turban and finally asked him to take it off. Gandhi demurred—Indian men wore turbans as a symbol of their manliness and thought it disrespectful to remove them in public—and quit the court. Outside, Dada Abdulla Sheth explained that in South Africa turbans were often treated like hats and removed in public, precisely in order not to be disrespectful. Gandhi said that he could not treat his turban like a hat, and that therefore he should perhaps get a hat. Dada Abdulla Sheth then told him that Indians in South Africa who wore hats and Western dress were usually Christian converts, worked in European restaurants as waiters, and were regarded by other Indians as outcastes. He went on to explain, however, that the forms of race prejudice in South Africa were quite haphazard and capricious, and that another English magistrate might not have regarded Gandhi's wearing his turban as disrespectful. Gandhi decided he would take his chances with his turban.

Gandhi left the port city by night train for Pretoria, some three hundred and fifty miles away. He was travelling first class. Before the train had gone very far, a European passenger ordered him out of the compartment, telling him he must travel in the van reserved for colored people, in the rear of the train. Gandhi appealed to a train official, informing the man that he had a first-class ticket, which had been bought for him from a European ticket clerk, and he refused to move. But the train official called a constable while the train was in the station at Maritzburg, and the constable forcibly removed Gandhi.

Gandhi spent the night alone, huddled up in a cold, dark waiting room in the station, too humiliated and confused to ask the stationmaster for his luggage, which contained his overcoat, and wondering whether he should proceed to Pretoria at all or return home to Rajkot; whether he should fight for his rights or let himself be insulted. He later came to regard his night in the Maritzburg station as one of the turning points of his life.

In the morning, he telegraphed Dada Abdulla Sheth and the railway authorities in Durban, and, thanks to their intervention, he was allowed to continue his journey in a first-class compartment. The train from Maritzburg took him as far as Charlestown, where he was obliged to change to a stagecoach. Its conductor, a Boer, would not let Gandhi sit inside with him and his other passengers, who all happened to be Europeans that day, but said he must sit next to the coachman, on the coach box. Gandhi protested but did as he was bidden. When the stagecoach stopped at a town called Pardekoph, the conductor ordered Gandhi to sit on the footboard, so that he himself could sit on the coach box for a while and have a smoke. "The insult was more than I could bear," Gandhi writes. "In fear and trembling I said to him, '. . . You would have me sit at your feet. I will not do so. . . .' The man came down upon me and began heavily to box my ears." The conductor heaped curses on Gandhi and tried to push him onto the footboard. But Gandhi held fast to his seat, and the other passengers finally took pity on him and made the conductor leave him alone. After several other humiliating encounters, during which Gandhi sometimes invoked and obtained the help of the authorities, he reached Pretoria.

Gandhi spent about six months working on Dada Abdulla Sheth's suit and became deeply involved in it. He gained the complete confidence of both parties and persuaded them to submit the suit to an arbitrator instead of continuing with expensive, prolonged, and bitter litigation. The arbitrator ruled in Dada Abdulla Sheth's favor, and awarded him thirty-seven thousand pounds. Gandhi then managed to persuade the merchant to let his relative pay the money in installments over a period of years, rather than ruin him by insisting on an immediate settlement. Gandhi was joyful at the success of his first job in South Africa, and concluded that the true function of a lawyer was not to exploit legal and adversary advantages but to promote compromise and reconciliation.

Within a few days of arriving in Pretoria, Gandhi, perhaps because of his humiliating journey, set up a series of regular meetings of all Indian residents, mostly petty traders, at the home of an Indian acquaintance of his to discuss their experiences of racial discrimination. He also started studying the so-called "disability laws" directed against Indians in the Transvaal. Indians were prohibited from owning property except in designated locations, and even there they could not have freeholds. They were not allowed to vote, and they were required to pay an annual head tax of three pounds. They were prohibited from being on the streets after 9 P.M. unless they were on business for Europeans, in which case they had to carry a pass stating the nature of the business. Individual government officials, all of whom were Europeans, exercised considerable personal discretion in enforcing the disability laws.

After Gandhi had been in Pretoria for about three months, he wrote to the *Natal Advertiser,* a newspaper published in Durban, "It seems, on the whole, that their [Indians'] simplicity, their total abstinence from intoxicants, their peaceful and above all their businesslike and frugal habits, which should serve as a recommendation, are really at the bottom of all this contempt and hatred of the poor Indian traders. And they are British subjects. Is this Christian-like, is this fair play, is this justice, is this civilization?"

In 1833, the British abolished slavery in their colonies, and this meant that the supply of cheap labor in vast and sparsely populated South Africa, where it had never been abundant, began to dry up just when South Africa's importance in world trade was growing. Since there was no Suez Canal at that time, most ships engaged in world trade were forced to circumnavigate South Africa. Moreover, there was a rapidly increasing demand for South African sugar, coffee, and tea. In the late eighteen-fifties, therefore, British South Africa worked out an arrangement with British India for importing Indian indentured laborers. Beginning in 1860, illiterate men, women, and children—victims of India's chronic poverty and devastating epidemics and famines, who had probably never before ventured out of their villages—were recruited by government agents from South Africa for five years' service at slave wages, were herded into ships, and, in South Africa, were delivered to European plantation owners. Many of these indentured laborers stayed on in South Africa after completing their service, primarily because prospects there seemed better. As their numbers grew, they attracted other Indian settlers—traders, shopkeepers, moneylenders, clerks, teachers, doctors—who also came in search of a better future, and by 1894 there were in Natal alone forty-three thousand Indians to forty thousand Europeans. (The native black population of Natal was about half a million.) But to the Europeans the Indians—whether they were in or out of indentured service, had been recruited or were volunteer immigrants, were rich or poor, had been transported from India or born in South Africa—were all "coolies," or hired laborers. Indian Muslims took to wearing robes with their turbans, so that they might be taken for Arabs—who, because they had all come to South Africa of their own free will, as entrepreneurs, enjoyed a higher status. Parsis passed themselves off as Persians. Indian converts to Christianity wore Western clothes. In these ways, Indians tried to hide their own regional, religious, and caste differences in order to gain a foothold in the class system of South Africa, but they rarely succeeded. To the Europeans, an Indian remained a "coolie": a "coolie trader," a "coolie shopkeeper," a "coolie moneylender," a "coolie clerk," a "coolie teacher," a "coolie doctor," a "coolie barrister."

The Europeans, too, were settlers, of course—mainly Dutch, or Boer, and British. The Boers began arriving in the seventeenth century, the British at the end of the eighteenth century. The Boers tended to be more rigid and ruthless in their treatment both of the native black population and of the Indians. The Boers perhaps took the attitude they did in part because they were Calvinists, believing in the doctrine of the elect and looking upon worldly inequities as preordained. They were also naturally conservative, being mainly small farmers, big plantation owners, or nomadic cattlemen living in isolation on the veldt. The British were more varied in their religious and social makeup— they included Nonconformists and evangelicals, and they were concentrated in the towns and cities, where they worked as artisans, traders, businessmen, government servants, doctors, and lawyers—and consequently there was more flexibility in their attitude toward nonwhites. Moreover, because of the demand for cheap plantation labor, the Indian population was increasing more rapidly in the Boer territories than in the British colonies. In any event, the disability laws in the Transvaal and the Orange Free State were much harsher than those in Natal and the Cape Colony.

When Gandhi's year in South Africa was over, he returned to Durban to board a ship for home, and Dada Abdulla Sheth made the day before Gandhi was to sail into a farewell party, to which he invited all the leading Indians in Durban. That day, as it happened, Gandhi picked up a newspaper, the *Natal Mercury,* and was shocked to read an article on a debate in the Natal Legislature over the Franchise Amendment Bill, which was about to be passed: it would remove all Indians in Natal from the voting roster. "The Asiatic comes of a race impregnated with an effete civilization with not an atom of knowledge of the principles or traditions of representative Government," the article read, in part. "As regards his instinct and training he is a political infant of the most backward type from whom it is an injustice to expect that he should . . . have any sympathy with our political aspirations." During the farewell party, Gandhi asked Dada Abdulla Sheth about the bill. "What can we understand in these matters?" Dada Abdulla Sheth said. "We can only understand things that affect our trade. . . . We are after all lame men, being unlettered. . . . What can we know of legislation?" Gandhi reminded Dada Abdulla Sheth that there were many Indians in Natal who were far from unlettered. Dada Abdulla Sheth rejoined that those educated Indians were not really Indians. They had been born and brought up in Natal and so were Christians, under the thumb of white clergy, who always went along with the government. Gandhi said that he thought the disenfranchisement would be a fatal blow to every Indian in Natal, whether Hindu, Muslim, or Christian. The guests, who had been listening to the conversation, were electrified.

They clamored for Gandhi to stay on in Durban for a time and help them mount a campaign against the bill. He allowed himself to be persuaded, and turned the farewell party into a working committee to plan the campaign.

In the days that followed, Gandhi drafted petitions, and collected signatures for them and for telegrams to be sent to the Speaker of the Legislative Assembly, the Attorney General, and the Premier, protesting the bill. He succeeded only in delaying the passage of the bill by five days. Gandhi now decided on the tactic of sending a "monster petition" to Lord Ripon, the Secretary of State for the Colonies. He insisted that the meaning and significance of the petition be explained to each Indian signatory individually. In a matter of two weeks, he succeeded in mobilizing Indians in Durban and the outlying villages— immigrants and Natal-born; freed indentured laborers; traders, shop-keepers, and clerks—and collecting ten thousand signatures.

Dada Abdulla Sheth and his merchant friends begged Gandhi to stay among them permanently and help them fight for their rights. Gandhi said he would, provided he could earn three hundred pounds a year, to permit him to live in a style worthy of a barrister. They offered to raise the sum annually through voluntary contributions, but Gandhi said he must earn the three hundred pounds solely in his professional capacity as a barrister, because he did not think that anyone should be paid for doing public service. The merchants therefore agreed to band together and retain him as their counsel, for three hundred pounds a year, to look after their business affairs.

Gandhi rented a two-story, five-bedroom house in the most fashionable European part of Durban, installed some furniture (bought for him by Dada Abdulla Sheth), engaged a cook, and moved in, with a couple of his clerks as boarders. The house, which was called Beach Grove Villa, had a balcony overlooking Durban Bay, and there was a back yard equipped with a swing and parallel bars. Gandhi rented a couple of rooms nearby to serve as his office, and could daily be seen walking to and from it, dressed in a lounge suit—a favorite one had faint blue stripes on a darker ground—and, of course, his turban.

As a barrister, Gandhi was entitled to appear in any high court in the Empire, and he applied for admission to the Natal Supreme Court. The Natal Law Society opposed his application in court—he was apparently the first Indian barrister ever known in Natal—but the chief justice ruled in his favor, observing from the bench, "The law makes no distinction between white and colored people." Gandhi was immediately sworn in. The chief justice thereupon ordered him to remove his turban. His Indian merchant friends who were sitting in the court, Dada Abdulla Sheth among them, expected him to refuse, as he had on his first visit to a South African court; they thought he would make a political issue of it. But Gandhi reasoned that now that he was an officer of the court he must comply with its customs, and he removed his turban. Many of his Indian merchant friends maintained that as a matter of racial pride he should not have given in. Gandhi granted that they had a point, but, as he wrote later, "I wanted to reserve my strength for fighting bigger battles."

Though the Franchise Amendment Bill had been passed, it required the royal assent to become law. Gandhi launched appeals to the British authorities in London. They were sympathetic, for, in the words of the historian Robert A. Huttenback, "if the Empire stood for equality, any attack on a particular group of the Queen's subjects by other members of the British family struck at the very roots of the imperial philosophy." But under the existing Constitutional arrangement with the colony they felt that if they tried to do more than moderate the excesses of the local government they would risk a "white revolt" and jeopardize their South African trade route to India and Australasia. The result was that the Franchise Amendment Bill eventually became law. In actuality, Natal as a British colony was prohibited from passing any overtly racial law, but it had complete freedom in all matters of administration, and so it was able to pass a series of loosely worded laws that could be used for racial discrimination. One, Law 25 of 1891, extended the term of indentured service of an Indian laborer from five to ten years; another, Act 17 of 1895, levied a prohibitive annual head tax of three pounds on a freed indentured laborer and on each of his dependents who chose to stay in Natal rather than be repatriated; still another was the Franchise Amendment Act, Act 8 of 1896. Other laws, even more stringent, were passed despite months of Indian agitation. (Act 14 of 1897 required prospective immigrants to show knowledge of a European language in an education test and made officials the sole judges of that knowledge; and Act 18 of 1897 required Indian merchants to renew their business licenses—which put them at the complete mercy of local officials.)

The protest movement against these laws lasted throughout the nineties. By 1896, Gandhi had become well known in the Natal English community for his frequent newspaper articles and open letters attacking racial legislation. "If He [Christ] came among us," he once wrote to the *Times of Natal,* "will He not say to many of us, 'I know you not?' . . . Will you re-read your New Testament? Will you ponder over your attitude towards the coloured population of the Colony? Will you then say you can reconcile it with the Bible teaching or the best British traditions?" At the same time that he berated the English, he exhorted the Indians to self-improvement: they must forget their religious and caste differences, he said, and reform their devious business ways, and change their insanitary habits, so that they could at least respect themselves. He established a permanent Indian political organization to fight for the rights of Indians and to act as a moral and social force for the reform of the Indian community, and called it the Natal Indian Congress, after the Indian National Congress, which was then agitating in India for similar causes. To the Indians in Natal, Gandhi was becoming known as Gandhibhai, meaning "Brother Gandhi," and sometimes simply as Bhai. They flocked to him in increasing numbers, with personal problems as well as legal ones.

One day, a man appeared in Gandhi's office in tattered clothes, his front teeth broken, his mouth bleeding. His name was Balasundaram, and he was an indentured laborer from Madras. Trembling and weeping, he told Gandhi that his master had beaten him and that he was afraid to go back to him. Gandhi took up his case and, after going to court, got him transferred to another European master. "The echoes of Balasundaram's case were heard in far off Madras," Gandhi writes. In fact, the echoes of Gandhi's work were beginning to be heard in many far-off places, and his name was becoming known in political circles in England as well as in India and in South Africa. He was still only in his mid-twenties.

Community Servant

THOUGH GANDHI WAS NOW EARNING A GOOD LIVING IN DURBAN and had a house of his own, he did not send for Kasturbai and their children. Instead, he sent for—of all people—Sheikh Mehtab to come and live with him. Sheikh Mehtab, who seems to have had nothing better to do, arrived in Durban shortly after he received the invitation. Gandhi installed him in Beach Grove Villa as a sort of majordomo, and gave him whatever money he wanted. Before very long, Sheikh Mehtab was stirring up domestic intrigues and entertaining prostitutes in the house. One day, Gandhi surprised him in the company of a prostitute and ordered him out of the house; he insolently refused to go until he was threatened with the police, but then he left, and never returned. (Sheikh Mehtab continued to live in Durban, eventually attaching himself to an Indian merchant, getting married, and becoming known as a reciter of romantic Urdu poetry.)

Gandhi never quite succeeded in explaining why he had sent for Sheikh Mehtab in the first place, or, for that matter, the exact nature of their relationship. Erik Erikson, in "Gandhi's Truth," a biographical exploration that he calls a "psycho-history," attaches considerable importance to their relationship, suggesting that perhaps it had a homosexual element, and also that perhaps "Mehtab played perfectly the personage on whom to project one's personal devil and thus became the personification of Mohandas' *negative identity,* that is, of everything in himself which he tried to isolate and subdue." In any event, Sheikh Mehtab's behavior brought Gandhi up short, and he immediately went to India to fetch Kasturbai and the children.

Gandhi spent six months in India, where he devoted himself mostly to publicizing the plight of the South African Indians. He wrote, and had privately printed and widely circulated, a pamphlet entitled "The Grievances of the British Indians in South Africa;" he contributed articles to newspapers; he addressed public meetings in the big cities; and he managed to enlist the support of both Lokamanya Tilak and Gopal Krishna Gokhale, the two preeminent but antagonistic leaders of the Indian nationalist movement. Exaggerated accounts of all these activities appeared in Natal newspapers; for example, Gandhi's pamphlet was falsely said to declare that "the Indians in Natal are robbed and assaulted, and treated like beasts."

Gandhi returned to Durban with his family at the end of 1896. They travelled with some four hundred other Indian immigrants on board the S. S. Courland, a ship owned by Dada Abdulla Sheth, and arrived in Durban at the same time as the S. S. Naderi, another ship carrying Indian immigrants to South Africa. Both ships had sailed from Bombay during an outbreak of the plague, and the Natal authorities therefore kept them anchored just outside Durban Harbor for the necessary observation and fumigation. They extended the normal plague quarantine from five days to sixteen, perhaps because they were as much afraid of the effect of Gandhi's return as they were of an epidemic of the plague. But the delay only exacerbated rumors, already circulating among Europeans in Durban, that Gandhi planned to swamp Natal with Indians. The authorities advised Gandhi to slip into Durban at night to avoid trouble, but his merchant friends, who were in touch with him by letter, said that such cowardly behavior would simply lend credence to the rumors, and that Gandhi must enter the city in broad daylight. That is what he did.

Arrangements were made for the Gandhis to stay with a Natal Indian Congress worker, Jivan Rustomji, until tempers in the European community cooled. As a further precaution, Kasturbai and the children set out from the dock in a carriage, and Gandhi, who followed on foot, was accompanied by one of Dada Abdulla Sheth's English attorneys, F. A. Laughton. The two men had not gone far when a group of European boys recognized Gandhi and started hurling insults at him. Laughton hailed a passing rickshaw, but the black rickshaw boy, sensing danger, fled. "Are you the man who wrote to the press?" someone shouted, kicking Gandhi from behind. The group grew into a crowd, which surged around Gandhi, separating him from Laughton. People pelted him with stones and brickbats, tore off his turban, and started punching him. Fortunately for Gandhi, who was on the point of fainting, the wife of the police superintendent of Durban, Mrs. R. C. Alexander, happened to be passing by on foot, and she rushed to Gandhi's aid. The crowd fell back, no doubt in deference to her sex and her position, and she stood beside Gandhi, using her parasol to protect his exposed head, until a few constables arrived. They escorted him to Rustomji's house, where Kasturbai and the children had arrived unmolested.

The crowd had followed Gandhi, however, and now surrounded the house and threatened to burn it down. Police Superintendent Alexander came and posted himself at the gate. He adopted the tactic of humoring the crowd by joining them in a lynching chant:

> Hang old Gandhi
> On the sour-apple tree.

Meanwhile, Gandhi's wounds were quickly bandaged, and the constables led him out through the back door. They jumped over fences, squeezed through railings, threaded their way down narrow lanes, and finally reached the sanctuary of the police station. Alexander announced to the crowd that Gandhi had slipped away, and it eventually dispersed.

In the days that followed, Gandhi was able to resume his normal life in his own house, having placated the European community by letting it be known that he would not press charges against his assailants, that reports of his political activities in India were malicious and mistaken, and that he had nothing whatever to do with the two shiploads of Indian immigrants, many of whom were bound for the Transvaal anyway.

The Gandhis had some difficulty adjusting to their new life at Beach Grove Villa. Gandhi and Kasturbai, in addition to their own two sons, now had charge of a ten-year-old nephew of Gandhi's named Gokuldas, who was Raliat's only child. The boy's father had died prematurely while Gandhi was in India. Gandhi had helped nurse his brother-in-law (whose name is lost to history) first in Bombay, where the brother-in-law was lying ill, and later in Rajkot, where he died. It is not known how the brother-in-law felt about being nursed by the family outcaste, or how or why the outcaste got custody of the child. In Durban, Gandhi once again had the children wear Western clothes, including shoes and stockings, although they complained constantly of discomfort. Yet he refused to send them to the local schools, because he thought they would only learn to ape European children. Instead, he sent Harilal and Gokuldas back home to a boarding school, but he recalled them within a few months, having decided that Indian schools were no better. Yet he himself did not have much time to teach them or Manilal, and so all three grew up without formal education or professional qualifications.

Gandhi, who had got very little out of his own schooling, was beginning to feel that formal education of any kind was less important than learning self-reliance, which was becoming the rule of life at Beach Grove Villa. Gandhi's several clerks and assistants lived with him in communal fashion, sharing the household tasks and eating with him, irrespective of their religion or caste. During his stay in Pretoria, an English barber had turned him away, whereupon he had taught himself to cut his own hair with the help of a mirror and a pair of clippers. Now, to save laundry money, he taught himself to wash and iron his own clothes, and even to starch his collars. He had dispensed with the services of the untouchable sweepers who generally did the scavenging work, because he was coming to believe that untouchability was an "excrescence" of Hinduism, and was not unlike the racist attitude of Europeans toward Indians and native Africans. The house had no running water or plumbing, and everyone, including Kasturbai, was expected to help with the latrine work. One day, Gandhi asked her to clean the chamber pot of a clerk who had been born an untouchable. She began to cry. Gandhi writes:

> I was far from being satisfied by her merely carrying the pot. I would have her do it cheerfully. So I said, raising my voice: "I will not stand this nonsense in my house. . . ."
> She shouted back: "Keep your house to yourself and let me go."
> . . . I caught her by the hand, dragged the helpless woman to the gate . . . and proceeded to open it with the intention of pushing her out. The tears were running down her cheeks in torrents, and she cried: "Have you no sense of shame? Must you so far forget your-

self? Where am I to go? I have no parents or relatives here to harbour me. Being your wife, you think I must put up with your cuffs and kicks? For Heaven's sake behave yourself, and shut the gate. . . ."

I . . . was really ashamed and shut the gate.

Gandhi, who had once thought of becoming a doctor, read popular health manuals and such books on nature cures as Ludwig Kühne's "The New Science of Healing" and Adolf Just's "Return to Nature," and gave free medical advice to his Indian clients and friends. When Kasturbai became pregnant again, he read a manual on obstetrics, and assisted in the delivery of their son Ramdas, born in Durban in 1897. Gandhi delivered their last child entirely by himself; this was Devadas, who was born in 1900, also in Durban.

As time went on, Gandhi put more faith in his nature cures than in medicines prescribed by doctors. In 1902, Manilal, who was ten years old, came down with typhoid complicated by pneumonia, and Gandhi felt he could cure him with a vegetarian diet and hydropathy. Manilal became so weak that the attending doctor said he would not be responsible for the boy's life if Gandhi persisted in refusing to give him chicken broth and eggs. Gandhi would have liked to have the child make his own choice between the two cures, but, reasoning that Manilal was too young to choose, Gandhi chose for him, and began treating him with his own cure. He wrapped the feverish boy in cold, wet sheets and covered him with blankets.

> I left Manilal in the charge of his mother [Gandhi writes] and went out for a walk. . . . "My honour is in Thy keeping, oh Lord, in this hour of trial," I repeated to myself. . . . After a short time I returned, my heart beating within my breast.
>
> No sooner had I entered the room than Manilal said, "You have returned, Bapu?"
>
> "Yes, darling."
>
> "Do please pull me out. I am burning."
>
> "Are you perspiring, my boy?"
>
> "I am simply soaked. Do please take me out."
>
> I felt his forehead. It was covered with beads of perspiration. The temperature was going down. I thanked God. . . .
>
> I undid the pack and dried his body. Father and son fell asleep in the same bed.

In 1886, gold was discovered in the Transvaal, setting off a gold rush. The gold mines, though they were in Boer territory, were financed and developed by British capitalists, who began demanding more and more say in the affairs of the Transvaal. The Boers, for their part, began agitating for complete control of the gold mines. The conflicting demands were largely responsible for the outbreak of the Boer War, in 1899. The South African Indians probably identified more with the pastoral ways of the Boers than with the industrial capitalism of the British, but most of them had no wish to take sides in the war, for fear of reprisals. Gandhi, however, felt so much loyalty to the British Crown that he wanted the Indians to go to war alongside the British. At the time, he was working two hours a day as a volunteer nurse in a small hospital for indentured laborers in Durban. He immediately sent the Natal government an offer to organize a volunteer ambulance corps of Indians for service in the front lines. "We do not know how to handle arms," he wrote to the Colonial Secretary of Natal. "It is perhaps our misfortune that we cannot. . . . The motive underlying this humble offer is to endeavor to prove that, in common with other subjects of the Queen-Empress in South Africa, the Indians, too, are ready to do duty for their Sovereign on the battlefield." The Natal government had such a low opinion of Indians that at first it refused Gandhi's offer. Later, however, after the British sustained heavy battle casualties, the offer was accepted.

Gandhi organized and led an ambulance corps of eleven hundred Indians—eight hundred of them indentured laborers—which served on many battle fronts, and, at the battle of Spion Kop, even went into the line of fire to remove the wounded. Afterward, the British decorated Gandhi and other corps leaders for their service to the Empire.

Gandhi felt that the lot of Indians in South Africa would improve as a result of their war service, and that, in any case, he could do more for them by going home and fighting the larger social and political battles of Indians in India. He consulted the Natal Indians, who were loath to see him leave South Africa but eventually gave their consent, on condition that he agree to return within a year if his services were required. They made farewell gifts to Gandhi and Kasturbai of gold, silver, and diamond ornaments. Gandhi had long believed that service was its own reward, and he now set about trying to make his family understand that. He knew that Kasturbai would not renounce the gifts easily, since jewelry was a Hindu wife's main insurance against bad times and was also a sign of respectability, so he first converted the children to his way of thinking, and then they all tackled Kasturbai. She cried and protested. "I can understand your not permitting me to wear them," Gandhi recalled her saying. "But what about my daughters-in-law? They will be sure to need them. And who knows what will happen tomorrow?" Gandhi said that she and the children had to learn to be self-reliant, and if they ever needed money they could ask him for it.

"Ask you? I know you by this time [she cried]. You deprived me of my ornaments, you would not leave me in peace with them. . . . You who are trying to make sadhus of my boys. . . . No, the ornaments will not be returned. And pray what right have you to my necklace?"

"But," I rejoined, "is the necklace given you for your service or for my service?"

". . . I have toiled and moiled for you day and night. Is that no service? You forced all and sundry on me, making me weep bitter tears, and I slaved for them!"

Gandhi remained firm, and finally got his way. He had all the gifts put into a trust for the service of the community.

In November, 1902, when Gandhi had been in India for nearly a year, he got cablegrams from Natal summoning him back. The Secretary of State for the Colonies, in London, Joseph Chamberlain, was expected in South Africa, to collect a "gift" of thirty-five million pounds—a sort of war debt—from the defeated Boers, and to further the idea of a union between the British colonies and the Boer territories; and the South African Indians wanted Gandhi to speak to Chamberlain on their behalf. Gandhi, true to his word, immediately set out for Durban, taking with him four or five educated young men who could speak English and might be able to continue his work in South Africa. Kasturbai and the children remained in India, because Gandhi intended to return after his meeting with Chamberlain—in a year, at most.

In Durban, Gandhi barely got a hearing from Chamberlain, who dismissed him, observing that the imperial government had little say in the affairs of self-governing colonies. (Chamberlain had come in order to exact that "gift" from the colonies, and he did not want anything to get in his way.) Gandhi now learned that South African Indians, in spite of their ambulance service in the war, were worse off than before: the Transvaal government was refusing to allow many Indians who had become refugees during the war to return to their homes and businesses in the Transvaal. He resolved not to go back to India but to settle in the Transvaal—in Johannesburg, the gold capital of South Africa. He rented a house in its European section and was soon earning four or five thousand pounds a year from his legal practice; in due course, he sent for Kasturbai and the children.

In 1904, plague broke out in Johannesburg's "coolie location." "Beyond arranging to clean the latrines in the location in a haphazard way, the Municipality [did] nothing to provide any sanitary facilities," Gandhi writes. As he was well aware, insanitary habits were second nature to Indians. He had been involved in trying to control the spread of plague in Rajkot in 1896 and in Durban in 1899, and had found that even the latrines of the most opulent houses were "dark and stinking and reeking with filth and worms," and that the sanitary arrangements of the holiest temples were no better. Gandhi now helped the Johannesburg authorities evacuate the "coolie location"—after which the authorities burned it down—and resettle the Indians in a camp outside the city. With his assistance, the Indians were persuaded to dig up silver and copper coins, amounting to some sixty thousand pounds, which they had buried in the old settlement for safekeeping, because they knew nothing of banks. The coins were sterilized and deposited in banks in the names of their owners, with Gandhi as a sort of custodian. In an old building near the camp, Gandhi nursed the plague victims, treating some of them with hydropathy. He had no fear of contagion, because during the years he had spent in South Africa he had come to believe that he was an instrument of God's will.

When Gandhi was alone in South Africa between 1893 and 1897, he often spent his Sundays with Christian evangelists, as he had in London. He attended their churches, discussed religion with them over Sunday lunches and teas in their homes, and went on long afternoon walks with them. They pressed him to read such books as Arthur T. Pierson's "Many Infallible Proofs," Joseph Butler's "Analogy of Religion," and Joseph Parker's "Commentary," and when he had read them they tried to claim him for Christianity. He was moved by their sincerity, but he found, he says, that "it was impossible for [him] to regard Christianity as a perfect religion or the greatest of all religions." In 1894, he started corresponding with his Christian friends in the London Vegetarian Society. One of them, Edward Maitland, got him interested in a move-ment Maitland had started—the Esoteric Christian Union, whose teach-ings, like those of the Theosophists, were an amalgam of Eastern and Western thought, a mystical response to the materialism of the indus-trial revolution. Gandhi became the South African representative of the Esoteric Christian Union, selling its literature through newspaper ad-vertisements, and proselytizing among his Christian friends. He reread the Bhagavad Gita and studied the Vedas and the Upanishads; he also studied the scriptures of his Muslim and Parsi friends—the Koran and the Avesta. In his religious explorations, he happened upon Leo Tol-stoy's Christian writings, and was inspired by Tolstoy's restless search for perfection and universal love. The thesis of one Tolstoy work, "The Kingdom of God Is Within You"—that all government is based on war and violence, and that one can counter these evils only through passive resistance—made a deep impression on him.

One day, Gandhi was having Sunday lunch with some European Christian friends who had a five-year-old son. The conversation turned to religion, and Gandhi began extolling the Buddha's love of all crea-tures, compared with Christ's love of man only; he praised the apple that he himself was eating, and disparaged the mutton that the boy was eating, since in the Buddha's eyes the sheep's life was as precious as the boy's. (In those days, Gandhi was eating nothing but fruit, uncooked rice and wheat, raw peas and potatoes, and nuts. Some say that citrus fruit may be what ruined his teeth and eventually left him toothless.) Gandhi writes that when he visited the family the following week, as usual, he found his hostess unhappy:

> "Mr. Gandhi," she said, "please don't take it ill if I feel obliged to tell you that my boy is none the better for your company. Every-day he hesitates to eat meat and asks for fruit, reminding me of your argument. . . . If he gives up meat, he is bound to get weak, if not

ill. . . . Your discussions should henceforth be only with us elders. . . ."

"Mrs. _____," I replied, ". . . what I eat and omit to eat is
bound to have a greater effect on the child than what I say. The best
way, therefore, is for me to stop these visits."

That is what he did.

In 1904, during a twenty-four-hour train journey from Johannesburg to Durban, Gandhi says, he became engrossed in Ruskin's book
"Unto This Last." Ruskin believed that the true basis of society was not
wealth, as the classical economists had it, but the "invisible gold" of
human companionship. The possession of wealth and power was selfish,
perpetuated social inequities and injustices, and had to be renounced
until there was enough for everyone—until, in Ruskin's words, "the
time come, and the kingdom, when Christ's gift of bread and bequest
of peace shall be unto this last as unto thee." To hasten the arrival of
that time, rich and poor were counselled to pursue simple pleasures and
inner tranquillity, "making the first of possessions, self-possession; and
honoring themselves in the harmless pride and calm pursuits of peace."
Gandhi says that the book confirmed his own growing conviction that
the simple life of a peasant or a craftsman was the ideal life.

A year earlier, before he had made his move from Durban to
Johannesburg, he, along with a couple of Indian friends, had started
publishing a four-page weekly called *Indian Opinion,* in English,
Gujarati, Tamil, and Hindi. A natural outcome of his pamphleteering
and newspaper writing, the weekly was intended to expose the
"blemishes" of South African Indians even as it insisted on their rights.
Indian Opinion was becoming his main preoccupation, and now, inspired by Ruskin, he bought, for a thousand pounds, a hundred acres
of land—mostly farmland—about fourteen miles from Durban, near
the town of Phoenix, and moved his printers and printers' assistants and
the press on which they printed *Indian Opinion* out there. He put an
English editor friend, Albert West, who had been helping him with the
weekly, in charge, and gradually organized a self-sufficient community
based on the religious and social principles of Tolstoy and Ruskin. At
first, the members had to make do with tents, but in due course they
put up simple huts of corrugated iron sheeting, and a number of them

settled there, tilling the land, editing the weekly, and running the presses.

Because of his law practice and his public commitments, Gandhi himself continued to live in or near Johannesburg, but he, Kasturbai, and the children would often visit Phoenix Farm, as it came to be called, taking a number of their Johannesburg friends with them. One of the friends was Henry Polak, an English newspaperman who did legal work in Gandhi's office, and who later edited *Indian Opinion* and became a well-known attorney. He had told Gandhi when they first met that he was waiting until he could earn enough money to send to England for his fiancée, Millie Graham. Gandhi, ever ready to take charge of other people's lives, immediately arranged for Millie to come out, and for Henry and Millie to get married (Gandhi was best man at their wedding) and settle in Johannesburg. Henry Polak came to play an increasingly important part in Gandhi's work in South Africa.

Early in 1906, a Zulu chieftain threw an assagai and killed a tax collector in Zululand. The incident set off violent disturbances. The British had annexed Zululand to Natal in 1887, and the spirited Zulus—whose main occupation was farming—did not like the arrangement. The Natal government now mounted a punitive expedition to put down what it called the Zulu Rebellion. As in the Boer War, Gandhi believed that Indians, as loyal subjects of the Empire, must side with the British, and he organized another volunteer ambulance corps.

When Gandhi and his corps got to Zululand, however, they discovered that the expeditionary force was quelling the "rebellion" by public hangings and public floggings. The wounded nursed by the corps were mostly Zulus. "We found that the wounded Zulus would have been left uncared for if we had not attended to them," Gandhi writes. "No European would help to dress their wounds. . . . We had to cleanse the wounds of several Zulus which had not been attended to for as many as five or six days and were therefore stinking horribly. We liked our work. The Zulus could not talk to us, but from their gestures and the expression of their eyes, they seemed to feel as if God had sent us to their succour." The conduct of the expeditionary force was such a scandal that the expedition was quickly called off, and Gandhi and his corps were returned to Johannesburg within six weeks.

Gandhi says that the suffering he witnessed in Zululand caused a profound and permanent change in his life, making him resolve to serve humanity with all his soul. To this end, within a few months of his return from Zululand he adopted three principles by which to live: brahmacharya, or celibacy, which was an ancient Hindu vow; satyagraha, or the force of truth and love, which was his own invention; and ahimsa, or nonviolence to all living things, which was an ancient Jain commandment. He says that his vow of celibacy was the most decisive break with his past; that, indeed, without it he could not have practiced the two other principles; and that although there were practical reasons for the vow (Kasturbai was in bad health and another pregnancy might have endangered her life, and he did not want any more children), the overriding reason was spiritual. For him, as a Hindu, sexual desire represented the source of all base and selfish human impulses—passion, anger, aggression—and sexual desire and the other impulses could be mastered only by renunciation of all interest in the outcome of any action. Action, as he had been learning all along from the Bhagavad Gita, had to be an end in itself, its own justification. He now started tacking up a couple of verses from the Bhagavad Gita on the bathroom wall every morning and memorizing them as he brushed his teeth. About this time, too, he initiated his lifelong practice of daily prayers and grew aware of an "inner voice," which thereafter became the main arbiter of all his important decisions.

Gandhi came to believe that his three principles required him to give up everything he owned, treat all people as part of his family, and contribute whatever he earned to community service. He wrote to Lakshmidas, in Rajkot, telling him he would therefore no longer have money to send home. Lakshmidas was incensed. "In stern language he explained to me my duty towards him," Gandhi writes. "I should not, he said, aspire to be wiser than our father. I must support the family as he did. I pointed out to him that . . . the meaning of 'family' had but to be slightly widened and the wisdom of my step would become clear." (Each brother held adamantly to his view, and Lakshmidas refused to have anything more to do with Gandhi. They were reconciled only when Lakshmidas was on his deathbed, seven years later.)

Satyagrahi in South Africa

IN 1906, THE TRANSVAAL GOVERNMENT INTRODUCED A NEW PIECE of anti-Indian legislation in the local legislature: the Asiatic Registration Bill (the bill also covered the Chinese, of whom there were a number), which was designed both to prevent Indians who had left the Transvaal during the Boer War from returning and to prevent any future Indian immigration. Under the bill, all Indians living in the Transvaal were to be fingerprinted and issued government registration certificates, which they were to have on their persons at all times, on pain of fine, imprisonment, or deportation. Only Indians actually residing in the Transvaal when the bill became law would be allowed to apply for registration. The resident Indians did not care for the idea of being fingerprinted like criminals and having to carry registration certificates around like dogs wearing license tags. Moreover, they feared that if the bill was passed it might one day be used to chase all Indians out of the Transvaal and eventually out of the whole of South Africa (there were then about thirteen thousand Indians in the Transvaal and about a hundred thousand in South Africa), and might also be imitated in other colonies.

Under Gandhi's leadership, the Indians living in the Transvaal decided to oppose the bill. They gathered in huge numbers in the old Empire Theatre in Johannesburg to work out a plan of action. During discussion of a resolution calling on Indians to resist the bill in the event that it became law, regardless of the penalties, one speaker passionately declared that, as God was his witness, he, for one, would never submit to registration. Gandhi was immediately struck by the speaker's invocation of God, and told the meeting that anyone who voted for the resolution by invoking God as his witness would in fact be making a solemn pledge, from which there could be no going back. "Resolutions of this nature cannot be passed by a majority vote," he said. "This pledge must not be taken with a view to producing an effect on outsiders. . . . Everyone must only search his own heart, and if the inner voice assures him that he has the requisite strength to carry him through, then only should he pledge himself and then only will his pledge bear fruit." All those assembled in the Empire Theatre stood up and declared en masse, with right hands raised, that, as God was their witness, they would never submit to registration. What had started out as a struggle for political rights was turning into a struggle for individual salvation. And this salvation, as Gandhi himself was beginning to define it, would be achieved only through truth and love—through the force of satyagraha, the principle that Gandhi spent the rest of his life refining.

Around that time, Gandhi wrote:

> Satyagraha is referred to in English as passive resistance. The term denotes the method of securing rights by personal suffering; it is the reverse of resistance by arms. When I refuse to do a thing that is repugnant to my conscience, I use soul-force. For instance, the Government of the day has passed a law which is applicable to me. I do not like it. If by using violence I force the Government to repeal the law, I am employing what may be termed body-force. If I do not obey the law and accept the penalty for its breach, I use soul-force. It involves sacrifice of self. . . . Moreover, if this kind of force is used in a cause that is unjust, only the person using it suffers.

Thereafter, political and religious aims became increasingly identified in Gandhi's mind, with the result that those who encountered him, whether as an opponent or as an ally, found him unpredictable but always disarming. Despite numerous resolutions, petitions, and representations against the Asiatic Registration Bill, the legislature passed it, and Gandhi went off to England to try to get the royal assent withheld. He called on prominent Indians and Englishmen, in their offices and chambers, in their houses and clubs, and returned to South Africa with assurances from the Secretary of State for the Colonies, who was now Lord Elgin, that the royal assent would not be given. But early in 1907 the Transvaal, under a new Constitutional arrangement that England had made with the former Boer territories and her old South African colonies, became empowered to enact any bill without the royal assent. The bill was promptly reintroduced, and became law.

Gandhi and his followers, stigmatizing the law as the "Black Act," formed the Passive Resistance Association (later called the Satyagraha Association), and refused to register. Gandhi and other leaders were put on trial and sent to jail for two months. As the days passed, resisters —all of them men, so far—began filling up the jails. General Jan Christiaan Smuts, the Minister in Charge of Indian Affairs, proposed a compromise to Gandhi: the government would not only release all the resisters but also repeal the law if Indians would register voluntarily. Gandhi says that after some hesitation he agreed to the compromise, because he felt that the resisters had scored a moral victory. He was let out of jail after serving only about two weeks of his sentence, and took the lead in applying for registration. Some of his followers, especially the fierce Pathans, felt that he had gone back on his pledge and betrayed their trust. One Pathan, Mir Alam, who had been Gandhi's client and had often gone to him for advice, swore that he would kill the first man to register. As Gandhi was about to enter the registration office, Mir Alam hit him on the head, knocking him unconscious, and, with some Pathan companions, proceeded to kick and beat him. Gandhi was finally rescued by passing Europeans and the police, and carried off to the office of an English friend, where, as soon as he regained consciousness, he insisted on registering, which the authorities allowed him to do from there. He spent the next ten days at the friend's house recovering from his injuries. (The friend was the Reverend Joseph J. Doke, who, with the publication of "M. K. Gandhi" a year later, in 1909, became Gandhi's first biographer.)

To Gandhi's embarrassment, Smuts announced that he would not repeal the "Black Act" after all, on the pretext that the Indians had failed to live up to their part of the bargain because every last one of them had not registered voluntarily. Gandhi and more than two thousand of his followers who had registered voluntarily thereupon gathered in the grounds of the Hamidia Mosque, in Johannesburg, and burned their registration certificates. A local correspondent for the London *Daily Mail* compared the event to the Boston Tea Party. It was the first of a series of public symbolic acts, which Gandhi used with ever-increasing effectiveness throughout his life to strengthen his causes.

Gandhi was again prosecuted and sentenced to two months in jail, along with scores of other resisters. As soon as they finished their jail terms, they began agitating against the "Black Act" all over again, and most of them were sent back to jail, this time for three months. Some were even deported to India.

When Gandhi was first sentenced to jail, he wondered what he would do there and how he would survive—what would become of his home, his legal practice, his public life. "How vain I was!" he writes. "I, who had asked the people to consider the prisons as His Majesty's hotels, the suffering consequent upon disobeying the 'Black Act' as perfect bliss, and the sacrifice of one's all and of life itself in resisting it as supreme enjoyment! Where had all this knowledge vanished to-day? . . . This . . . train of thought acted upon me as a bracing tonic, and I began to laugh at my own folly." He found that a simple, chaste, abstemious life of privation and prayer was perfectly suited to jail. Many resisters were locked up together in one cell and were allowed after a time to cook their own fare, and under those circumstances he worked out a regimen of exercising and cooking and of reading and writing. He translated "Unto This Last" into Gujarati, for wider dissemination among his followers, and read for the first time Henry David Thoreau's "Civil Disobedience," which reinforced ideas he had already arrived at for himself: that it was more honorable to be right than to be law-abiding; that it was every man's right—indeed, his duty—to resist a tyrannical government; and that a minority of one could bring about a change in the government.

In the next two years, there was something of a lull in what Gandhi often described as the war between the ants and the elephants, because the governments of Natal, the Transvaal, the Cape Colony, and the Orange Free State all became preoccupied with the establishment of the federal Union of South Africa. Since the new Union was to have dominion status within the British Empire, its Constitution had to be approved by the British government, and in 1909 Gandhi again went to London, in the hope that the British government could be persuaded to help Indians obtain rights of citizenship in the new Union which would be—in some respects, at least—on a par with the Europeans' rights. His mission proved, in his words, "thankless and fruitless." When the Union of South Africa was established, in 1910, the British colonies and the former Boer territories, now provinces in the new Union, all kept their old racial laws in force.

Gandhi's mission to England, however, did result in his writing a manifesto entitled "Indian Home Rule." An astonishingly violent defense of nonviolence, the manifesto is a kind of Socratic dialogue between a "reader" (a composite of Indians whom Gandhi had met on this visit to England), who advocates violent overthrow of the Empire, and an "editor" (Gandhi himself), who vehemently opposes violent political action. He lashes out at other Indian leaders and their ideas as outdated; at the British Parliament as sterile; at the free press as dishonest; at doctors and lawyers trained in Western ways for exploiting the Indian people; at railways for spreading the curse of Western civilization; and at Western civilization itself, which is materialistic and encourages the pursuit of pleasure without religion or morality. He offers in its place the ideal of the simple, golden life of ancient India, which he imagines to have been much more in tune with the spirit of satyagraha. By his manifesto, Gandhi at one stroke disowned both the British establishment in India and the Indian Congress establishment opposing it.

As the struggle over the "Black Act" grew, Gandhi saw a need for a large community in the Transvaal on the model of Phoenix Farm—a community where the resisters and their families might live, work to support themselves, and, in the process, rediscover that simple, golden life. Most of the resisters—or satyagrahis, as they were now generally called—were very poor men, and had to leave their families practically without resources when they went to prison. "Even a satyagrahi may be excused if he feels troubled at heart from want of his daily bread," Gandhi writes. "There cannot be many in the world who would fight the good fight in spite of being compelled to condemn their nearest and dearest to the same starvation which they suffered in their own person." In 1910, Hermann Kallenbach, a successful architect of German-Jewish origins, who had no family of his own, and who had become one of Gandhi's most ardent followers, bought some eleven hundred acres of land twenty-one miles from Johannesburg and gave it to Gandhi, rent free, for his second community. Gandhi called this one Tolstoy Farm, not after the Tolstoy of "War and Peace" but after the later, cranky, fanatically religious Tolstoy of "The Kingdom of God Is Within You": the Tolstoy who turned his back on his own artistic achievements; who abandoned his estate and his family; who didn't believe in owning property; who thought money was tainted; who gave up smoking and drinking; who didn't believe in killing living things, in hunting, or in eating meat; who espoused manual labor; who wandered the Russian countryside in the plain smock and trousers of a muzhik; and who inveighed against the Russian Orthodox Church as a worldly force whose aim was to crush Christ, and against civilization, which was based on violence, since governments were kept in power by huge standing armies. This Tolstoy taught that man's highest duty was to love his fellow-man and resist evil and violence—to live like Christ.

Men, women, and children lived at Tolstoy Farm in the manner of a joint family, and were schooled there in fearlessness, self-reliance, self-denial, self-sacrifice, and suffering; in embracing poverty and living in harmony with other people and with nature—so that they could learn to practice brahmacharya, satyagraha, and ahimsa, and thus do battle indefinitely with the corrupt society and the government. They got up at dawn. They walked everywhere they had to go, however far; Gandhi would often get up at two o'clock in the morning, walk the twenty-one miles to Johannesburg, attend to his law practice, and walk back to the farm in the afternoon. They didn't kill anything—not even snakes. They grew their own food, ground their own wheat, baked their own bread, and toasted some of the wheat to make caffeine-free "caramel" coffee according to a recipe provided by Gandhi. They made their own furniture, clothes, and sandals. They met every day with Gandhi to read the Bhagavad Gita, to pray, and to sing hymns of many religions. Gandhi had begun a number of these practices at Phoenix Farm, and now, at Tolstoy Farm, he made them into a way of life.

Gandhi felt that children were naturally moral and were corrupted by society, so he advocated, among other things, that boys and girls not be segregated but live and play together. They even bathed together— always, however, under his watchful eye. Once, he learned that a boy and a girl had had sexual intercourse, and he immediately cut off the girl's hair to make her "sexless." At the same time, he himself observed a seven-day fast as a penance for their moral lapse. The boy and girl repeated their offense some time later, whereupon he observed a four-teen-day fast. Hindu ascetics had always observed fasts for self-purification. Gandhi was now observing them for the purification not only of himself but also of others. Believing that there was no boundary between public and private morality in any society, he had concluded that he could expiate the sins of others by taking them on himself—a notion that had the effect of binding the immediate community (and, subsequently, his ever-increasing circle of disciples and followers) more tightly to him.

Gandhi started fasting regularly, for a week at a time, because the Bhagavad Gita said:

> For a man who is fasting his senses
> Outwardly, the sense-objects disappear,
> Leaving the yearning behind; but when
> He has seen the Highest,
> Even the yearning disappears.

During the first several fasts he undertook, he had a tendency to lose his voice, and when he broke the fast he would have difficulty in swallowing or in keeping food or drink down, and would experience some pain in walking, because his legs and feet had grown weak through lack of use. (He stayed in bed while he was fasting.) In time, he discovered that he could control such effects by swallowing a little water when he fasted, and doing exercises in bed. He would have liked to do away with food entirely, he says, because it inevitably involved some sort of himsa, or violence, against animal or plant life. He says he realized, however, that without some himsa there could be no social order—in fact, no life. The best he could do, he felt, was to reduce his needs to the minimum, and so do as little himsa as possible. He took a vow against drinking cow's milk, because he had read that some dairymen mistreated their cows to get the last drop of milk from them, and he lived for a time only on uncooked cereals, bananas, dates, oranges, lemons, groundnuts, and olive oil. "Medically there may be two opinions as to the value of this diet, but morally I have no doubt that all self-denial is good for the soul," he writes.

In the autumn of 1912, in response to repeated urging by Gandhi, the Indian nationalist leader Gopal Krishna Gokhale paid a brief visit to South Africa, to see for himself the conditions of the South African Indians and to try to bring pressure on the Union government to repeal the two main anti-Indian laws—the "Black Act" in the Transvaal, and the annual three-pound head tax on freed indentured laborers and their dependents in Natal, for the head tax was prohibitive for most Indian laborers. Gokhale received assurances from Smuts and the Union

Prime Minister, General Louis Botha, that both laws would be rescinded within a year or so. But nothing came of these assurances.

In March, 1913, a case involving the right of Bai Mariam, the wife of a Muslim immigrant to the Cape, to join her husband came before Justice Malcolm Searle, in the Cape Supreme Court. The Justice handed down the ruling that marriages that had not been solemnized according to Christian rites and had not been registered by the Union Registrar of Marriages had no legal status in the Union. (Hindu, Muslim, and Parsi marriages had never been registered anywhere and were governed mainly by religious traditions that allowed polygamy.) Bai Mariam was not allowed to land and was ordered to return to India. (As it happened, the Searle decision coincided with the passage of the Union Immigration Restriction Act, which, modelled on the Natal Act 14 of 1897, in effect barred any future Indian immigration into South Africa; such a bill had been proposed almost from the establishment of the Union, and had immediately become a rallying point of the Indian protest movement.)

Gandhi felt that the Searle decision had instantaneously made all Indian wives except Christian ones concubines or common-law wives, and their children illegitimate; the wives had no legal right to enter, let alone live in, the Union of South Africa, and were there solely by the grace of the government. Up to then, Gandhi had restricted his satyagraha movement to the Transvaal and its "Black Act," because he felt that it should concentrate on one simple, basic moral issue at a time, and had restricted it to men, because he felt that it was unmanly to call on mothers, wives, and daughters to endure the travails of a satyagrahi. But now, in the Searle decision, Gandhi had a simple, basic moral issue that touched the lives of Indian men and women alike, throughout South Africa. His advocacy of the repeal of the head tax had brought the Indian poor into politics; now his advocacy of the validity of Indian marriages brought women into politics. Women and the poor, who had been left out of the élitist politics usual in that day, became the rank and file of Gandhi's movement in South Africa, as their counterparts did later in India.

Later in the year, Gandhi decided he would try to fill the jails of the Union with Indians and so expose the immorality of the anti-Indian laws, in the hope of bringing about a moral transformation of the whole of South African society. Sixteen of his relatives and close friends from

Phoenix Farm, including Kasturbai, courted arrest by crossing the border from Natal into the Transvaal without the required immigration permits. The government, playing into their hands, arrested and jailed them all. A few days later, eleven "sisters" from Tolstoy Farm also courted arrest by crossing the border without the required immigration permits, this time from the Transvaal into Natal. But the government chose not to arrest them, and so, in accordance with Gandhi's plan, they marched on for thirty-six miles to Newcastle, where five thousand indentured Indian laborers worked European-owned coal mines. There the eleven women succeeded in persuading all the miners to go out on strike to protest the head tax and the Searle decision. Gandhi then rushed to Newcastle and took up residence with an Indian Christian couple, Mr. and Mrs. D. M. Lazarus. The mine owners tried to intimidate the strikers by shutting off the water and electricity in the company-owned dwellings where they lived and by beating some of them up. Gandhi promptly told the strikers to leave their dwellings and come and camp on the plot of land around the Lazaruses' house. Thousands of miners, accompanied by their wives and children and outfitted with only the clothes on their backs and a blanket for bedding, crowded onto the plot and started camping there, supported by whatever food and utensils the Newcastle Indian merchants could spare. Gandhi was at a loss to know what to do next. How was he going to continue to feed them, let alone take care of their other needs—especially if the strike dragged on? He felt that his only hope was to get them all arrested and so make them charges of the government. He therefore decided to march them all into the Transvaal without the required immigration permits. He warned them of the horrors of being Indian prisoners in European-run jails and encouraged any waverers to return to their dwellings. They all stayed.

On October 28th, Gandhi set out with his straggly "army of peace," numbering five or six thousand, for Charlestown, a small town just inside the Natal border, where the army camped for a week, living off the hospitality of local Indian merchants and European sympathizers. It was no easy business managing so many soldiers. "I found that when the men had a little leisure, they occupied it with internal squabbles," Gandhi writes. "What was worse, there were cases of adultery. There was terrible overcrowding, and men and women had to be kept together. Animal passion knows no shame. As soon as the cases occurred, I arrived on the scene. The guilty parties were abashed, and they were segregated. But who can say how many such cases occurred which never came to my knowledge?" Gandhi, Kallenbach, and the other lieutenants of the army used the week in Charlestown to plan their protest march into the Transvaal. At the same time, they put the government on notice of their intention to break the immigration laws, hoping to get the government to rescind the "Black Act" and the head tax at last and reverse the Searle decision or else to arrest them all. The government, however, did nothing. Since Gandhi could no longer count on room and board at "His Majesty's hotels" for all the satyagrahis, he decided to march them into the Transvaal and on to Tolstoy Farm.

On November 6th, Gandhi, leading two thousand and thirty-seven men, a hundred and twenty-seven women, and fifty-seven children, crossed the Natal border. (He does not say what happened to the rest of the satyagrahis or why he left them behind; they probably stayed on in the camp in Charlestown.) The marchers got as far as Palmford, a town eight miles inside the Transvaal, on the first day. As they were settling down to sleep after finishing a small meal of bread and sugar that Gandhi had been able to arrange for them, the police finally arrived, but with orders to arrest only Gandhi. Gandhi instructed his lieutenants to continue the march to Tolstoy Farm, which was still a hundred and fifty miles away. He then went off with the police, but after only one night in jail he was released on bail, because the government needed time to prepare a case against him. He rejoined the marchers.

In the next three days, he was arrested twice more—once in the town of Standerton, where he was also released in a very short time, apparently because the government could not make up its mind how to proceed against him, and once at Teakworth, near Johannesburg, where he was charged with inducing indentured laborers to leave Natal. Kallenbach and Polak had been arrested in Charlestown at about the same time and were both sentenced to three months' hard labor in jail; Gandhi was sentenced to nine months in jail or a sixty-pound fine. He chose jail. The satyagrahis had meanwhile continued marching, but when they reached the town of Balfour the government finally stopped them. All of them were herded onto three special trains and taken back to Natal, where the authorities, having no jails to accommodate them,

improvised jails by surrounding the mine compounds with wire netting. The satyagrahis, imprisoned behind the wire netting, were forced
to work the mines, with the mine staffs acting as jailers. When other
Indian laborers—there were now about sixty thousand in South Africa
as a whole—heard of these indignities, thousands of them went out on
strike.

The march had made headlines in England and in India. Gandhi
had seen to it that the government in London and the Indian nationalist
leaders knew what was going on almost from day to day, by sending
them cablegrams and by making statements to the press. The British
government was genuinely shocked, and the Indian nationalist leaders
clamored for the Viceroy to do something. Pressure was put on the
Union government to release Gandhi and his associates and to set up
a commission of inquiry. Gandhi was convinced that the commission
was just a way for the government to buy time and end up doing
nothing—since not only were there no Indians on it but some of its
members were notoriously anti-Indian—so he made ready for another
protest march, this one against the commission. Just at that time, as it
happened, European railway workers went on strike throughout South
Africa, threatening the survival of Botha's government. Gandhi immediately called off his protest march, on the ground that a satyagrahi
did not take advantage of his adversary's weakness. Gandhi reports:

> One of the secretaries of General Smuts jocularly said: "I do not
> like your people, and do not care to assist them at all. But what am
> I to do? You help us in our days of need. How can we lay hands upon
> you? I often wish you took to violence like the English strikers, and
> then we would know at once how to dispose of you. But you will
> not injure even the enemy. You desire victory by self-suffering alone
> and never transgress your self-imposed limits of courtesy and chiv-
> alry. And that is what reduces us to sheer helplessness."

In June, 1914, through a number of letters and conversations,
Gandhi, representing no government and holding no office, negotiated
an agreement with General Smuts as if he were on an equal footing with
him. All Indian marriages solemnized by Hindu, Muslim, or Parsi
tradition were recognized as valid, and the head tax was abolished and
arrears cancelled. The Union Immigration Restriction Act, however,
remained in force, except that as a gesture the government allowed six

educated Indians to immigrate to South Africa every year. And no more indentured Indian laborers were to be allowed to enter after 1920. The main provision of the "Black Act" also remained in force: Indians were not permitted to move freely from province to province. The agreement was a compromise, but Gandhi considered it a victory for his satyagraha movement.

A fortnight later, Gandhi left South Africa for good. "I sailed for England, to meet Gokhale, on my way back to India, with mixed feelings of pleasure and regret," he writes. "Pleasure because I was returning home after many years and eagerly looked forward to serving the country under Gokhale's guidance, regret because it was a great wrench for me to leave South Africa, where I had passed twenty-one years of my life sharing to the full in the sweets and bitters of human experience, and where I had realized my vocation in life." Gandhi spent the rest of his life refining and deepening the ideas he had formed in South Africa. His South African experience as a whole had brought about in him a religious conversion that was unique in that it was not a sudden revelation but a gradual realization of God. The experience had also left him somewhat disenchanted with the British Empire, for which he had at one time had so much enthusiasm. He now had certain reservations about it, having seen that Britain had sacrificed the interests of its Indian subjects in South Africa for mere trade advantages.

Satyagrahi in India

GANDHI HAD ARRIVED IN LONDON FROM SOUTH AFRICA IN August, 1914, just after the outbreak of the First World War. Radical Indian friends of his in London wanted India to take advantage of the war to wrest political concessions from England, but Gandhi still considered himself a loyal subject of the Empire; besides, he believed that a satyagrahi who had not tried to prevent a war could not avoid taking part in it without being cowardly. (He was constantly introducing and developing new variations on the theme of satyagraha.) While he was in London, he again organized—with the reluctant consent of the British government—a small ambulance corps of Indian volunteers, but it never got to the front, and merely did some token nursing in England. It disintegrated within a few months, partly because Gandhi had fallen out with the military authorities by refusing to let his corps function as part of the Army, and partly because he succumbed to the damp, inhospitable English climate and contracted pleurisy. A friend advised him to seek a warmer climate, and he sailed for India, reaching Bombay in January, 1915, his health considerably restored by the voyage. He was now forty-five.

Accepting an offer of financial help from some textile merchants in his native region of Gujarat, Gandhi in 1915 established his first permanent community in India, near Ahmedabad, on the west bank of the Sabarmati River. Ahmedabad was one of the most ancient and beautiful cities of India, dotted with old mosques and medieval ruins, but it was also the center of India's textile industry—a place of belching smokestacks surrounded by filthy lanes and squalid shanties. Gandhi called his community Sabarmati Ashram. In the ancient Hindu tradition, an ashram was a retreat where a group of devout people lived, meditated, and mortified the flesh, waiting to free themselves from the body, the bondage of worldly existence. But the Sabarmati Ashram was a religious community only in a very loose sense. Gandhi carried over to Sabarmati Ashram the daily regimen perfected at Phoenix and Tolstoy Farms and added to it spinning and weaving. He did, however, ask its members—many of whom had followed him there from Phoenix Farm —to live by a number of simple vows that had both political and religious aims: to practice brahmacharya, satyagraha, and ahimsa; to discipline their palates; to possess nothing; to cultivate fearlessness; to boycott imported English cloth; and to accept untouchables as equals. Some fifty or sixty million people—one-fifth of India's population— were untouchables, but the vow regarding them immediately threatened the survival of the ashram.

Gandhi had begun to fulfill his vow by accepting a family of untouchables—a father, mother, and baby daughter, whose names were Duda, Dani, and Lakshmi—into the ashram community. The other ashramites, however much they sought to follow Gandhi's precepts, found the family's presence humiliating and defiling, and avoided their company. The man in charge of the communal well balked at allowing the family to draw water from it, and cursed them and Gandhi. The Ahmedabad community as a whole threatened to stop all dealings with the ashram and drive the residents out. The textile merchants on whose charity the ashram depended for its very existence withdrew their support. Gandhi prepared to move his community to the section of the city where only untouchables lived, and have its members earn their livelihood doing the work of untouchables. But the ashram was saved when a man drove up in a big car and handed Gandhi thirteen thousand rupees. The donor, who wished his identity kept secret, was revealed later to have been the leading textile merchant of Ahmedabad, Ambalal Sarabhai.

Gokhale had strongly criticized Gandhi's manifesto "Indian Home Rule" as crude, ill conceived, and indicative of how Gandhi had lost touch with Indian politics. He had extracted from Gandhi a promise to refrain from direct political activities and pronouncements until he had spent at least a year reacquainting himself with the country. Gokhale died shortly after Gandhi's return to India. Gandhi resolved to go barefoot for a time to mourn his mentor, and, to reacquaint himself with the country, he began travelling through Indian by train, always going third class, with the poor. Third-class compartments had almost unrestricted ticket sales and no reserved seats—only uncushioned benches—and the compartments were crowded not only with people but with their bedrolls, bundles, trunks, baskets, and rubbish. Sometimes Gandhi had barely enough room to stand, and occasionally he was forced to sleep standing up. Everywhere he went, he saw poverty, filth, and disease. He stopped at Hardwar, on the Ganges, among the holiest of the holy places of pilgrimage for Hindus, and was aghast to find it as badly befouled as the rest of the country. As an act of atonement, he resolved that thereafter he would restrict his diet in any given twenty-four hours to only five articles of food.

In December, 1916, when Gandhi had been back in India for almost two years, he attended a session of the Indian National Congress, in Lucknow, which had on its agenda, among other subjects, agrarian discontent in Champaran. Gandhi knew nothing about Champaran and took no part in the debate, but afterward he was approached by a poor farmer who pleaded with him to go there and see for himself how the tenant farmers were being exploited by their English landlords. Champaran was such a remote district—in the foothills of the Himalayas, in the province of Bihar—that Gandhi had never heard of it, and he put the farmer off. But the farmer persisted, and followed him wherever he went—to Cawnpore, to Ahmedabad, to Calcutta—and at last Gandhi agreed to make the journey. In April, 1917, Gandhi and the farmer left Calcutta for Champaran.

They stopped in Muzaffarpur, which was the town nearest to Champaran, and there Gandhi learned from the local vakils that most of the arable land in the area was owned by Englishmen and cultivated by Indian tenant farmers. Under the tenancy system, each farmer had been obliged to set aside fifteen per cent of his land for growing indigo—once Bihar's most profitable crop—and turn over all the indigo to the landlord as rent. The English landlords had the crop processed in local factories into the deep-blue dye, which they then shipped to Europe for sale. At the beginning of the century, however, the Germans had discovered a method of making a synthetic blue dye, which eventually became so inexpensive that no one wanted to buy natural indigo any-more. The landlords, taking advantage of the farmers' ignorance of the German discovery, had thereupon demanded that they pay their rent in cash. When the farmers finally realized that they were growing an unmarketable crop, they felt that they had been cheated and robbed. They banded together and engaged vakils to sue for a full refund of the cash they had paid as rent. Gandhi concluded that litigation would only impoverish the poor farmers further, and he said that what the vakils should do instead was to go into the villages and, as the first step in reforming the whole tenancy system, collect testimony from the farmers about all their grievances. Gandhi was so persuasive that many vakils took his advice, even though by doing so they risked imprison-ment as political agitators. When Gandhi tried to talk to the landlords in Champaran, they would have nothing to do with him. As far as they knew, he was nothing but an interloper and a troublemaker.

In Champaran, Gandhi himself began collecting testimony from the farmers. Local English officials soon served him with an order to quit the district, but he refused to obey the order and was summoned to appear before a magistrate. Gandhi telegraphed these developments to the Viceroy and to various prominent friends. Moreover, word spread locally that a champion of the helpless was going on trial in Motihari, the district headquarters, and poor, emaciated farmers flocked there on foot or by bullock cart from surrounding villages, as if Gandhi's mere presence had liberated them from their old fear of landlords and officials. Gandhi told the magistrate that he had not disturbed the peace in any way but that since he could not obey the order he was guilty as charged. "I have disregarded the order served upon me," he said, "not for want of respect for lawful authority, but in obedience to the higher law of our being, the voice of conscience." Before Gandhi came up for sentencing, however, the authorities in Delhi, realizing that the local officials had bungled by making him into a hero, ordered that the charge against him be dropped and that he be allowed to proceed with his work undisturbed.

With the help of vakils and other recruits, Gandhi succeeded in collecting testimony from some eight thousand farmers throughout Champaran. "We may look on Mr. Gandhi as an idealist, a fanatic, or a revolutionary according to our particular opinions," a young British civil servant in Champaran reported at the time. "But to the *raiyats* [farmers] he is their liberator, and they credit him with extraordinary powers. He moves about in the villages asking them to lay their grievances before him, and he is transfiguring the imaginations of masses of ignorant men with visions of an early millennium." Gandhi was hailed as a "liberator" because he had imparted to the farmers, for the first time in their long history of exploitation by landlords, some hope of relief. Eventually, at the insistence of the Viceroy, Lord Chelmsford, a Champaran Agrarian Enquiry Committee was set up to investigate the local tenancy system, and Gandhi was given a seat on it. The farmers expected him to hold out for a full refund of their cash payments, but the committee unanimously recommended that the landlords refund only twenty-five per cent of the cash. On this particular issue, Gandhi had compromised because he felt that any repayment was an acknowledgment that the landlords had wronged the farmers and because he was more interested in the triumph of principle than in the rout of an adversary. He writes, "The superstition that the stain of indigo could never be washed out was exploded."

Gandhi stayed in Champaran for several more months and, with the help of volunteers recruited from as far away as Bombay, set about trying to teach the villagers rudimentary methods of hygiene and sanitation. Most of them suffered from chronic dysentery and chronic malaria, and from boils and scabies. They were introduced to simple medicaments—quinine and sulphur ointment—along with nature cures. They were taught how to keep their huts tidy and well swept, and their lanes clear of filth. Schools were improvised in huts, and soup kitchens set up in many villages to feed the poor and teach them the virtues of eating nutritious meals at regular hours. But at the end of 1917 Gandhi was called to Ahmedabad to help settle a labor dispute. Without his inspiring presence, the volunteer workers left, and the villagers reverted to their old ways.

In July, 1917, plague had broken out in Ahmedabad, and people had begun fleeing the city, abandoning their dwellings and shops. The mill owners, afraid of losing business to their competitors in Bombay, started paying the miserably poor unskilled mill hands "plague bonuses," amounting to as much as eighty per cent of their wages, to keep them in the city. No such bonuses were paid to the skilled mill hands, who were expected to stay in any case because they enjoyed certain small privileges at the mills. They began negotiating for a "dearness allowance," pleading that the war had doubled the prices of most necessities. When the plague epidemic abated, a few months later, the mill owners stopped the bonuses and cut short all discussion of the "dearness allowance." Together, the skilled and unskilled mill hands numbered some ten thousand, and now—even though they all lived virtually from hand to mouth, belonged to no unions, and had no bargaining power to speak of, since they could easily be replaced—they started talking, for the first time, of striking against the mill owners.

Gandhi received a call for help in the labor dispute from Anasuya-behn Sarabhai, who was a sister of the mill owner Ambalal Sarabhai but was championing the mill hands' cause. Gandhi had many friends among the mill owners and was well known to the mill hands as the sadhu who lived in the local ashram. He agreed to help, and quickly became the spokesman for the mill hands, who were asking for a fifty-per-cent increase in the wages they had been earning when the plague broke out; the mill owners, acting together, were offering twenty per cent. Gandhi recommended as a compromise a thirty-five-per-cent increase, but the mill owners turned it down.

On February 21st, a small group of mill hands actually went on strike, and the mill owners, who were experiencing shortages of materials because of the war, used the occasion to close down all the mills, declaring that the mill hands could go back to work only when they accepted the twenty-per-cent increase. Gandhi now started meeting every day with the mill hands under a babul tree on the east bank of the Sabarmati River, just outside the city, to pray with them and to exhort them to remain united and firm in their demand. The mill hands, after four days of no work and little to eat, began to think of settling on the mill owners' terms, but at the meeting on the fifth day of the lockout Gandhi persuaded them to make a pledge that, regardless of the consequences, they would not return to their jobs without the thirty-five-per-cent increase, and that they would not beg or steal, loot or damage property, or resort to violence of any kind. The daily meetings continued, and the babul tree was soon dubbed the Keep the Pledge Tree.

Gandhi, Anasuyabehn, and other volunteers visited the huts of the mill hands daily and tried to provide them with a little food and keep them occupied in constructive work—repairing huts, cleaning roads, and putting up buildings across the river in the Sabarmati Ashram. But as the days passed, the mill hands grew more and more desperate, attendance at the meetings became smaller and smaller, and it began to look as if the starving mill hands would go back on their pledge—especially since, after the lockout had been going on for three weeks, the mill owners again announced that the men could return to their jobs if they accepted the twenty-per-cent wage increase.

At the Keep the Pledge Tree meeting on March 15th, Gandhi, in an effort to rally the strikers' spirits, declared that he would not touch food until either the mill owners accepted binding arbitration or the mill hands quit their jobs for good. "While I was still groping and unable to see my way clearly, the light came to me," Gandhi writes. "Unbidden and all by themselves the words came to my lips." Gandhi had never before undertaken a fast for a public cause, but, he says, he now saw that it could be an important weapon for a satyagrahi, provided that the motive for using it was disinterested and pure, and the issue involved so critical that death was preferable to capitulation. Yet, he says, he was instantly filled with self-doubt. The mill owners might capitulate not because of the justice of the cause but because of their affection for him, their concern for his well-being, or even their fear of the consequences if he should die. He tried to convince himself that his fast was true to his principle of satyagraha, but he could not overcome the feeling that it might actually turn out to be a betrayal of it. Still, having committed himself to a fast, he felt he had no choice but to go through with it. Three days later, on March 18th, the mill owners agreed to arbitration. Gandhi called off his fast, the mill hands returned to work, and eventually, through arbitration, they received the thirty-five-per-cent increase. The Ahmedabad strike was the first such organized effort by any workers in India. (Two years later, Gandhi inaugurated the Ahmedabad Textile Labor Association and so helped launch India's trade-union movement.) Gandhi's fast was in the Hindu tradition, for Hindus often used fasts to exert pressure on their opponents, but in justifying his own fast in Ahmedabad he later drew a distinction between a fast in the service of what he considered a "creative idea" —in this case, binding arbitration—and a fast for private gain or for the intimidation of an adversary. "I can fast against my father to cure him of a vice, but I may not in order to get from him an inheritance," he explained. In the course of the next thirty years, he used the weapon of public fasting seventeen times.

At about the time of the Ahmedabad strike-*cum*-lockout, the peasants in the Kheda district, near Ahmedabad, were claiming that the damage to their crops from adverse weather in 1917 was so great that it called for remission of their annual revenue assessment, which they were not required to pay if the harvest fell twenty-five per cent below the yield for a normal year. The local officials were disputing the extent of the damage and insisting that the assessment be paid. In late March of 1918, Gandhi agreed to go to the Kheda district, and there he addressed a meeting of some five thousand peasants. He urged them not to pay the assessment, and "to fight it out." Inspired by Gandhi's call, many educated men and women in the area gave up the practice of their professions and went with him from village to village encouraging the peasants to overcome their fear of authority and refuse to pay the assessment. They were eagerly received, and were helped along the way with offers of bullock carts and food and shelter. The local officials retaliated by attaching the peasants' land and cattle, but then they realized that they had gone too far—that their retaliatory measures had boomeranged. A compromise was arranged: the richer peasants had to pay the assessment; the poorer were let off. The effort in the Kheda district was Gandhi's first large-scale satyagraha movement in India. It brought him into contact with influential people in the area, who became stalwarts of his future campaigns, and it established him as a leader in a populous countryside, from which his fame quickly spread. The foundations of his national leadership and national satyagraha campaign were thus laid in his native Gujarat.

In April of 1918, Gandhi received an invitation from the Viceroy to attend a conference in New Delhi on recruiting Indians for service at the front. About eight hundred thousand Indians were already fighting in the British Army. Nationalist leaders like Lokamanya Tilak and Annie Besant objected to any recruitment in India without firm guarantees from the British that India would be granted home rule, or dominion status, when the war was over. Gandhi, in contrast, still felt that Indians, as loyal subjects of the Empire, were duty-bound to help Britain in the war. (English officials had been taunting him by saying that so far all that he himself had done for the war as a loyal subject of the Empire was to harass them in Champaran and Kheda.) But since he was also committed to satyagraha and ahimsa, he went to the conference reluctantly. Nevertheless, once there, he allowed himself to be persuaded by the Viceroy to become an active recruiting agent. He wrote at the time to a Christian missionary friend, Esther Faering, "Indians have a double duty to perform. If they are to preach the mission of peace, they must first prove their ability in war. . . . A nation that is unfit to fight cannot from experience prove the virtue of not fighting." All the same, his decision was condemned both by his co-workers and by most of the nationalist leaders.

Gandhi started recruiting in familiar territory, in Kheda. The district contained six hundred villages, and he hoped to recruit at least twenty able-bodied men from each, but he found that the peasants who had so recently cheered him shunned him now as a turncoat. Some days, he would walk as much as twenty miles without getting anyone even to listen to him, let alone enlist. He became weak and dispirited— at the time he was living mostly on groundnut butter and lemon juice—and in August, while he was stopping over at Sabarmati Ashram, he contracted dysentery. He tried to cure himself by fasting, but, he says, he became so hungry that when Kasturbai gave him porridge and lentils he overate, and made his dysentery worse. Nevertheless, he set off by train with a co-worker, Sardar Vallabhbhai Patel, for Nadiad, a town in Kheda twenty-nine miles from Ahmedabad, to carry on the recruiting campaign. They reached Nadiad around ten o'clock in the evening and had to walk about half a mile from the station to the ashram where they were to spend the night. "It was as good as ten [miles] for me," Gandhi writes. "I somehow managed to reach the quarters, but the griping pain was steadily increasing." He developed a fever, became delirious, and, he says, lost his will to live. He was taken back to Ahmedabad, where Ambalal and Anasuyabehn Sarabhai nursed him in their home. He was convinced that he was going to die, and he wanted to die in his own ashram, so he was moved there. The doctors pressed meat broth, eggs, and milk upon him, but he spurned them. Kasturbai, however, persuaded him to drink goat's milk by arguing that his vow against milk applied only to cow's milk. He says that the goat's milk,

together with the news that Germany had been defeated and the war
was over, helped him to start getting better.

In March, 1919, the British government passed the Rowlatt Act, which
kept in force in India such stringent emergency wartime measures as
press censorship and summary justice for political agitators, and extin-
guished any lingering hopes for dominion status. Gandhi, who had put
his trust in the good intentions of the British, felt betrayed. He says he
had a waking dream that he should call for a twenty-four-hour hartal,
or general strike, as a satyagraha protest against the Rowlatt Act. During the hartal, all work would stop and the entire country would pray
and fast for self-purification. He called for a day of hartal to be observed, and eventually fixed April 6th as the date. The idea of a hartal
against the widely unpopular Rowlatt Act was eagerly taken up by the
nationalists, and on April 6th work in a number of towns and cities
came to a standstill. People pledged that, regardless of the consequences, they would not submit to the Rowlatt Act. Some prayed and
fasted, but others took to violence: officials were attacked, government
buildings burned, shops and houses plundered, trains stopped and
looted, telephone and telegraph wires cut. Many people died in the
rioting. Gandhi, horrified, called for an end to the hartal, but the
violence continued. On April 10th, in the city of Amritsar, in the
Punjab—the scene of the worst violence—an English schoolteacher was
assaulted by a mob. Although she escaped being killed, Brigadier General Reginald Edward Harry Dyer, a veteran of the First World War
who had also fought in Burma and on India's northwest frontier, arrived in Amritsar on April 11th, and the next day he proclaimed a ban
on public meetings and processions. On April 13th, some five thousand
of the city's residents, in defiance of the ban, held a meeting at Jallianwalla Bagh, a tract of land mostly walled in by buildings. General Dyer
blocked the main entrance with troops and ordered them to open fire.
The panic-stricken crowd, trapped and unarmed, surged in all directions. Within ten minutes, at least four hundred people were dead and
twelve hundred maimed or wounded. The following day, General
Dyer decreed that all Indians passing along the street on which the
English schoolteacher had been assaulted must crawl on all fours as
penance for the crime. He further decreed that any Indian who failed

to show proper respect for the British—by getting down from his bullock cart to salute a passing Englishman, for instance—would be publicly flogged. Some time later, when word of the massacre and Dyer's other excesses finally reached Gandhi (any violence against Europeans or Anglo-Indians was widely publicized, but news of the massacre was censored), he concluded that the British would stop at nothing to keep India subjugated, but he blamed himself for the outbreaks of violence, because it was he who had called the hartal in the first place. He felt his mistake to be of such proportions that he referred to it as his "Himalayan blunder." He had miscalculated the forces of evil in Indian society, he said, and had summoned his people to satyagraha before they were ready for it.

In any event, the government swiftly countermanded the crawling order and appointed Lord Hunter, a distinguished jurist, to head a committee of investigation. His report was thorough and fair, but the Jallianwalla Bagh massacre, though it was exceptional in the history of the British raj, became a byword for British brutality.

Late in 1919, the British proposed to grant Indians, among other things, more places in the Indian Civil Service and greater participation in the provincial legislative assemblies and ministries. Gandhi dismissed the proposals, known as the Montagu-Chelmsford Reforms, as a "subtle method of emasculation," and said that Indians should have nothing more to do with the British or the government. In fact, he said, they should observe a whole program of "non-cooperation"—not only stay out of the Civil Service and legislative assemblies but also boycott English (the official language), the courts, British-run schools and colleges, and British goods, including textiles. And they should volunteer their services for nationalist causes, speak their mother tongues, set up Indian arbitration boards to settle their court cases, enter Indian-run schools and colleges, and, above all, wear khadi as an expression of their nationalism. Gandhi believed that he had found in non-cooperation yet another powerful weapon for satyagrahis—one that could achieve *swaraj* (literally, "self-rule") for India in a year, at most. He was vague about what form *swaraj* would take, speaking of it, variously, as a people's democracy, spiritual and political freedom, and the millennium.

Non-cooperation was at once attacked by other nationalists as a creed of "negation, exclusiveness, and despair;" as an anarchist scheme to undermine respect for law and authority, for persons and property; as a doomed attempt to build a "Chinese wall" between India and the West. Nevertheless, in 1920 non-cooperation was narrowly adopted by the Indian National Congress, India's chief political party, as its national program. The Congress, from its founding, in 1885, had been the preserve of the upper and middle classes—of Anglicized lawyers educated in British-run schools and universities, who wore Western-style suits, spoke English among themselves, and were more interested in becoming partners of the British than in overthrowing them. Party meetings were likely to be devoted to rhetorical debate rather than to serious discussion. But since 1918, in view of Britain's failure to grant India any kind of home rule, the Congress had become more nationalistic and more radical. Now, in 1920, it adopted a new Constitution, drafted by Gandhi, which was designed to refashion it into a militant grass-roots movement, with village, district, provincial, and national committees, all democratically elected. Anyone who could afford the subscription of four annas, or one-fourth of a rupee, a year could become a member. Gandhi's success in the Congress was due in part to his ability to influence its Muslim minority—an ability he possessed because at around that time he had lent his support to the most important Muslim political and religious issue of the day. This was the Caliphate—or, as it was called in India, the Khilafat—Movement, an attempt by the Indian Muslims to save the defeated sultan of Turkey as the caliph of Islam. It was a hopeless undertaking, because the caliphate had long been as moribund an institution as the Turkish Empire. Gandhi espoused this exclusively Muslim cause for the sake of Hindu-Muslim unity; and thereby won widespread Muslim backing for the first —and also the last—time in his life. (The Khilafat Movement fizzled out in 1924, when the Turks themselves—having previously banished the sultan and declared Turkey a republic—abolished the caliphate.)

In 1921, Gandhi began a dizzying tour of the country, travelling to the most remote villages to meet, direct, and advise Congress workers and recruit new ones. He now always wore a white khadi dhoti—the mendicant's or fakir's garb. Villagers who got word that he was coming mobbed his train in country station after country station simply to catch sight of him—to receive his darshana. He would often say a few words about satyagraha and ahimsa, or about his experiences in South Africa. He became renowned for his voluntary poverty, his humility, and his simple, saintly life, and began to be called Mahatma.

The British at first did not take non-cooperation seriously, dismissing it as a foolish, hysterical scheme, which would soon destroy itself. But as non-cooperation gathered momentum, they came to realize that it posed a threat to their entire system of law and administration. The government began to watch Gandhi's movements closely. In November, 1921, when the Prince of Wales arrived in Bombay on a visit to India, his arrival was boycotted by the local residents, and there were also outbreaks of rioting and arson. Thereafter, in Indian cities, meetings and processions were forcibly dispersed, midnight searches were made of Congress offices for seditious material, and by January, 1922, as many as thirty thousand Congress workers had been put in jail.

In February, Gandhi came under pressure from his Congress colleagues to lead the country in mass civil disobedience. He resisted at first, because he could not think of one basic issue capable of mobilizing the whole country and he feared that the people would again resort to violence, as they had during the agitation against the Rowlatt Act. Then he decided to experiment briefly with civil disobedience in the county of Bardoli, in Gujarat, by directing peasants to refuse payment of the land-revenue tax. If it worked there, he intended to raise the same issue and fight it in the same way in district after district, until the whole country was striking against the payment of the tax. But, as he had feared, shortly after he launched his Bardoli campaign, on February 5th, rioting broke out—in Chauri Chaura, a little, out-of-the-way village in the nearby United Provinces. He called off the experiment and abandoned all thought of a national campaign, thus confounding his colleagues and followers.

Nevertheless, on March 10th, at ten-thirty in the evening, a police officer arrived at Sabarmati Ashram and arrested Gandhi. A week later, Gandhi was tried in Ahmedabad on a charge of writing three seditious articles in his weekly *Young India*. "I am satisfied that many English and Indian officials honestly believe that they are administering one of the best systems devised in the world and that India is making steady though slow progress," Gandhi said in his statement to the court. "They do not know that a subtle but effective system of terrorism and an organized display of force on the one hand, and the deprivation of all powers of retaliation or self-defense on the other, have emasculated the people and induced in them the habit of stimulation. . . . I believe that I have rendered a service to India and England by showing in non-cooperation the way out of the unnatural state in which both are living. In my humble opinion, non-cooperation with evil is as much a duty as is cooperation with good. . . . I am here, therefore, to invite and submit cheerfully to the highest penalty that can be inflicted upon me for what in law is a deliberate crime and what appears to me to be the highest duty of a citizen. The only course open to you, the Judge, is either to resign your post and thus dissociate yourself from evil, if you feel that the law you are called upon to administer is an evil and that in reality I am innocent; or to inflict on me the severest penalty if you believe that the system and the law you are assisting to administer are good for the people of this country and that my activity is, therefore, injurious to the public weal.''

The judge sentenced Gandhi to six years in jail, adding that "no one would be better pleased than I'' if the government later saw fit to reduce the sentence. Two days later, Gandhi was taken by special train to Yeravda Central Jail, in Poona, a hill station about three hundred and fifty miles south of Ahmedabad. He served only twenty-two months of his sentence, partly because in 1924 he had to undergo an operation for appendicitis. Not only did this leave him weak and exhausted but the non-cooperation movement was now in complete disarray, so the government decided to release him. For the next three or four years, he mostly stayed out of politics.

Then, in 1928, the government increased the land-revenue tax by twenty-two per cent—in, as it happened, Bardoli. Gandhi was persuaded to help organize a second civil-disobedience campaign there. The peasants refused to pay the tax, and the government retaliated by arresting many of them and attaching their property. This time, there was no rioting; the peasants stoically bore the indignities heaped upon them, and, as a consequence, the government was obliged to yield. It rescinded the tax increase, released the prisoners, and restored the property. But two more years passed before Gandhi, disillusioned by British attempts at Constitutional reform, finally launched a national civil-disobedience campaign.

Early in 1928, the Conservative Government of Stanley Baldwin had sent a commission, under the chairmanship of Sir John Simon, to India to review its Constitutional status—a move called for in the Montagu-Chelmsford Reforms of 1919. Gandhi and other Congress leaders boycotted the Simon Commission, on the grounds that no Indians had been appointed to it and that, in any case, the appointment of a commission was a charade, given the imperialist attitude of the Conservative Government. Both the Government and the commission were denounced at protest meetings across the country. The meetings were often forcibly dispersed by lathi charges. (A lathi is a large, heavy, ironbound stick commonly carried by policemen in India.) During a lathi charge in Lahore, Lala Lajpat Rai, the best-known Punjabi nationalist—he was popularly called the Lion of the Punjab—was fatally injured. In revenge, a Punjabi named Bhagat Singh assassinated the assistant superintendent of police in Lahore and later bombed the Legislative Assembly in New Delhi. Once again, to Gandhi's horror, a peaceful protest had turned violent.

In December of 1928, Gandhi was prevailed upon to come out of his relative political seclusion to attend the annual session of the Congress, in Calcutta. The Congress leaders were bitterly divided over the question of whether India should demand dominion status or press for all-out independence, and they looked to Gandhi for an answer. Gandhi, who still preferred accommodation with the British to a complete break, and so favored dominion status, came up with a compromise: if at the end of one year the government still refused to grant India dominion status, then he himself would lead a national civil-disobedience campaign for all-out independence.

Meanwhile, in June, 1929, the Labour Government of Ramsay MacDonald had succeeded Baldwin's Conservative Government, and after due deliberation it proposed a Round Table Conference in London between British and Indian representatives to debate whether India could be granted dominion status and, if so, when and how. The members of the Congress decided to boycott the conference, ostensibly on the ground that they had demanded immediate dominion status, not more talk on the whether, when, and how, but actually because they knew they would have a poor negotiating position. All over India, people were divided not only on the question of dominion status versus independence but also on the questions of the disposition of some six hundred practically autonomous princely states—the so-called Indian

India—and of the protection of the Muslim minority. Some Indians even wished India to continue under British rule or to receive dominion status in stages. Therefore, neither the Congress nor Gandhi could claim to speak for all Indians, and so neither was in a position to make a "national demand" at the conference. Instead, on January 1, 1930, Congress defiantly unfurled a flag for independent India and so opened its campaign for all-out independence.

Everyone in the Congress now looked to Gandhi to find an issue around which the whole country could be rallied nonviolently, and within two months he did find one. His "inner voice" told him to lead a civil-disobedience campaign against the salt-tax laws, on the model of his 1913 satyagraha campaign in South Africa. First, he wrote to Lord Irwin, the Viceroy:

> The iniquities [of the tax laws in general and the salt laws in particular] . . . are maintained in order to carry on a foreign administration, demonstrably the most expensive in the world. Take your own salary. . . . You are getting over 700 rupees per day against India's average income of less than two annas per day. . . . Thus you are getting much over five thousand times India's average income. . . . On bended knee, I ask you to ponder over this phenomenon. I have taken a personal illustration to drive home a painful truth. I have too great a regard for you as a man to wish to hurt your feelings. . . .
>
> But a system that provides for such an arrangement deserves to be summarily scrapped; . . . nothing but unadulterated non-violence can check the organized violence of the British government. . . .
>
> But if you cannot see your way to deal with these evils and my letter makes no appeal to your heart, on the eleventh day of this month, I shall proceed with such co-workers of the ashram as I can take, to disregard the provisions of the salt laws.

The Viceroy, rather than enter into a discussion with Gandhi or arrest him, contented himself with having his secretary write a formal acknowledgment of Gandhi's letter.

Under the salt laws, the government enjoyed a monopoly on salt mining, levied a sales tax on salt, and forbade Indians to make their own salt or to use contraband salt. A large number of Indians lived on plains not far from the sea and could easily have made their own salt by drying out seawater in the sun. For the Indians, salt was as essential as air and water: most of them labored long hours in the fields in blistering heat and ate only lentils, bread, and salt. Gandhi came to look upon the salt tax as a tax on Indian sweat and blood.

On March 12, 1930, Gandhi—accompanied by scores of ashram residents; workers in what he had named his Constructive Programme, a movement for social reform; and press correspondents—set out for Dandi, a coastal town two hundred miles south of the ashram, where he planned to publicly flout the salt laws, vowing that he would not return to the Sabarmati Ashram until they had been repealed. Every day, he marched about twelve miles, then stopped for the night in a village, where he held a prayer meeting and gave a talk about the salt laws and the Constructive Programme, on occasion mentioning the second Bardoli campaign as an inspiring example of both the potency of nonviolence and his countrymen's capacity for it. Every evening, too, he found time to do an hour's spinning and to keep his diary and correspondence up to date. Some villagers joined the march; others sprinkled water along Gandhi's path to settle the dust, and strewed leaves and flower petals before him.

Gandhi's journey to Dandi was compared by his disciples and followers to Jesus's journey to Jerusalem; many Hindus who could read bought copies of the Bible and read it. Gandhi himself apparently thought that he might have to die in Dandi, as Jesus died in Jerusalem. He and his followers arrived there on April 5th and spent the night praying on the beach. In the morning, he walked into the sea to bathe and purify himself. Then he and his followers went through the process of making salt from seawater and so became criminals in the eyes of the law. He and his followers camped near Dandi for the next month, making and selling small quantities of salt, and waiting to see what the government would do. At first, the government did nothing, in the expectation that Gandhi's bizarre campaign would spend itself. But the story of the salt march and Gandhi's illicit activities was reported around the world, and in India more and more people began going on symbolic salt marches of their own. Up and down the coasts, on the beaches, and on the banks of brackish streams—wherever there was salt to be found—people became satyagrahis and broke the law. Scarcely any violence was reported. The satyagrahis waded into the sea, collected salt water in pans, watched it evaporate in the sun, and shared the precious salt left behind. The authorities, completely underestimating the symbolic power of Gandhi's action, ridiculed the idea that the British raj could be dissolved in pans of seawater. Not much salt was actually produced, but stories of selling and using contraband salt were widely told to dramatize the evils of the British system. Civil disobedience spread to other forms of protest and soon far surpassed the non-cooperation campaign of 1920 and 1921. In fact, the 1930 effort became the largest protest movement that Gandhi ever led.

The government had continued to follow a policy of restraint in the hope of diffusing the force of the movement, but at last it decided to act, and on May 5th, in the middle of the night, the police appeared at Gandhi's camp and arrested him. His arrest was followed by government action against practically anyone who was involved in an important way in the civil-disobedience campaign. Webb Miller, a United Press correspondent, described what happened on May 21st to a march designed to raid the government's Dharasana Salt Works, a hundred and fifty miles north of Bombay:

> Suddenly at a word of command, scores of native policemen rushed upon the advancing marchers and rained blows on their heads with their steel-shod lathis. Not one of the marchers even raised an arm to fend off the blows. They went down like ten-pins. From where I stood I heard the sickening whack of the clubs on unprotected skulls. The waiting crowd of marchers groaned and sucked in their breath in sympathetic pain at every blow. . . . They marched steadily, with heads up, without the encouragement of music or cheering or any possibility that they might escape serious injury or death. The police rushed out and methodically and mechanically beat down the second column. There was no fight, no struggle; the marchers simply walked forward till struck down.

By midsummer, according to one estimate, as many as a hundred thousand satyagrahis, including most of the major and minor Congress leaders, were in jail.

Civil disobedience nevertheless continued in India, and it was against that background that, in November, the Round Table Conference was convened in London. Britain was represented by delegates from the Labour, Conservative, and Liberal Parties, and, except for the Congress, practically all important sections of Indian opinion were represented, in the persons of some of the most important potentates of the Indian princely states and preeminent leaders of the All-India Muslim League—a minority religious party that from its founding, in 1906, had dedicated itself to greater representation of Muslims in the government. The conference lasted over two months and ended with unanimous agreement on a new system of federal government for India, which would grant Indians some measure of responsible self-government both in the provinces and at the center. The princes agreed to the federation partly because they were afraid of the effects of the civil-disobedience movement in their states; the Muslim Leaguers agreed to it partly because they looked upon the Indian princes—whether Hindu or Muslim—as allies against rule by the Congress, which amounted to populist Hindu domination; and the British agreed to it partly because they saw in the federation a way of safeguarding minority interests while allowing greater Indian participation in the government. The agreement had the effect of making many Hindus, including members of the Congress, abandon their civil disobedience, and at the same time raised the expectations of Muslim Leaguers about their role in any future Indian government. When the conference adjourned, Prime Minister MacDonald expressed the hope that the Congress would participate in a second Round Table Conference. In January, 1931, Gandhi and many other Congress leaders were therefore released from jail, and Gandhi was invited to New Delhi for preliminary discussions with the Viceroy.

In New Delhi, Gandhi often went five miles on foot from a friend's house, where he was staying, to the Viceroy's palace for the discussions. In England, Winston Churchill, among other upholders of the Empire, declared himself humiliated and revolted by the "spectacle of this one-time Inner Temple lawyer, now seditious fakir, striding half-naked up the steps of the Viceroy's palace, there to negotiate and to parley on equal terms with the representative of the King-Emperor." Between February 17th and March 4th, Gandhi and the Viceroy, Lord Irwin, met eight times, for a total of twenty-four hours. During the discussions, Gandhi had very much in mind the precedent of his successful negotiations with General Smuts in 1914, in the far more racially tense atmosphere of South Africa, after which the two had parted as friends with mutual esteem. Irwin, for his part, was well disposed toward Gandhi and genuinely interested in Constitutional reforms for India. The two finally concluded what came to be called the Irwin-Gandhi

Pact, in which Gandhi agreed to go to the Second Round Table Conference, without any prior commitment concerning independence, and to
call off all protest against the salt laws and every other form of civil
disobedience, while Irwin agreed to release most civil-disobedience
prisoners and to grant Indians living on the coast permission to manufacture salt. Both Gandhi and Irwin had yielded much more than they
wanted to, but each was looking to the second conference for further
political gains. (The salt laws were never completely repealed, so
Gandhi never returned to Sabarmati Ashram to live. When he was not
travelling or in jail, he lived at Sevagram Ashram, which he had
established in 1936 near the village of Segaon, in Central India, dedi-
cating it to the carrying out of the ideals of the Constructive Programme.)

The Congress elected Gandhi as its sole representative to the Second Round Table Conference, and he sailed for England late in August
of 1931, accompanied by, among others, Mahadev Desai, Mirabehn,
Pyarelal, Devadas Gandhi, and Sarojini Naidu, who together had made
up for many years what was a kind of informal secretariat. Gandhi and
his entourage stayed in a settlement house called Kingsley Hall, in the
East End of London, about five miles from St. James's Palace, where
the Second Round Table Conference was held, but Gandhi was prevailed upon to maintain an office in Knightsbridge for the convenience
of his English friends and admirers and also of many well-to-do Indians
living in England who were eager to talk with him.

Gandhi's visit created a great stir in England, and he made the most
of it. He went to Oxford colleges and Lancashire cotton mills. He met
Charlie Chaplin and George Bernard Shaw, and gave interviews to
journalists from all around the world. In his encounters, he often returned to the simplistic, romantic themes he had introduced in "Indian
Home Rule": that through much of history the West had been governed by the laws of force and violence, imperialism and aggression,
while the East, in contrast, had been governed by love and spirituality,
by ahimsa and satyagraha, and that he was the evangelist from the East
to the West.

The Second Round Table Conference met under less propitious
circumstances than the first. Although the Muslim League and the
princely states were once again represented, the Labour Government

had been replaced by the National Government, which, though still led by Ramsay MacDonald, was dominated by the Conservatives. At the conference table, Gandhi argued passionately for independence, or, at the least, a partnership of equals between India and England, but the National Government, for all its interest in setting up a responsible federal government in India, was far from ready to give up the Empire. Moreover, the conference further exposed the underlying differences between the Congress, on the one hand, and the Muslim League and the princes, on the other, and both the latter feared more than ever that if the British departed without first guaranteeing their interests they would be overwhelmed by the Congress. Gandhi returned to India in December, 1931, a disappointed man, recognizing that he would now have to contend for independence not only with the British but also with his own countrymen; indeed, he now despaired of ever achieving independence through negotiation. He and his followers in the Congress tried to launch another civil-disobedience movement for independence, but this time they were arrested at once, and were again sent to jail. They were released about a year and a half later. Gandhi called off the movement, which had lost much of its momentum, and gave up his membership in the Congress, and for the rest of the thirties he had little to do formally with politics.

In 1937, the British finally put into effect a new Constitution for India—the product of many years of debate and agitation, dating back to the Simon Commission. India was to be granted its long-awaited self-rule in stages, beginning with the transfer of most powers to the popularly elected provincial governments. The Congress was divided in its reception of the Constitution. One faction regarded it as, among other things, a means of realizing the goals of Gandhi's Constructive Programme, and urged cooperation; the other faction, one of whose leaders was Jawaharlal Nehru, regarded it as "a charter of slavery" (Nehru's phrase), and urged non-cooperation. (Nehru, who had first met Gandhi in 1916, was an aristocrat of modern Western outlook, while Gandhi, in some respects, pictured himself as a peasant of medieval outlook. They became very close but continued to espouse opposing political principles.) In part because the Congress didn't want to leave the field open to the Muslim League, and in part because it was seduced by the prospect of power, those who urged cooperation even-

tually prevailed, and the Congress participated in provincial elections
held under the Constitution in 1937.

Gandhi was drawn back into politics by the spectacle of Indians' being
forced to fight in the Second World War as subjects of the British
Empire. Though he had tried to follow the political events in Europe
leading to the war, he seems never to have quite grasped the
phenomena of Nazism and Fascism or to have seen the war, when it
came, as much more than a clash of imperialistic interests. Some of the
leaders in the Congress, asserting that Indians should fight only as free
people in defense of their homeland—which, as part of the British Empire, was then threatened by the possibility of a Japanese invasion—
and only in support of the cause of freedom, instead of as subjugated
people, now urged Gandhi to lead a mass civil-disobedience campaign
for independence. But Gandhi, although he was opposed to war in any
form, did not want to stab the British in the back. He therefore came
up with a strategy that at once satisfied the Congress and avoided
undermining the British war effort: a succession of individual acts of
civil disobedience in place of mass civil disobedience. In line with this
strategy, he designated one satyagrahi at a time to court arrest by
breaking the law—for instance, by spreading anti-war propaganda. His
first choice was Vinoba Bhave, a brahmachari resident of his ashrams,
whom he considered the most saintly of his followers and therefore the
purest of sacrifices. Bhave was arrested in October, 1940, tried, and
sentenced to three months in jail. Gandhi's second choice was Nehru,
who was also arrested, tried, and sentenced—to four years in jail—and
so it went, over a period of about a year, until there were some twenty-
three thousand Congress workers in jail. Gandhi himself stayed out of
jail to manage the campaign.

Late in 1941, a few days before the surprise attack on Pearl Harbor,
Winston Churchill, faced with the prospect of an imminent Japanese
invasion of India and pressured by anti-colonial sentiment not only in
the Labour Party but also in the United States, released all the important Congress prisoners. Then, in March, 1942, he sent Sir Stafford
Cripps—a left-wing Labour Member of Parliament, a nephew of Bea-
trice Webb, and, as it happened, a vegetarian—to India to make another attempt to work out a Constitutional arrangement acceptable to

Gandhi and the Congress. Cripps proposed immediate Indian participation in the government (including matters of defense), but under the Viceroy's direction, and full self-government after the war—even the right to secede from the Commonwealth—but with the proviso that any Indian province, princely state, or religious minority could, if it chose, negotiate a separate relationship with Britain. Though Congress took the offer very seriously, Gandhi saw in it not the promise of a free, united India but the threat of several separate Indias. In any event, negotiations eventually broke down over the nature of Indian participation in the government and in the war effort. The British blamed Gandhi for the breakdown. At the Lord Mayor's Banquet in London that November, Churchill made his famous quip "I have not become the King's First Minister in order to preside over the liquidation of the British Empire." As B. R. Nanda, in his "Mahatma Gandhi"—the biography perhaps most familiar to Indian readers—suggests, each British proposal for reform and self-government "tended to become out-of-date by the time it was actually granted." He explains, "The Reforms of 1919 might well have appeased political India in 1909; the Reforms of 1935 would have evoked enthusiasm in 1919; and an equivalent of the Cripps offer in 1940 could [in 1935] have opened a new chapter in Indo-British relations, halted the process of estrangement between the Congress and the Government and between Hindus and Muslims."

In August, 1942, Gandhi at last felt impelled to launch the mass civil-disobedience campaign, demanding that the British "quit India," which he had been trying to avoid for the past two years. He told Congress workers to consider themselves thenceforth free of British rule. The government promptly arrested all the Congress leaders. Gandhi and his closest followers were imprisoned in the abandoned palace of the Aga Khan in the vicinity of Poona—quarters improvised as a jail expressly for them. Outside the jail, Gandhi's mass civil-disobedience campaign quickly degenerated into mass violence, this time abetted by Marxist revolutionaries in the left wing of the Congress.

Lord Linlithgow, who was now the Viceroy, said that Gandhi was responsible for the violence. Gandhi, shocked by the accusation, wrote a stream of letters to him from jail, maintaining that it was the government's precipitate arrest of him and other Congress leaders which had excited popular passions and provoked the violence. But Lord Linlithgow, in his replies, persisted in blaming Gandhi. And so in February, 1943, when Gandhi was seventy-three years old, he undertook a twenty-one-day fast as an appeal to God to help him settle what he called his "misunderstanding" with Lord Linlithgow. Lord Linlithgow, for his part, allowed Gandhi to be attended by teams of doctors but continued to refuse to admit that he himself had been in any way responsible for the violence. He condemned Gandhi's fast as political blackmail, as a form of personal violence, and as a denial of Gandhi's own pronouncements over twenty-five years that fasts should be used only for self-purification and for disinterested ends. Gandhi survived the fast, but his health was seriously impaired. In subsequent months, he came down with a succession of diseases—malaria, amoebic dysentery, hookworm, and acute anemia. All across the country, there was considerable agitation for his release, and it intensified after Kasturbai died, in jail, on February 22, 1944. On May 6, 1944, Gandhi was finally released. By then, he had spent some five and a half years in British jails in India, much of that time as a result of his three major civil-disobedience movements—the non-cooperation movement of 1920–22, the salt movement of 1930–32, and the individual and mass satyagraha movement of 1940–42. He was never to go to jail again.

Constructive Worker

BETWEEN 1924 AND 1940, GANDHI HAD DEVOTED HIMSELF mostly to the social, economic, and spiritual regeneration of the country, which he came to believe would be achieved not by Constitutional concessions and reforms, political debates and resolutions, but by the efforts of the people themselves. As the years passed, he put more and more emphasis on what he had originally conceived of as "spiritual socialism"—the positive counterpart of non-cooperation and civil disobedience—and eventually called the Constructive Programme. The authorities, the Congress members, and the intellectuals all dismissed the Constructive Programme as anemic, visionary, a sort of diversion from the main political struggle, but for Gandhi the Constructive Programme was really another form of satyagraha, which could bring about a nonviolent agrarian revolution—in fact, was the only road to economic development for a poor country like India. The Constructive Programme was intended to ameliorate conditions in the bleak, disease-ridden villages in which most Indians lived—to revitalize the old relationships between the cultivator and the soil, the herdsman and his animals, the craftsman and his craft. Gandhi simply wanted to give Indians the opportunity to live in modest circumstances with a certain amount of dignity and decency—to make it possible for hundreds of millions who were going naked or in rags, were hungry or undernourished, and could find little or no work, to be clothed, fed, and provided with useful occupations. He called on all Indians to breed cattle, so that there would be milk for nourishment, dung for fertilizer and fuel, and bullocks for pulling the plows and drawing water from the wells; to take up some form of handicraft, so that no one would be a burden on society; to rediscover man's original relationship to nature,

because divorce from nature, he believed, was the source of all ills; to
educate themselves in the rudiments of sanitation and hygiene, so that
they could halt the spread of filth and disease; to engage in such activities as forestry and beekeeping, pottery and papermaking, so that no
one would be without food, utensils, or books; to promote basic education through work-and-study schools, so that children would grow up
knowing how to read and write and do manual labor; to raise cotton
and to spin and weave it, so that there would be no shortage of khadi;
to participate in village assemblies and thereby learn to solve local
problems; to form economic cooperatives, so that no one would profit
unfairly from another's labor; to extend equal rights to the tribal peoples oppressed for centuries as untouchables; to accord lepers the respect due them as human beings and to work for the eradication of
leprosy; to abolish hereditary bars to learning, so that knowledge
would not be the preserve of the Brahmans; to work for the total
prohibition of alcohol, which was the curse of the poor, and especially
of the untouchables; to abolish purdah and grant equal rights to
women; to overcome religious hatred, so that Hindus, Muslims, Sikhs,
Christians, and members of all other faiths could live together in harmony; and to learn Hindi, so that there would be a common language
for the whole country. In these ways, Gandhi believed, each village
could overcome its social and economic divisions, of which untouchability was the most extreme example; discover a new sense of identity
and a new interdependence; and, in the end, make the whole of India
into an association of religious village republics working harmoniously
together.

A few illustrations will serve to show how Gandhi tried to put the
Constructive Programme into practice.

One of the main causes of religious antipathy between Hindus and
Muslims was as old as the Persian invasion of India in the eleventh
century, which first brought the two religions into real contact: Hindus
had always worshipped the cow as a symbol of motherhood, and ab-
stained from eating beef for fear of spiritual pollution; Muslims slaugh-
tered cows, and beef was a staple of their diet. But other causes of
antipathy between the two communities had their beginnings under the
British rule. In 1909, ostensibly to protect the rights of Muslims, who

were outnumbered five to one by Hindus, the British instituted a separate Muslim electorate, and then, in 1922, they reinforced the separation by reserving special places for Muslims in the Indian Civil Service. "Since the economic backwardness of India made government employment one of the major, if not the major industry of the country," Fischer writes, "the reservation of official jobs for Mohammedans remained a festering sore as long as British rule lasted." Gandhi, the evangelist of universal brotherhood, who often romanticized India's past, imagined that Hindus and Muslims had lived together like brothers until the advent of the British, and, left to themselves, would do so again. In fact, he himself had succeeded in bringing them together when he joined the non-cooperation movement to that of the Khilafat, but this alliance soon fell apart. Nanda writes:

> A number of Hindu leaders . . . felt that the Muslim masses had received a dangerous awakening through the coalescence of the Khilafat and non-cooperation movements, and that it was necessary for Hindus to adopt measures of self-defense against Muslim communalism, which was the more dangerous because it appeared to them to have the backing of the British Government. Many Muslim politicians who had been in the forefront of the Khilafat movement had also second thoughts and felt that they had too readily joined hands with the Congress, in fighting for a new order in which the position of the Muslim community was not likely to be too secure.

When Gandhi came out of jail in 1924, he discovered that non-cooperation was being directed not against the government but against other Indians, and, what was worse, that it had unleashed unusually violent and widespread Hindu-Muslim riots. Extremists in the two communities were gaining the upper hand everywhere. Gandhi blamed himself, for he felt he had helped to awaken the masses politically by his campaigns for the non-cooperation movement and the Khilafat. "Have I not been instrumental in bringing into being the vast energy of the people?" he wrote after one such riot. "I must find the remedy, if the energy proved self-destructive. . . . Have I erred, have I been impatient, have I compromised with evil? . . . If real non-violence and truth had been practiced by the people, the gory duelling that is now going on would have been impossible." In order to stem the influence of Hindu and Muslim extremists and regain his power over the people, he undertook a twenty-one-day fast at the home of a Muslim friend in Delhi, entrusting himself to the care of Muslim doctors. He understood that his fasts had a great emotional effect, because the news of his suffering and possible death quickly travelled far and wide, and people who were unable to read or to understand complex issues readily grasped the symbolic importance of his fasting. By now, Gandhi had worked out a regimen for surviving a long fast—drinking a lot of water, sometimes with salt in it, having enemas twice a day to remove toxins from his body, and remaining in bed.

Impelled to action by the possibility of Gandhi's death, Hindu and Muslim leaders met in Delhi, papered over their differences, and affirmed the right to freedom of conscience and religion. Gandhi broke his fast to his followers' singing of "Lead, Kindly Light" and to their reading from Hindu and Muslim scriptures.

Ever since writing his "Indian Home Rule," Gandhi had romantically imagined that Indians had been spinning and weaving their own cloth for centuries before the British came to India, and that British textile mills had deprived the native clothmakers of work and turned them into half-naked consumers. (In reality, the spinning wheel and loom had been unknown in many parts of India, and long before the British came many Indians went half-naked.) He condemned the British for carrying much of India's cotton off to Lancashire mills and making it into cloth, which they then brought back to India and sold at prices that few could afford. He believed that industrialism, by divorcing man from handicrafts and manual "bread" labor—from nature itself—had robbed him of his identity and made him prey to exploitation and enslavement. He argued that man could regain his heritage and freedom only by rediscovering the value of "bread" labor, and particularly of the spinning wheel and the hand loom. At the time Gandhi started wearing dhotis, they were rarely made of khadi, which came in inadequate widths and was coarse and rough to the touch. He let it be known that he would wear the khadi dhotis anyhow, until wider and better-quality khadi became available. It soon did. In fact, the Sabarmati Ashram was conceived partly as a challenge to the textile mills of Ahmedabad, which was referred to as the Little Lancashire of India. Soon Gandhi was spinning in the Sabarmati Ashram for an hour or two every day, taking solace in the monotonous, undulating whine and buzz of the spinning wheel, and even attributing some healing powers to the sounds when he fell sick in 1918. In due course, spinning and hand-weaving became part of the daily routine of his ashram, and "slivers," "pirns," "counts," and "carding strips" part of the daily speech. Nationalists had long used the boycott of British cloth as a means of political protest, but its main beneficiaries before Gandhi came along had been Indian mill owners, who took advantage of the artificial scarcity to raise the prices of their cloth. During the non-cooperation campaign of 1920–22, Gandhi had hoped to make the boycott permanent, and to put an end to profiteering by Indian mill owners, by teaching everyone to use a spinning wheel.

Before Gandhi got very far, however, he was sent to jail. He took up the cause again in 1925 and spent that entire year touring the country and preaching the virtues of the spinning wheel. He now travelled in second-class compartments, so that his entourage could accompany him and he could have peace and quiet to read and write. But he also walked long distances through thorn and thicket, mud and water, to penetrate the deepest interior of India. Everywhere, he was greeted by crowds. He urged them to ply the spinning wheel, and talked at length about "the khadi franchise," "yarn currency," and "the thread of destiny." He told them that their enslavement was the result of their weakness, not of British might. He told them that they could become strong by taking pride in a simple, frugal, chaste life, by praying, by eating unspiced food, by wearing simple clothes, and by treating Muslims, untouchables, women, and other oppressed minorities as equals. He succeeded in making "spinning wheel" a byword for economic independence and nonviolent revolution, and "Lancashire mills" a byword for economic imperialism and oppression.

Despite his constant disavowals, people began worshipping Gandhi as a god, as a divine manifestation, like Krishna or Buddha, and claiming that his touch or his mere presence had cured them of disease or spared them death. They tried to get close to him and touch his feet, if not with their hands, then with their staffs. In consequence, his feet and legs were often bruised, and his attendants massaged them with ghi. Inspired by his presence, people promised to dedicate themselves to the Constructive Programme, but they lapsed into their old ways after he had gone; well-to-do women who stripped off their jewels—

bangles, necklaces, earrings, nose rings, anklets—and donated them to his cause went home and donned others. Critics who had all along attacked the Constructive Programme as "anti-modern," "backward-looking," and "utopian," and who called khadi "monotonous white shrouds," were quick to point to the fickleness of its supporters.

In 1926, Gandhi, worn out by his travels, retreated to the Sabarmati Ashram to rest his voice, to meditate, and to read and write.

On September 20, 1932, Gandhi, who was again in Yeravda Central Jail for seditious activities, took what he considered might be his last glass of hot water with lemon juice and honey, and embarked on a fast "unto death." This time, he was protesting against a provision of the proposed new Constitution for India which, among other things, granted untouchables a separate electorate, permitting them to elect untouchable representatives to the provincial legislatures. The government, Gandhi's followers, and the leaders of the untouchables were all surprised at his opposition to the provision, since, as a renowned champion of untouchables, he was expected to applaud favored treatment for them. All three groups condemned his fast, which they felt would play into the hands of orthodox Hindus who wanted to perpetuate the old religious and social disabilities of the untouchables. Gandhi, however, saw in the Constitutional provision a further British attempt to stoke minority discontent in order to keep India subjugated. First the Muslims had been given a separate electorate, and now the untouchables. Who would be next? He felt, moreover, that religious and social disabilities could not be legislated out of existence but could only be set aside by a change of heart. "I believe that if untouchability is really rooted out, it will not only purge Hinduism of a terrible blot but its repercussions will be worldwide," he said in a press interview a few hours after beginning his fast. "My fight against untouchability is a fight against the impure in humanity. . . . The very best in the human family will come to my assistance if I have embarked on this thing with a heart . . . free of impurity, free of all malice, and all anger. . . . You will, therefore, see that my fast is based first of all in the cause of faith in the Hindu community, faith in human nature itself, and faith even in the official world. . . . My cry will rise to the throne of the Almighty God."

News of Gandhi's fast spread quickly, and everywhere people

prayed for his life and observed a day's fast in sympathy. The fast so dramatized the plight of the untouchables that all across the country Hindus opened temple doors to them and allowed them to walk on public roads reserved for caste Hindus, and, in some cases, even touched them and broke bread with them. The government opened the gates of the jail, so that Gandhi and his followers, the untouchables' leaders, and orthodox Hindus could settle the issue among themselves. Several days of intense negotiation followed, with Gandhi lying on an iron cot under a mango tree in the jail yard, his health failing rapidly. The negotiators reached the so-called Poona Agreement, or Yeravda Pact, which gave untouchables the right to elect more representatives to the provincial legislatures than were allowed for in the British proposal but also gave caste Hindus a role in selecting the representatives. The British government agreed to the change, and on the seventh day of the fast Gandhi broke it by drinking a glass of orange juice.

The fast, however, failed to bring about any lasting change in the lot of the untouchables, whom Gandhi had started calling Harijans, or "children of God," and in 1934 he attributed a calamitous earthquake in Bihar to the persistent Hindu oppression of them. Even some of his admirers, like Nehru, and the poet Rabindranath Tagore, reproached him for linking cosmic and human events and so fostering superstition, but he continued to make the point for days as he walked from village to village consoling and nursing the earthquake victims.

In 1930, when Gandhi was serving an earlier sentence in Yeravda Central Jail (he jocularly called it "Yeravda Temple"), he started sending a weekly letter to his disciples in the Sabarmati Ashram. The letters, which were read at the evening prayer meeting in place of the short discourses he usually gave, all illustrate his preoccupation with the monastic dedication required of ashram residents and Constructive Workers alike—to truth, to nonviolence, to celibacy, to poverty, to scripture reading, to control of the palate, to humility, to devotion, to sacrifice, to honesty, to fearlessness.

He vowed to seek after the Truth. For Gandhi, Truth was God, as distinguished from "God is Truth." He believed that the existence of Truth/God could not be proved, only experienced. "There is an indefinable mysterious power which pervades everything," he writes. "I feel it, though I do not see it." Truth/God was not a personal being but an eternal principle, and each person had an inborn sense of it. Truth/God could not be perceived through the senses, which deceived us, but only through the soul, which was the divine in us.

He vowed to practice nonviolence. For Gandhi, the way to holiness and to yoga, or union with God, lay not in withdrawal from the world (jnana-yoga, or philosophical contemplation) but in immersion in the world (karma-yoga, or action)—the way celebrated by the Bhagavad Gita. All action of necessity involved the search for Truth/God. Each person would find a different Truth/God, but if he searched honestly and took care not to violate or injure another person's Truth/God, then he would be right, whatever he believed and however he acted. By thus making the means and the end virtually identical, Gandhi tried to get around the dilemma of means and ends which especially bedevils religious men in politics.

He vowed to dedicate his life to celibacy. For Gandhi, selfless service was the holiest action, and chastity, in body, speech, and mind, was the best armor for such action. Since marriage ordinarily meant, in Gandhi's words, "we two first and the devil take the rest," a husband and wife were to relegate sex to the function of procreation only, and were otherwise to live, like brother and sister, for the ideal of service.

He vowed to own nothing. For Gandhi, possessions had no value—and, in fact, were encumbrances to service. He believed that in life everyone should travel light—that, for example, a person saving for the future of his children was living in fear when he should be trusting his welfare and his family's to Truth/God.

And so on. In a sense, Gandhi had been experimenting with and perfecting these principles of the Constructive Programme for most of his adult life.

Although by his mid-thirties Gandhi was committed to an ascetic life, he was unlike many ascetics in that he continued to discharge his family responsibilities. As time went on, however, he came to see these responsibilities simply as part of a larger responsibility, to his farms in South Africa and to his ashrams in India—to all his followers, wherever they were—and he found it more difficult to be a husband to his wife and a father to his sons than to be a surrogate husband and father to his larger family. Exasperating as he found it, no matter how hard he tried to wean Kasturbai away from possessions and money, she continued for much of her life to yearn for them, and no matter how many geography lessons he gave her, she continued to think until the end of her life that Calcutta was a province whose capital was Lahore. Fischer, who spent a week with Gandhi and Kasturbai in 1942, two years before she died, writes, "Kasturbai, with sunken face, straight mouth, and square jaw, seemed to listen attentively, but I did not hear or see her say a single word to her husband during the entire week, nor him to her."

Gandhi urged his sons to live lives of godliness and poverty, accepting the moral principles that he himself had arrived at only after formal study, considerable self-indulgence, and the pursuit of worldly ambition, and had systematized in the Constructive Programme. At one time or another, all four sons tried to live up to their father's expectations of them, but each, in his own way, failed, and in Gandhi's attitude toward their failure there was, by his own testimony, an element of guilt for sexual excesses in his childhood marriage. When his eldest son, Harilal, disappointed him, he would say, "I was a slave of my passions when Harilal was conceived," or "I led a carnal and luxurious life during Harilal's childhood." Gandhi's sons, for their part, resented being made the victims of their father's theories—by, for example, not being given a formal education, which would have provided them with their own way of earning a living.

Harilal had received some formal education in India; when the rest of the family joined Gandhi in South Africa in 1905, Harilal was left behind in order that he might go on with his schooling, as the ward of a lawyer, Haridas Vakatchand Vora. Harilal fell in love with the lawyer's daughter, Gulab, and later married her. When Gandhi learned of the marriage, he all but disowned his son. Harilal, being eager to rehabilitate himself in his father's eyes, later accepted a challenge from Gandhi to go to South Africa and join in his struggle. Harilal arrived in Johannesburg, with his wife, in 1907, threw himself into the fight against the "Black Act," and was jailed several times. He also lived on Tolstoy Farm. But he longed for a university education and legal training in England. He frequently quarrelled with his father for denying him the necessary money, and said that without a legal education his father himself would never have been able to do what he had done. But Gandhi insisted that what was important in life was moral education, not a slavish academic education. The upshot was that in 1911 Harilal left a letter for his father saying he was breaking all ties, and disappeared. He lived for a couple of months under an assumed name in Portuguese East Africa. Later, returning to Ahmedabad, he continued his schooling for a time, dabbling in Sanskrit and French. He lived there quietly, with his wife and four children, not attracting much notice or taking any part in politics. Then, in 1918, Gulab died in the influenza epidemic. Harilal never quite recovered from her death. He became notorious for doing nearly everything his father disapproved of. He became a meat eater, an alcoholic, a gambler, a philanderer. He was converted to Islam, and he began using his father's name for shady business dealings even as he reviled his father and his father's way of life. He embezzled thirty thousand rupees from a Madrasi merchant; he played at being a successful Calcutta businessman, accumulating large debts; on one occasion, in 1925, he bilked a Muslim businessman out of an investment. The Muslim businessman did not prosecute, because of his regard for Gandhi, but, instead, wrote a letter to Gandhi appealing for the money. Gandhi responded not by repaying the man but by publishing the letter in *Young India,* along with his reply, which warned people against being swayed by big names in their transactions, and noted that "men may be good, not necessarily their children." Harilal gave himself over completely to a dissolute life and was rarely seen sober. He quarrelled with his brothers, calling them charlatans for trying to emulate their father. He wrote long, accusatory letters to his father and threatened to send them to newspapers for publication, but generally he contented himself with circulating them among his father's friends. For years, the family did not know where or how he lived. He was seen in various parts of India, in rags—gaunt, sick, and penniless. In his later years, he mostly divided his time between Calcutta, where he had old friends; Delhi, where Devadas settled; and Bombay, where his eldest son, Kantilal, lived.

Kasturbai generally took her son's side, and suffered much despair on account of the quarrels between father and son. She dictated a letter to Harilal in 1936 when she heard he had been arrested yet again for drunken, disorderly conduct. (She had already been exposed to many newspaper accounts of his debauches.) "You know that he [Gandhi] attaches the greatest importance to purity of conduct," she wrote. "For sheer shame, I am unable to move about among my friends or strangers. . . . Every morning I rise with a shudder to think what fresh news of disgrace the newspapers will bring. . . . You are my eldest son and nearly fifty years old. I am even afraid of approaching you, lest you humiliate me." When Kasturbai was dying, Harilal was brought to her bedside in the Aga Khan Palace jail, but he arrived drunk. She beat her forehead in despair. She died the next day, Harilal also appeared at his father's funeral, in 1948, but he arrived late, long after the cremation, and looked so much like a derelict that only a few people recognized him, and then belatedly. Several months later, he died, of tuberculosis, in a sanatorium.

In 1944, Gandhi established in the village of Uruli, near Poona, a small nature-cure clinic, thereby institutionalizing his system of spiritual medicine and putting into practice another element of the Constructive Programme. In 1901, by following the nature cures of Kühne and Just— a regimen of hip baths, mud poultices, and long walks—he had been able to cure himself of the headaches, constipation, and physical lassitude from which he had long suffered. A few years later, Kasturbai had started hemorrhaging from a serious gynecological disorder. (We don't know what it was.) She had been operated on in a hospital and was so weak that the attending doctor refused to accept responsibility for her life unless he was allowed to give her at least meat broth. Gandhi promptly dismissed the doctor, removed her from the hospital, and nursed her back to health with hydropathy and other Kühne and Just remedies, one of which was to deny her salt and lentils, the principal items of her diet. Thereafter, Gandhi came to believe, with Kühne and Just, that man's disharmony with nature was the cause of all his physical and mental illnesses; that God had provided in earth, water, and air the means of tending the body; that the best way of keeping fit was to avoid everything artificial, to eat no meat or other rich foods, and to discipline oneself against lethargic ways. He believed that thanks to his practice of the nature cure he had a strong constitution and would live to be a hundred and twenty-five years old—the traditional life span of a Hindu sage.

Gandhi carried his concept of nonviolence so far that after the Nazis came to power in Germany he wanted the Jews, whom he called the "untouchables of Christianity," to resist Hitler nonviolently. In 1938, he wrote in *Harijan:*

> If there ever could be a justifiable war in the name of and for humanity, war against Germany to prevent the wanton persecution of a whole race would be completely justified. But I do not believe in any war.... If I were a Jew and were born in Germany and earned my livelihood there, I would claim Germany as my home even as the tallest gentile German might, and challenge him to shoot me or cast me in the dungeon.... For to the God-fearing, death has no terror. ... The Jews of Germany can offer satyagraha under infinitely better auspices than the Indians of South Africa. The Jews are a compact, homogeneous community in Germany. They are far more gifted than the Indians of South Africa. And they have organized world opinion behind them. I am convinced that if someone with courage and vision can arise among them to lead them in non-violent action, the winter of their despair can in the twinkling of an eye be turned into the summer of hope. And what has today become a degrading manhunt can be turned into a calm and determined stand offered by unarmed men and women possessing the strength of suffering given to them by Jehovah.... The German Jews will score a lasting victory over the German gentiles in the sense that they will have converted the latter to an appreciation of human dignity.

Gandhi thus urged a program of mass civil disobedience on the Jews, even if it led to mass martyrdom, for he was confident that if they went to their deaths voluntarily, their martyrdom would have such an effect on public opinion that in the end the Jews would triumph over Hitler. He could not have foreseen that a modern, mechanized state would be able to dispatch six million people in secret, but after he learned of their fate, he continued to insist that if the Jews had followed his counsel of total nonviolence, and gone to their deaths voluntarily, they would have scored a moral victory even though their fate would have been no different. He maintained that moral courage in the long run would always triumph over tyrants like Hitler, who would come and go, and who could win only small, tactical battles, not the big moral battles, which were the only ones that counted.

Martyr

THE SECOND WORLD WAR AND THE ANTI-IMPERIALIST FORCES IT
brought to the fore made Indian independence all but inevitable. Yet
it began to look increasingly as though the independent India for which
Gandhi and his Hindu and Muslim followers had been striving for
some twenty-five years would be not the secular, united country of their
dreams, in which religious toleration would reign, but a country parti-
tioned by religious strife into two warring parts—the predominantly
Hindu India and the predominantly Muslim Pakistan. This ominous
prospect (eventually the reality) haunted Gandhi's last years and re-
duced him to despair about his entire life's work. He put the primary
blame for that outcome on Muhammad Ali Jinnah, who became the
founder of Pakistan.

Jinnah, who came to be known among his followers as Qaid-e-
Azam, or Great Leader, was born in 1876 into a merchant family in
Karachi, on the Arabian Sea. He married in his teens, studied at the
Inns of Court, was called to the bar, lost his mother while he was in
England, spent ten years in India building up a flourishing legal prac-
tice, and then entered politics as a staunch nationalist—a Congress
follower of Gokhale. Here any parallels between Gandhi's life and
Jinnah's cease. By temperament, Jinnah was haughty, punctilious, and
worldly—a city dweller who often dressed like an English gentleman
and modelled himself on the political élite of Britain. Jinnah left the
Congress in 1920, just when—and, in fact, because—Gandhi was rising
to power in it and transforming it into a mass movement. He disdained
Gandhi's religious attitude toward politics, his civil-disobedience campaigns, his fasts and marches, because of their appeal to the masses. He
himself had little in common with the orthodox of his religion: he

167

seldom went to the mosque; he never learned to read the Koran in the original Arabic; he married out of his religion (his child bride had died while he was studying law in England, and his second wife was a Parsi heiress); and he drank, smoked, and ate pork—all taboo to Muslims. He nevertheless became the spokesman for politically ambitious middle-class city Muslims, who came to regard Gandhi's pleas for Hindu-Muslim toleration as a means of perpetuating Hindu domination. (Jinnah's idea of a Muslim nation was, of course, abhorrent to Gandhi, but it also seemed visionary and impractical, since the Muslims in India were outnumbered five to one by the Hindus and were dispersed all over the country; Gandhi's idea of Hindu-Muslim toleration seemed visionary and impractical to Jinnah, especially since Gandhi sometimes referred to independent India as the Hindu Ram Rajya, or Ram's Kingdom.) Jinnah went on to become the moving force behind the Muslim League, which in 1940 voted for the partition of India. The arrest of Gandhi and the Congress leaders in 1942 left Jinnah and the Muslim League free to consolidate their position in the country.

By 1944, Jinnah had acquired such a large following among Muslims and, with his demand that the British secure a separate homeland for Muslims before leaving India, had become such a powerful obstacle to independence that Gandhi was impelled to go to him and plead with him to moderate his demand. Gandhi met with him several times in Bombay, where Jinnah had a palatial seaside home, and proposed a number of compromises, among them the right of Muslims to take a separate vote after independence on the part they wanted to play in India. But Jinnah was adamant in his demand for Pakistan, and the talks broke down.

Gandhi had had many previous adversaries in his life, but none of them had ever aroused his passion or made him despair as Jinnah did. Up to then, in everything Gandhi had said, done, or written there had been a current of optimism, which flowed out of his unshakable faith that Providence guided human destiny. That optimism had begun to diminish. He stopped talking about living to be a hundred and twenty-five, and started calling himself such things as a "spent bullet." He was losing his will to live.

In 1945, Clement Attlee's Labour Party was elected to office and expressed its willingness to transfer power to India as soon as the Indians agreed among themselves what form their independence would take. Hindu and Muslim chauvinists in many cities resorted to violence, making it the more urgent to resolve the problem of whether there should be one nation or two. At the same time, the violence posed for Gandhi the question of whether he had been right in ever thinking that Hindus and Muslims could live like brothers, that his people could master his principles of satyagraha and ahimsa, that he understood the role of violence in human nature.

In March, 1946, Attlee sent a Cabinet Mission to India to determine how best to transfer power. The Mission listened to all the politicians, and then recommended a three-tiered governmental structure: a weak central union to deal with foreign affairs, defense, and communications; semi-autonomous regional groups of provinces and states—one group predominantly Hindu, one predominantly Muslim, and one more or less balanced between the two religions—to deal with other matters of common concern; and individual provinces and states within the groups to deal with all local matters. Gandhi felt that any regional division along religious lines was "sinful" and a first step toward Jinnah's Pakistan, yet after several days of studying the scheme and searching his heart he declared, "It is the best document the British government could have produced in the circumstances." The Constitutional scheme was necessarily vague—on, for instance, whether or not the semi-autonomous regional groups were "optional"—but precisely because of its vagueness it was at first acceptable to both the Congress and the Muslim League. It foundered on the basic question it was intended to resolve: how to reconcile the differences between the advocates of one nation and the advocates of two. Many members of the Congress began saying that the regional groups were optional, and Nehru said that they would never come into being; Jinnah, taking his cue from the Congress and Nehru, rejected the whole notion of central union.

In August, 1946, Jinnah initiated what he called a direct-action program for the creation of Pakistan, and, however unwittingly, touched off a long religious civil war. Hindus and Sikhs, on the one hand, and Muslims, on the other, began striking out at each other from Calcutta to Lahore—burning and looting bazaars, torturing and murdering their neighbors, and turning whole communities into refugees. One of the worst outbreaks of violence occurred in the predominantly Muslim district of Noakhali, in Bengal; previously, the violence had been restricted to cities, but here it spread to the villages. Gandhi did personal penance for the violence, trudging barefoot through the mud and swamps of Noakhali and preaching a message of total nonviolence, which was marred, as always, by inconsistencies; for example, although he believed that suicide was immoral, he counselled women to take their lives rather than sacrifice their virtue by being raped.

In London and New Delhi, the Congress, the Muslim League, and Labour Party leaders continued to debate the ramifications and modifications of the Constitutional scheme. The British felt they could not coerce any section of the country into accepting it. The Muslim League, citing the religious violence as evidence of a natural enmity between Hindus and Muslims, refused to compromise in any way on the demand for Pakistan. As for the Congress, alarmed by the growing violence in the country, it finally, in January, 1947, acceded to the demand, thereby implicitly accepting Jinnah's premise that Hindus and Muslims could not live together, and rejecting Gandhi's premise that they could. Gandhi felt betrayed and confused: on the one hand, he blamed Jinnah for inflaming religious passions, although he had to concede that the passions must have been present in the first place to be inflamed; on the other, he blamed the Congress for acting precipitately and out of fear, since if it had remained adamant against partition the British would sooner or later have had no choice but to transfer power to it as the majority party. Instinct told him to organize a civil-disobedience campaign in protest against partition, but he did nothing—because, he writes, his reason told him that the British were acting in good faith and a civil-disobedience campaign against them would be unfair. He seems to have lost his old confidence in the right course of action and in his ability to understand and lead the people. The opportunity for civil disobedience was soon lost in the onrush of events.

In February, Attlee stated in the House of Commons, in effect, that Britain was ready to transfer power to India, united or not. In March, Lord Louis Mountbatten, a great-grandson of Queen Victoria, arrived in New Delhi as Viceroy to supervise the transfer of power. In June, the new Viceroy announced a procedure for legislators and their leaders to vote for or against a partition whereby two areas of the country—West Punjab (along with Sind, the Northwest Frontier Province, and Baluchistan) and East Bengal, where there were sizable majorities of Muslims—would become Pakistan, even though they were separated by about a thousand miles. After intensive negotiations, both the Congress and the Muslim League voted for partition. J. B. Kripalani, president of the Congress and an eminent Gandhian, addressing his Congress colleagues after they had accepted partition, observed, "Some members have accused us that we have taken this decision out of fear. I must admit the truth of this charge. . . . The fear is that if we go on . . . retaliating and heaping indignities on each other, we shall progressively reduce ourselves to a state of cannibalism. . . . I have been with Gandhiji for the last thirty years. . . . Why then am I not with him [now]? It is because I feel that he has as yet found no way of tackling the problem [of Hindu-Muslim violence] on a mass basis."

On August 15th, India celebrated its independence, and Pakistan its birth. Gandhi took no part in the independence celebration. He felt that his thirty-two years of work for independence had come to "an inglorious end." In October, he observed his seventy-eighth birthday, saying to well-wishers, "Where do congratulations come in? Would it not be more appropriate to send condolences? . . . Time was, whatever I said, the masses followed. Today, mine is a lone voice."

In the months after independence, the religious war continued with redoubled violence as Hindus and Sikhs fled for their lives from Pakistan and Muslims from India. "The battlefield was everywhere, in village, town, road, temple and mosque," writes the Canadian political scientist Michael Brecher. "In sheer numbers it [the cross-migration] was the greatest in history, probably about twelve million, equally divided between Hindus and Sikhs fleeing from West Punjab and Muslims from [East Punjab]. Before the year was out half a million people died, or were murdered." A similar battlefield was opened up in Pakistani East Bengal and Indian West Bengal. The violence was becoming a war of extermination.

Gandhi twice fasted "unto death" for a restoration of religious toleration in independent India. The first fast, in Calcutta, at the moment of independence, has been called his last great achievement, because he served, in Mountbatten's words, as a "one-man boundary force" to stop the Hindu and Muslim communities in Calcutta from repeating the massacres of the previous year. He broke each of his fasts only after receiving pledges from Hindu, Muslim, and Sikh leaders that they would try to make their people live with each other amicably. The pledges had a miraculous short-term effect, but in the end they did not stem the growing violence. Moreover, Gandhi became disillusioned with the Congress government, which, he felt, was like that of the British: monolithic, élitist, out of touch with the masses, and pursuing policies abhorrent to him—Westernizing, industrializing, and modernizing India, and so continuing the process, started under the British raj, of dividing the city from the village, the urban middle class from the rural poor, the government from the religious life of the people. Gandhi's two principal lieutenants—Nehru, a latter-day Fabian Socialist, who was now the first Prime Minister of India, and Patel, a Bismarckian conservative, who was now the Deputy Prime Minister—were always at loggerheads over whether to take a "soft line" or a "hard line" on a problem, such as how to treat the forty million Muslims still living in India. Gandhi would somehow manage to settle their differences on one matter, only to see the two men fall out over another. He came to realize that the Congress rank and file were as corrupt and greedy in power as they had been idealistic and self-sacrificing out of power. Gandhi could probably have become head of the government and ruled the country through his Constructive Workers, but that was not his way. He had spent his public life opposing the government in power, and now he continued to oppose the government in power, appealing directly to the people, and organizing his disciples and followers to be the "conscience" of the government by striving to attain the social and economic goals of the Constructive Programme.

Gandhi's allegorical interpretation of the Bhagavad Gita—that man was a battlefield for good and evil—was fundamental to his view of politics. It made him spend most of his life battling the government in power with an extremist's zeal, since to cooperate with evil in any form was to compromise one's goodness. But it also made him think that one's opponents and enemies—the Jinnahs, and even the Hitlers—could be reconciled and won over, and, indeed, redeemed, by appeals to their good impulses through the goodness of one's own impulses and sacrifices. He once wrote, "You must never despair of human nature."

The date was January 30, 1948; the place, a room in a house in New Delhi owned by Ghanshyam Das Birla; the time, four-thirty in the afternoon. Gandhi sat on the floor eating his customary evening meal and talking with Patel in an attempt to settle yet another of Patel's differences with Nehru. Abha Gandhi interrupted the talk by pointing to the large pocket watch pinned to Gandhi's dhoti. Gandhi rose, visited the bathroom, and then went out of the house, supporting himself on the shoulders of Abha and another young woman relative, Manu Gandhi. They walked briskly to a nearby terrace, where a congregation of about five hundred had assembled for Gandhi's evening prayer meeting. People rushed forward into his path to get his darshana and to touch his feet. Gandhi removed his hands from the women's shoulders and greeted the people by bringing his hands together in the traditional Hindu manner. When he was a few yards away from the wooden platform where he was to sit, a thickset man with close-cropped hair and heavy-lidded eyes, wearing a blue sweater and a khaki bush jacket, pushed forward in front of him as if to make obeisance. Instead, he fired three shots from a small pistol. Gandhi fell to the ground and died within minutes. In the ensuing shock, tumult, and hubbub, Gandhi's disciples managed to carry his body into Birla House. They laid him on the floor of the room where he had spent his last few days.

Nehru, in a choked voice, announced on All-India Radio, "The light has gone out of our lives and there is darkness everywhere and I do not quite know what to tell you and how to say it. Our beloved leader, Bapu, as we call him, the father of our nation, is no more. . . . The light that has illumined this country for these many years will illumine this country for many more years, and a thousand years later that light will still be seen . . . and it will give solace to innumerable hearts."

The frantic crowd outside Birla House demanded Gandhi's darshana, so his body was taken to the roof and placed under a searchlight. Over the weeping and wailing of the crowd could be heard the chanting of the Bhagavad Gita. Gandhi's body was returned to his room later in the evening, and mourners inside and outside Birla House kept vigil all night long.

Early the next morning, Gandhi's followers bathed and draped his body and put a garland of khadi fragments and a string of beads around his neck, and then carried him back to the roof for another public darshana. At eleven o'clock, the body was placed on a bier and draped with the saffron-green-and-white flag of independent India. The bier, attended by Gandhi's sons Devadas and Ramdas (Manilal was in South Africa) and by Nehru, Patel, and other leaders and disciples, was placed on a gun carriage. Accompanied by units of the cavalry and other troops, it was drawn through the streets of New Delhi by two hundred men from the Army, Navy, and Air Force. (All the arrangements for the funeral had been entrusted to the Ministry of Defense.) Millions of people joined the cortege or watched its progress from vantage points in trees or on rooftops or monuments, intoning sacred Sanskrit chants and calling out *"Mahatma Gandhi ki jai!"* Armored cars were strategically dotted along the route to prevent violence; planes flew overhead, tipping their wings in salute and scattering rose petals.

It took nearly five hours for the cortege to reach the cremation site, on the west bank of the sacred river Jumna, five and a half miles from Birla House. There Gandhi's body was laid on a low, flat sandalwood funeral pyre. At four-forty-five in the afternoon, as Brahmans chanted Vedic mantras, Ramdas put a torch to the pyre.

On February 12th, after thirteen days of national mourning, Gandhi's ashes, which had been brought by special train to Allahabad, were, in accordance with Hindu rites, ceremoniously committed to the confluence of the sacred rivers Jumna and Ganges.

Gandhi's assassin, a thirty-seven-year-old Brahman bachelor named Nathuram Vinayak Godse, was captured at the prayer meeting by some bystanders. Gandhi's disciples saved him from being lynched by the angry crowd. Godse was from Poona and had been brought up in the surrounding Maharashtran region—the region of Gokhale and Tilak, which was traditionally known for its fiery Hindu chauvinism. He belonged to the Hindu Mahasabha, a right-wing orthodox Hindu party, which was the Hindu counterpart of the Muslim League. He never finished high school, yet he thought of himself as something of an intellectual and ideologue. He was the founder, editor, and publisher of the Marathi *Agrani* and the English *Hindu Rashtra*, two extremist tabloids crusading for Hindu rule. Godse also fancied himself a student of Hindu scriptures, and particularly of the Bhagavad Gita, but his interpretation was literal and fundamentalist—quite the opposite of Gandhi's. For Godse, the Bhagavad Gita was a historical document, describing a real battle at Kurukshetra, at which the god Krishna actually counselled Arjuna that it was his moral duty to fight and kill his blood cousins—in contrast to Gandhi's belief that the battlefield of

Kurukshetra was the soul, in which the forces of good and evil were constantly at war. Godse went on to conclude that it was *his* moral duty to kill Gandhi. He believed that Gandhi and his work for religious toleration and nonviolence had already made the Hindus lose the battle for Hindu India and cede Pakistan to the Muslims, and that if Gandhi and his ideas were not checked they would bring about the destruction of Hindu India altogether, since, even in the face of widespread massacres of Hindus and Sikhs in Pakistan, Gandhi persisted in preaching nonviolence. In Godse's opinion, the only answer to violent aggression was violent self-defense.

Police investigation showed that Godse had not acted alone but had conspired with a number of other extremist Hindus. On May 27, 1948, in the case of Rex v. Nathuram Vinayak Godse & Others, Godse, his principal co-conspirator, Narayan Apte (the manager of *Hindu Rashtra*), and seven more conspirators were brought to trial at the Red Fort, in Delhi. The case was heard in an upper room of a barracks put up by the British during the Victorian period on the grounds of the old Moghul palace within the fort.

At one point in the trial, which lasted nine months, Godse said, "I sat brooding intensely on the atrocities perpetrated on Hinduism and its dark and deadly future if left to face Islam outside and Gandhi inside, and . . . I decided all of a sudden to take the extreme step against Gandhi." In a lengthy statement in defense of his crime, he insisted he had no personal hatred of Gandhi as a man; that, in fact, he revered him and had bowed to him in obeisance before firing his pistol. He said that, like Gandhi, he instinctively venerated everything about Hindu religion, Hindu history, and Hindu culture, yet, again like Gandhi, rejected many of the superstitious elements of Hinduism, such as the caste system and its curse of untouchability. He said that Gandhi, however, had betrayed his Hindu religion and culture by supporting Muslims at the expense of Hindus, and so had become an unwitting instrument of British imperialism and its policy of "divide and rule." He went on to say:

> I firmly believed that the teachings of absolute ahimsa as advocated by Gandhiji would ultimately result in the emasculation of the Hindu Community and thus make the community incapable of resisting the aggression or inroads of other communities, especially

the Muslims. . . . To imagine that the bulk of mankind is or can ever become capable of scrupulous adherence to these lofty principles in its normal life from day to day is a mere dream. . . . In the Mahabharata, Arjuna had to fight and slay quite a number of his friends and relations, including the revered Bhishma, because the latter was on the side of the aggressor. It is my firm belief that . . . [to call] Rama, Krishna, and Arjuna guilty of violence is to betray a total ignorance of the springs of human action. . . . Each of the heroes in his time resisted aggression on our country, protected the people against the atrocities and outrages by alien fanatics, and won back the motherland from the invader.

Nathuram Godse and Narayan Apte were found guilty as charged, and, although Gandhi's disciples and followers urged that the assassins' lives be spared, Godse and Apte were hanged, on November 15, 1949, in the Punjab—in the courtyard of a jail in Ambala, near Kurukshetra.

I I I

The Company They Keep

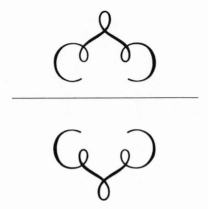

Nonviolence: Brahmacharya

and Goat's Milk

PERHAPS THE MOST CELEBRATED PASSAGE IN GANDHI'S AUTOBIOG-
raphy reads:

> The dreadful night came. . . . It was 10:30 or 11 P.M. I was
> giving the massage [to his father]. My uncle offered to relieve me.
> I was glad and went straight to the bedroom. My wife, poor thing,
> was fast asleep. But how could she sleep when I was there? I woke
> her up. In five or six minutes, however, the servant knocked at the
> door. I started with alarm. "Get up," he said. . . .
> "What is the matter?" . . .
> "Father is no more." . . .
> I felt deeply ashamed and miserable. I ran to my father's room.
> I saw that, if animal passion had not blinded me, I should have been
> spared the torture of separation from my father during his last mo-
> ments. I should have been massaging him, and he would have died
> in my arms. . . .
> The shame . . . of my carnal desire even at the critical hour of
> my father's death . . . is a blot I have never been able to efface or
> forget. . . . Although my devotion to my parents knew no bounds
> . . . it was weighed and found unpardonably wanting because my
> mind was at the same moment in the grip of lust. . . . It took me long
> to get free from the shackles of lust, and I had to pass through many
> ordeals before I could overcome it.

179

This incident occurred in 1885, when Gandhi was sixteen and had been married for three years. Kasturbai was in an advanced stage of pregnancy, and Gandhi says he felt that this, quite apart from his father's illness, should have led him to refrain from sexual intercourse. But it was not until some fifteen years later, after the birth of his fifth child, that he began in earnest to try to restrain his sexual needs. He did not want any more children, and he had long believed that abstinence was the only morally defensible method of birth control. He started sleeping apart from his wife and retiring only when he was utterly exhausted. Yet he was still not able to master his sexual needs. Because he was growing more and more preoccupied with what became his lifelong search for God, he resolved to take a vow of brahmacharya, or celibacy, which among Hindu mystics and ascetics is considered the ultimate act of self-sacrifice and personal renunciation—the surest way of avoiding all temptation and of finding God. But five years more passed before he actually found the strength to take the vow. By that time, he was thirty-six years old and had been married for twenty-four years. "The elimination of carnal relationship with one's wife seemed then a strange thing," he writes. "But I launched forth with faith in the sustaining power of God."

According to ancient Hindu scriptures, the conservation of semen—or "vital force," as it is called—is essential for physical, mental, and spiritual strength, and its loss is the cause of all infirmity and disease. Strict rules are set down to help a brahmachari keep his vow: the brahmachari must not look at women, must not sit on the same mat as women, must not take women as pupils, must not allow himself any physical stimulants like milk, curds, ghi, hot baths, or massages with oil, and must avoid not just women but also eunuchs and animals. Gandhi, while accepting the basic teaching about "vital force," rejected the rules, which in his opinion made the brahmachari concentrate all his efforts on controlling his erections and seminal discharges, and so neglect the concomitant search for spiritual strength and for God. He maintained that the brahmachari who had developed complete self-control need never be afraid of mixing freely with women and of taking daily baths and massages, and that the best ways to develop such self-control were by regarding every woman as a blood relative, by exercising regularly and doing physical work, by avoiding erotic literature and indecent talk, by filling the mind with good and useful ideas, and by constantly repeating the name of God. "The full and correct meaning of brahmacharya is search for the Brahman," Gandhi writes. In Hindu philosophy, Brahman is the religious principle that involves the realization of Brahma, and Brahma, in its various manifestations—Creator, Preserver, and Destroyer—is the Supreme Being, from which everything comes and to which everything, through the cycle of incarnation and reincarnation, strives to be reunited. "As the Brahman is immanent in everyone, it can be known through contemplation and the inner illumination resulting from it," Gandhi continues. "This illumination is not possible without complete control over the senses. Hence, brahmacharya means control in thought, speech and action of all senses, at all places and at all times. The man or woman who observes such perfect brahmacharya is totally free from disease and, therefore, he or she lives ever in the presence of God, is like God."

Nevertheless, Gandhi says, he found mastering his sexual needs a daily struggle, like "walking on the sword's edge." He eventually came to blame his diet for his daily struggle; like most Hindus, he believed that the palate, the source of an infant's first gratification, was the source of all pleasures. He had always been a vegetarian, and over the years he had renounced stimulants of the palate, like spices, but, as other vegetarians did, he had continued to rely on certain animal products— milk, curds, and ghi—as the staples of his diet. He now came to believe that these were responsible for his animal passion. But, try as he might, he could not give them up. Then, in 1912, he read that some Indian dairymen were in the habit of blowing hot liquid through a pipe into a cow's uterus, a process that somehow enabled them to extract the last drops of milk, and his compassion for the cow at last gave him the strength to take a vow that he would never drink milk again. But doing without milk did not bring him relief from his struggle. He continued to have sexual dreams and an occasional illness. In 1918, when he was in Ahmedabad, he had a severe attack of dysentery. He writes in his autobiography about a visit from a doctor:

He said: "I cannot rebuild your body unless you take milk. If in addition you would take iron and arsenic injections, I would guarantee fully to renovate your constitution."

"You can give me the injections," I replied, "but milk is a different question; I have a vow against it." . . . Kasturbai was standing near my bed listening all the time to this conversation.

"But surely you cannot have any objection to goat's milk then," she interposed.

The doctor too took up the strain. "If you will take goat's milk, it will be enough for me," he said.

I succumbed. . . . For although I had only the milk of the cow and the she-buffalo in mind when I took the vow, by natural implication it covered the milk of all animals. . . . The memory of this action even now rankles in my breast and fills me with remorse, and I am constantly thinking how to give up goat's milk.

Although, in efforts to find a substitute, Gandhi experimented with groundnut oil, soybean oil, and coconut milk, he was not able to give up goat's milk. He continued to feel guilty about his shortcomings as a brahmachari, and blamed them on one occasion for his coming down with appendicitis and at other times for seminal discharges, one of which particularly disturbed him, because at the time he was sixty-six years old and was unwell. Gandhi finally came to believe that if he was ever to grow into a perfect brahmachari—achieve universality and union with God—he must, like some Hindu brahmachari mystics, become physically and spiritually more like a woman, or, rather, embrace in his person both male and female attributes. The nineteenth-century Hindu mystic Ramakrishna was thought to have identified himself so closely with women that he was able to "menstruate" by having periodic discharges of blood through the pores of his skin. Describing the perfect brahmachari, Gandhi writes, "Even his sexual organs will begin to look different. . . . It is said that . . . impotent [men] . . . desire erection but they fail to get it and yet have seminal discharges. . . . But the cultivated impotency of the man whose sexual desire has been burnt up and whose sexual secretions are being converted into vital force . . . is to be desired by everybody." In Gandhi's view, women were altogether nobler than men. Their interest in sex was submissive and self-sacrificing. (Gandhi assumed that women got no pleasure from sex.) Their love was selfless and motherly, stemming from the demands of childbearing and child rearing. They were more virtuous than men, because they had a greater capacity for suffering, for faith, and for renunciation—in fact, for nonviolence. They were therefore better qualified than men to teach "the art of peace to the warring world."

They were the incarnation of ahimsa and the natural leaders of satyagraha.

Ahimsa—"love-force," or "nonviolent force"—involving reverence for all life, is a notion with a long religious history and has been interpreted to mean either that men and women should avoid evil by withdrawing from the world or that they should fight evil by doing good deeds in the world. For Gandhi, "ahimsa . . . is not merely a negative state of harmlessness but . . . a positive state of love, of doing good even to the evil-doer." He believed that only love, or nonviolence, would conquer evil wherever it was found—in people or in laws, in society or in government. The notion of satyagraha—"truth-force," or "soul-force"—was Gandhi's own and came to him spontaneously, he says, about a month after he took his vow of brahmacharya. According to Gandhi, a satyagrahi, or votary of satyagraha, is governed by the belief that the soul can be saved from evil in the world, and so helped along in its search for Brahma, by truth and truth alone. The satyagrahi practices ahimsa truthfully at all times and cheerfully accepts whatever suffering may result from his truthfulness. Gandhi felt that a brahmachari, being without worldly desires and attachments, was best equipped to practice ahimsa and satyagraha. For Gandhi, the vow of brahmacharya was not a form of emasculation but the greatest source of inner strength. "In India there is not only no love but hatred due to emasculation," he wrote in 1917. "There is the strongest desire to fight and kill side by side with utter helplessness. This desire must be satisfied by restoring the capacity for fighting. Then comes the choice. . . . Immediately you cease to fear, you are ready for your choice—to strike or to refrain. To refrain is proof of awakening of the soul in man; to strike is proof of body-force. The ability to strike must be present when the power of the soul is demonstrated. This does not mean that we must be bodily superior to the adversary." Yet it is hard to imagine that he didn't see some connection between nonviolence and the absence of masculinity, for why else would he have considered the submissive and self-sacrificing character of women better suited than the "brute" and selfish character of men to the practice of nonviolence?

Although truth and nonviolence were the forces governing all Gandhi's civil-disobedience campaigns against injustice, oppression, and religious strife in South Africa and India, his belief in their power was put to its most severe test in 1946 in Noakhali, a remote, swampy rural district lying in the delta formed by the Ganges and Brahmaputra rivers, in what was then Indian East Bengal and is now Bangladesh. At the time, eighteen per cent of Noakhali's population of two and a half million was Hindu and eighty-two per cent Muslim, but a small number of Hindus owned three-quarters of the land, and most Muslims were little better than serfs. In October of that year, Muslims started torturing and killing Hindus, raping and kidnapping Hindu women, looting and burning Hindu shops and dwellings, smashing temple idols, and forcing Hindus to recite the Koran and to slaughter and eat their own cows. It was one of the most savage outbreaks of the religious rioting that accompanied the partition of India and the creation of Pakistan, and it marked the first time that the religious violence had reached into a rural area. This was especially alarming to Gandhi. He had always taken pride in his knowledge of India's villages—where most Indians lived—and he now thought that if he could get the Noakhali Hindus to go back to their villages and could persuade the Muslims to accept them and love them as brothers he might have a hope of preventing and containing violence, and so prevail on India to stay united in religious toleration. Therefore, with a band of disciples and dedicated volunteers, he set out for Noakhali on a mission of peace and reconciliation, despite his age (he was then seventy-seven), and despite warnings from the Indian authorities and some of his followers that the Noakhali Muslims, always orthodox, had turned fanatic, and that he would almost certainly be assassinated—an event that would engulf the entire subcontinent in the very violence he hoped to quell. "I am prepared for any eventuality," he wrote his cousin Narandas Gandhi from Noakhali. " 'Do or Die' has to be put to the test here. 'Do' here means Hindus and Mussulmans should learn to live together in peace and amity. Otherwise, I should die in the attempt."

Charu Chowdhury, a Bengali Hindu brahmachari, who made most of the arrangements for Gandhi's tour through Noakhali and was at his side during much of it, is, like most of Gandhi's disciples, old now. More than a quarter century after Gandhi's pilgrimage, he still lives not far from Noakhali—in Dacca, the capital of Bangladesh. He makes his home in the Ramakrishna Mission, which is the principal Hindu cultural and educational institution in the predominantly Muslim country. The mission is situated in a sort of compound off a narrow, crowded lane lined with dingy shops. In the compound are rows of low white barrackslike buildings, each with open doors on two sides; an evil-smelling, stagnant pond; a few banana trees; and a large white temple, inside which a man is just visible in the late-afternoon light, sitting in the Hindu lotus position and lost in meditation in front of an altar.

When I arrive at the mission, it's four o'clock in the afternoon. I am shown into a small room in one of the white buildings. The room has white walls, a gray concrete floor, and a single window with brown wooden shutters over it, and it is crammed with objects. There are two beds, a wooden cupboard with wire-mesh doors, two wooden straight chairs, a green wicker armchair, a table covered with a green cloth, a large, shallow wicker basket, a burlap bag, and a gray water jug. Clothes hang on a line over the two beds, and on shelves behind one of the beds are some dusty bedrolls, old suitcases, old biscuit tins, and bags of food. Piles of books and papers are everywhere. There is no fan, and the air is thick with large, heavy-bodied, vicious mosquitoes.

Two men—who prove to be fully dressed—peep out from under the covers on the beds. One of them greets me warmly, bids me sit down, gets up, and goes out with the water jug. He soon returns, and gives the jug to the other man, who now goes out with it, and the first man draws a chair up to the table and sits down. He has a square face with heavy jowls, a bulbous nose, rather thin lips, discolored teeth, short, thinning dark-gray hair, and small, parched, wrinkled hands. He is dressed in a kurta and lungi (a saronglike garment) of white khadi, has a white khadi scarf around his neck, and is wearing glasses with heavy black frames. He looks to be about seventy. He is Charu Chow-dhury—or Charu Babu, as he is more generally known, Babu being an honorific title in Bengali.

"When Bapu was in Noakhali, Muslims used to come and harass him at prayer meetings," Charu Babu says. "They would ask him such questions as 'Why are you here in Noakhali when Muslims are dying in Bihar and in Delhi? Why don't you go there with your peace mission?' Then, one day, when Bapu had been in Noakhali for about four months, he actually received a message from the government of Bihar saying, 'You come to Bihar at once and talk peace here.' I went with him as far as Calcutta and put him on a train for Bihar. As I bowed goodbye, he said, 'What are you going to do?' I said, 'You are not taking me to Bihar. What more have I got to do?' He said, 'You go back to Noakhali and carry on my work until I come back.' He never came back—he was shot in Delhi. But I stayed on in Noakhali, through all the changes. First it was Pakistan. Then it was Bangladesh. But I stayed on. That's what Bapu told me to do.''

I ask him about Gandhi's tour through Noakhali.

"I had been working for Bapu for many years in his Constructive Programme, for the development of khadi and village industries in Bengal, when Bapu decided to go to Noakhali. Some of my friends and I went there immediately, as an advance party, to make arrangements for him. The monsoon had just ended, and streams and canals were overflowing with water and sludge. In some places the water was knee high, in other places breast high. It was almost impossible to get around. But Bapu came. I remember Bapu walking through village after village. I remember the broken glass, brambles, and filth sometimes deliberately strewn in his path. Yet Bapu always went barefoot. He said it was part of his penance. I remember Bapu wading through water, trudging through bogs, sometimes crossing canals in boats that had to be pushed and punted through weeds. Bapu saw the Hindu refugees—thousands of men, women, and children, all crying uncontrollably. Bapu saw the streams and canals filled with human and animal bodies. Bapu saw the burned and rotting crops. Bapu saw the ashes of huts and shrines. Bapu went from village to village collecting testimony of individual sufferings and assessing the amount of food and money needed for rehabilitation. Bapu tried to strengthen the Hindus spiritually, so that they would be prepared to sacrifice even their lives in order to bring about a change of heart in their Muslim persecutors. Bapu begged the Hindus to return and rebuild their villages. He tried to get the Muslims to rediscover the goodness that was within them. He begged the Muslims to stop persecuting their Hindu brethren. He fasted for the Hindu-Muslim violence. But neither Hindus nor Muslims had any use for him or his nonviolent methods. Then, one damp, chilly morning, after Bapu had been in Noakhali less than two weeks, he gathered all of us around him in our camp in the village of Kazirkhil. Bapu had decided to leave us all and go and live in Srirampur. Srirampur was a small, ravaged village four miles away, from which almost all Hindus had fled. He said, 'All the while I have been looking for the light in Noakhali, I have been groping in the dark. I know now what I must do. It's time for yajna—for yet another kind of penitential sacrifice. Father and daughter, brother and sister, husband and wife must part company and work alone. We must all renounce each other.' We protested, and said we would all be killed if we didn't stay together. But Bapu insisted that only by being more on his own could he find his bearings and test his faith not just in truth and nonviolence but also in God. He counselled us to do the same—to go and live in riot-torn villages, too, and work for our own salvation and that of Noakhali and Mother India. We said a short prayer; we sang a hymn; we wept.''

A boy servant comes in with tea, and Charu Babu strokes the boy's chin.

"Of course, Bapu wasn't completely alone in Srirampur," he continues, taking some tea. "He did have three attendants with him. But he wasn't happy there. He seemed to feel that he was not making any progress in his solitary quest, and so he decided to resume his tour of the devastated Noakhali countryside. He was old, restless, weak, and dispirited, and not able to walk much at a stretch, so we arranged for overnight stops in villages a few miles apart, to make it possible for him to go from one village to the next as his morning walk. Since all the paraphernalia he needed—the buckets, the bathtubs, the commode, the syringes, and whatnot—had to come with us, it was no easy task getting from village to village.''

Charu Babu is a sociable, irrepressible man, and he holds my hand as he talks. Like other brahmacharis I have met, he seems to feel the need to touch, as if the austere practice of brahmacharya were insupportable without some form of physical communion.

"Does anyone in Noakhali remember Gandhi today?" I ask.

"No," he says. "There are no monuments to Bapu anywhere in this region, except for a Gandhi ashram in the village of Jayag, in Noakhali—and there's little enough of that. The ashram's four custodians—they were Hindus—were butchered by the Pakistanis in 1971, during the struggle for the independence of Bangladesh. I would have been butchered, too, if I hadn't been in prison at the time. I was considered Pakistan's Enemy No. 1 and spent twelve years in a Pakistani jail. But I was treated well, because I was a model prisoner and spent my time reading and tending a garden, just as Bapu would have done. I was very proud of my garden.''

The other man returns, puts down the water jug, and silently begins sorting some papers. He is about forty, gaunt, with shoulder-length curly brown hair going gray and a small beard and mustache. He has heavy-lidded eyes and a wary expression, and wears a white khadi lungi, a white khadi kurta, and, around his elbow, a chain hung with tiny metal prayer drums and other charms.

"This is my friend, and he was considered Pakistan's Enemy No. 2," Charu Babu says, as though that were the man's name. "We were in jail together. He owned textile mills and was a millionaire before all his property was confiscated by the Pakistani government."

An old man with a boyish face, short white hair, large eyes, and few teeth now joins us. He carries a large umbrella and is also dressed in white khadi.

"This is Pakistan's Enemy No. 3," Charu Babu says cheerfully. "Bapu lit a little lamp here and we 'enemies' have tried to keep it burning through all the years of Pakistani persecution. Now, thank God, we have Bangladesh. The new state doesn't think of us as 'enemies'—not yet, anyway."

With Charu Babu as my guide, I drive in a jeep to the house of M. A. Abdullah, who was one of the few Muslims in Noakhali to take Gandhi's message of religious toleration to heart and, after the partition of India, to give hope to the "enemies of Pakistan" that Gandhi's pilgrimage would one day bear fruit. At the time of Gandhi's pilgrimage, he was Superintendent of Police in Noakhali, and was therefore responsible for protecting Gandhi's life. "Mr. Abdullah rose to be Deputy Inspector General of Police of all of East Pakistan," Charu Babu tells me. "He would have been named Inspector General if the Pakistani government had not suspected him of being a Hindu sympathizer. After they retired him, although he was in his fifties, he became a student, qualified as a lawyer, and devoted his energies to the betterment of the poor. He's been a bachelor all his life and as good as a brahmachari. He's really one of us."

We drive for what seems like hours down a narrow main street, which must originally have been designed for horse carts and is now one long traffic jam of buses, lorries, cars, bicycle rickshaws, and wooden wagons loaded with sacks of flour and drawn by ghostly men covered with flour from head to toe. Hundreds of tiny shops are packed together, and merchants, children, cows, mules, and goats jostle for whatever space they can get.

The jeep stops abruptly, and Charu Babu hails an impressive-looking, large-boned, wizened old man wrapped in a long blue shawl who is walking along the street. "This is Munindro Bhattachary," Charu Babu says. "He's a true Gandhian, and he's carrying on the work of Gandhi's pilgrimage all by himself. He walks at least twenty miles a day, all over Dacca, preaching nonviolence and brotherly love."

Munindro Bhattachary launches into what turns out to be a speech that Gandhi gave on satyagraha in 1920. He has a squeaky voice but is something of an orator. He recites the speech in its entirety and then, without another word, stumps off.

Abdullah lives on the ground floor of a large old yellow house off a narrow alley in the noisy, congested center of Dacca. He is lying propped on one elbow on a charpoy without any bedclothes, in the middle of a large, open, but musty room, which smells of sickness. He is sixty-seven but looks older. He is bald, with small eyes, and has an enormous growth on his forehead, and a funguslike skin disease on one foot. He wears a white undershirt and dhoti. In the room are several trunks, a dusty radio, clothes hanging on a line, a bicycle leaning against a wall, and books and yellowing papers all over, on shelves and on the floor. Through the open door, an immense and menacing black beehive can be seen hanging from a branch of a large tree in the courtyard.

"Partition was caused by hatred," Abdullah says. "Hatred was of this world. Gandhiji was of the other world. Common men could not put his ideals into practice. I never thought of myself as a Muslim, a Hindu, a Christian, or a Parsi—only as a policeman."

Abdullah's voice is indistinct and hesitant; he seems to be in pain and talks with his eyes closed. (I learned later that he was dying.) "There is no position I can lie in comfortably," he says. "The whole of my insides shake and rattle when I breathe."

"What was it like trying to protect Gandhi in Noakhali?" I ask.

"I had a good number of policemen to help me do the job," he says. "And the government of Bengal had also assigned eighteen or twenty armed soldiers to protect him. We all moved along with Gandhiji from village to village, but Gandhiji had no use for us and moved freely in hostile crowds. Any madman could have assassinated him at any time, but we all took it for granted that no one ever would, so in a way we were all responsible ultimately for his assassination."

Abdullah probably shouldn't be talking at all, but during his reminiscing his voice becomes animated. "Noakhali is a long story, and it will take a long time to tell," he says. "Leave me your address, and I'll write to you."

At the time Gandhi decided to leave his followers and go and live in Srirampur, he wrote, "Truth and ahimsa, by which I swear and which have to my knowledge sustained me for sixty years, seem to fail. . . . To test them or, better, to test myself, I am . . . cutting myself away from those who have been with me all these years, and who have made life easy for me. . . . I do not propose to leave East Bengal till I am satisfied that mutual trust has been established between the two communities and the two have resumed the even tenor of their life in their villages. Without this there is neither Pakistan nor Hindustan—only slavery awaits India, torn asunder by mutual strife and engrossed in barbarity." Gandhi had lost his will to live, lost all hope for a united, free, and peaceful India, lost confidence in his ability ever to become a perfect instrument for the practice of satyagraha and ahimsa, and therefore of brahmacharya. He was often heard to mutter, *"Kya karun? Kya karun?* [What shall I do? What shall I do?]"

The most reliable firsthand account of Gandhi's personal crisis in Noakhali is to be found in a book entitled "My Days with Gandhi." It was written by Gandhi's Bengali interpreter, Nirmal Kumar Bose, who accompanied Gandhi even to Srirampur and lived there with him. Bose was unique among Gandhi's attendants in that he was not a longtime disciple but a left-wing intellectual, who had taken a leave of absence from a teaching post at the University of Calcutta in order to accompany Gandhi to Noakhali as his interpreter. He was consequently a more detached observer than any of the other attendants. In Noakhali, Bose says, Gandhi was apt to wake up in the middle of the night shivering. He would ask the attendant sleeping next to him—usually a woman—to hold him for five or ten minutes, until the shivering stopped. "He sometimes asked women to share his bed and even the cover which he used," Bose reports, "and then tried to ascertain if even the least trace of sensual feeling had been evoked in himself or his companion." In Gandhi's view, such contacts with women were "experiments in brahmacharya," an essential part of his aspiration to become "God's eunuch," as he put it, but in Bose's view they were a form of exploitation, however unconscious, since the women being used in the experiments were in a sense being treated as inferiors. He says he noticed that each of the women around Gandhi considered herself to have a special relationship with him and was so jealous of her place in his affections, so fearful of losing it, that the slightest sign of rejection from him made her "hysterical." Bose remarks, "Whatever may be the value of the *prayog* [experiment] in Gandhiji's own case, it does leave a mark of injury on the personality of others . . . for whom sharing in Gandhiji's experiment is no spiritual necessity." When Bose confronted Gandhi with what he considered the unhealthy results of the brahmacharya experiments, Gandhi replied that the women had assured him that holding him or sleeping next to him had no ill effect on them. Gandhi maintained that his brahmacharya experiments were a crucial test of his renunciation of sex, a necessary part of his yajna for the violence of Noakhali. He charged Bose with "unwarranted assumptions" concerning his relationship with the women. Bose became so troubled about the issue that he abruptly left Gandhi's service and returned to Calcutta, but the argument continued through correspondence, which Bose reprints in his book. Gandhi wrote to him:

> I do not call that brahmacharya that means not to touch a woman. What I do today is nothing new for me. . . . I am amazed at your assumption that my experiment implied any assumption of woman's inferiority. She would be, if I looked upon her with lust with or without her consent. . . . My wife was "inferior" when she was the instrument of my lust. She ceased to be that when she lay with me naked as my sister. . . . Should there be difference if it is not my wife, as she once was, but some other sister? I do hope you will acquit me of having any lustful designs upon women or girls who have been naked with me. A or B's hysteria [Bose omits names] had nothing to do with my experiment, I hope. They were before the experiment what they are today, if they [are] not less of it.

Bose was anything but convinced, and wrote back that, according to Freud, "we . . . are often motivated and carried away by unconscious desires in directions other than those to which we consciously subscribe." Gandhi replied that he didn't know anything about Freud or his writings, and that he had heard the name mentioned only once before, and then, too, by a professor. Gandhi said he wanted to know more about Freud, but Bose apparently never pursued the matter with him.

Bose is seventy-two years old at the time of my visit, and although he is convalescing from an operation for cancer, he is eager to see me and talk about Gandhi. The taxi taking me to his house, in the old part of Calcutta, plunges off a major thoroughfare into a gully, or narrow lane, and winds through several more gullies, past once elegant but now dilapidated private houses. We pass a dead horse lying on its side, its mouth fixed in agony, and pull up in front of a beige stucco house with louvred shutters. A hammer and sickle has been stencilled on the wall. There is a gate leading into a lovely inner courtyard filled with large tropical potted plants, and a delicate wrought-iron spiral staircase ascends from the courtyard to Bose's apartment, which has a wrought-iron balcony supported by Corinthian columns.

A young, plump, dark-skinned servant boy with a shaven head and wearing only a green lungi opens the door and shows me into Bose's study, which has French windows; the calls of hawkers rise from the street below. In the study are a table stacked with books in Bengali, a couple of armchairs, and a large writing desk, which has on it the Concise Oxford Dictionary, Fowler's "Modern English Usage," "How to Teach Yourself Assamese," an alarm clock in a cardboard box, a small bronze turtle, a pink plastic letter opener, and a pot of glue, along with polished stones used as paperweights—a Gandhian trademark—and a calendar with Gandhi's picture on it. One wall is covered with well-stocked bookshelves, and another is lined with tall metal cupboards.

Bose comes in, attended by a pretty young woman, and they sit down together at the desk. He has large, weary-looking brown eyes and yellowish pale skin. He is slender and clean-shaven, with short, wispy gray hair, a straight nose, and very fine-boned hands. He is wearing a white khadi dhoti and a short-sleeved white khadi shirt buttoned down the back. The young woman has long, curly black hair and is wearing a white sari with pastel stripes.

"This is my niece," he says, adding wryly, "She looks after her bachelor uncle in the Gandhian tradition of secretary-nurses."

"Were you Gandhi's secretary-nurse as well as his Bengali interpreter?" I ask.

"Yes, of course," he says. "As a student, I had read a lot of
Tolstoy and Kropotkin and other political anarchists, and thought of
myself as one of them. Then I came upon the writings of Gandhiji. I
felt that he was in the same anarchist tradition but that he was also a
heroic figure, like Socrates or Jesus, prepared to lay down his life for
truth as he saw it. I was very excited, and started compiling an anthol-
ogy of Gandhiji's economic and political writings. In 1934, a friend
introduced me to him, but my interest in him remained academic
until 1946, when he asked me to go with him to Noakhali and act as
his Bengali interpreter. I went, although I was sure we wouldn't
come out alive. In no time at all, I was doing everything for him—
nursing him, massaging him, bathing him. Wherever he was, he kept
rigidly to his daily routine. He was so much preoccupied with the
physical details of his daily life because mastering his physical self was
part of his program of mastering his spiritual self. I remember once
during the morning walk we came upon a child suffering from fever
lying in the sun outside a hut. Gandhiji examined the child and told
the parents that he would be back with a syringe to administer a
saline enema. I said to Gandhiji, 'You must let me do it. If it gets into
the papers that I allowed you to administer an enema to a child when
I was with you and could have done it, I would lose face wherever
my name is known.' So Gandhiji wrote out for me the whole prescription—how much salt to use, how much water, what the temperature of the water should be, and so on. It is preserved with the rest of
my papers, which are now in the archives of the Asiatic Society here.
I printed it in 'My Days with Gandhi'—which, by the way, I published at my own expense, because after Gandhiji's death everyone
wanted to suppress all further discussion of the brahmacharya experiments." (Bose says in the preface to his book that when he submitted
the manuscript to the Navajivan Press, which owns the copyright to
all Gandhi's writings, and which functions both as the center of the
Gandhi industry and as an arbiter of what is written about Gandhi, its
managing trustee wrote back, "I am of opinion that you be better
advised to leave out of the book Bapu's experiments in sex or brah-

macharya and reconstitute the book to say about Bapu's great work in Noakhali.")

"Have you told all you know about the brahmacharya experiments?" I ask.

"I was never able to find out very much," he says. "None of the girls would talk to me—I'm considered an apostate. Anyway, the wish to be truthful died in our country with Gandhiji. It was never very strong, even among his disciples. Since Gandhiji never had any privacy—and in the camp everyone slept in one room—there could be no question of impropriety. Once, when he had been pestering the girls about how they felt about holding him during his shivering fits, I asked him, 'What's so special about hugging an old man of seventy-seven to comfort him in the night?' He gave me the standard reply that he wanted to be so pure that he would be above arousing impure thoughts in anyone else."

"Why didn't you pursue the subject of Freud with him?" I ask.

"Gandhiji died about a year after I left Noakhali," he says. "And, anyhow, I was far from being an authority on Freud."

"Do you think Gandhi ever succeeded in becoming completely sexless? Did he ever, in your opinion, become a perfect brachmachari?"

"I don't think he succeeded in identifying completely with women—in reaching the bisexual state of, say, a Ramakrishna. If he had, I don't think he would have been so concerned about what the women who lay next to him were feeling. I do think, however, that there was something saintly, almost supernatural, about him."

Bose motions weakly to his niece, and she leaves the room, returns with a key, unlocks one of the metal cupboards, and takes down a book. It is Vincent Sheean's "Lead, Kindly Light." She opens it at a certain page and hands it to him. The passage he reads, which concerns Gandhi's assassination, strikes me as Sheean at his most sentimental, but Bose seems genuinely affected by it. Bose reads:

Inside my own head there occurred a wavelike disturbance which I can only compare to a storm at sea—wind and wave surging tremendously back and forth. . . . I recoiled upon the brick wall and leaned against it, bent almost in two. I felt the consciousness of the

Mahatma leave me then. . . . The storm inside my head continued for some little time. . . . Then I was aware of two things at once, a burning and stinging in the fingers of my right hand and a similar burning and stinging in my eyes. In the eyes it was tears, although of some more acid mixture than I had known, and on my fingers I did not know for a while what it was, because I put them in my mouth (like a child) to ease the burning. . . . I looked at my fingers. On the third and fourth fingers of my right hand blisters had appeared. They were facing each other, on the sides of those fingers which touch. The blister on the third finger was rather large and was already filled with water. The blister on the fourth or little finger was smaller. They had not been there before I heard the shots.

In Noakhali, Gandhi publicly disclosed the fact that he had been taking naked girls to bed with him for years but had tried to keep the practice secret in order to avoid public controversy. He said he believed that his secrecy, which amounted to untruthfulness, had been a serious error—an impediment to his becoming a perfect brahmachari. He is even reported to have boasted that if he could just be successful in his brahmacharya experiments, just prove how potent—physically, mentally, and spiritually—he had become through seminal continence, he would be able to vanquish Muhammad Ali Jinnah himself, the father of Pakistan, through nonviolence, and foil Jinnah's plans for partition. Orthodox Hindus had always condemned Gandhi for his unorthodox brahmacharya practices, such as his long daily baths and massages, often administered by girls, and his daily walks with his hands on the shoulders of girls, saying that they set a bad example to other brahmacharis, "offended the accepted notions of decency," and were "a cloak" to hide his "sensuality." Nor had they been convinced by Gandhi's protestations that there was no privacy about his baths and massages, during which, he said, he often read or fell asleep; that he considered himself a parent to the girls who served him and walked with him; that his brahmacharya vow had nothing to do with orthodox laws and therefore he was free to frame his own rules as he went along, provided they did not violate his principles. His public revelations, in the name of truth and nonviolence, about his brahmacharya experiments shocked not

only orthodox Hindus but also some of his closest disciples, who, like
Bose, attacked him and parted company with him on account of
them.

Gandhi, however, continued his brahmacharya experiments
through what were to be the last months of his life, in Noakhali and
in the suburbs of Delhi, as he tried to stem the tide of religious violence
and turmoil, of retaliation and counter-retaliation spreading through
the entire subcontinent. He continued to defend his brahmacharya
experiments with such statements as "I have called my present venture
a yajna—a sacrifice, a penance. . . . How can there be that self-purification when in my mind I entertain a thing which I dare not put openly
into practice?" And "My meaning of brahmacharya is this: 'One . . .
who, by constant attendance upon God, has become . . . capable of lying
naked with naked women, however beautiful they may be, without
being in any manner whatsoever sexually excited.' " And "When the
gopis [milkmaids] were stripped of their clothes by Krishna, the legend
says, they showed no sign of embarrassment or sex-consciousness but
stood before the Lord in rapt devotion." And "The whole world may
forsake me but I dare not leave what I hold is the truth for me. It may
be a delusion and a snare. If so, I must realize it myself."

Whatever the spiritual source of Gandhi's brahmacharya experiments, Bose, for one, maintains in his book that their psychological
source was "repression of the sexual instinct," prompted by a self-
imposed penance for "having proved untrue to his father during the
last moments of his life" and for not having nursed his father as a
mother would have. Erik Erikson, in his book "Gandhi's Truth,"
agrees, and, in his discussion of the brahmacharya experiments, goes
on to develop the theme of Gandhi's maternalism:

> The whole episode, as Bose brilliantly recognized at the time,
> points to a persistent importance in Gandhi's life of the theme of
> motherhood, both in the sense of a need to be a perfect and pure
> mother, and in the sense of a much less acknowledged need to be
> held and reassured, especially at the time of his finite loneliness. In
> this last crisis the Mahatma appears to have been almost anxiously
> eager to know what those who had studied the "philosophy" of that
> doctor in Vienna might say about him, although he probably could
> do little with the interpretation offered by one of his friends, namely
> that his shivering was an orgasm-equivalent. . . .

As to the Mahatma's public private life, all we can say is that here was a man who both lived and wondered aloud, and with equal intensity and depth, about a multiformity of inclinations which other men hide and bury in strenuous consistency. At the end, great confusion can be a mark of greatness, too, especially if it results from the inescapable conflicts of existence. Gandhi . . . had wanted to purify his relationship to his father by nursing and mothering him; and he had wanted to be an immaculate mother. But when, at the end, he was defeated in his aspiration to be the founding father of a united India, he may well have needed maternal solace himself.

The women who may have given and received this "maternal solace" have, with one exception, passed into the Gandhi biographies and memoirs as no more than letters of the alphabet, and everyone, including Erikson and Bose, has assumed that the story of the experiments will never be fully told. The exception is Manu Gandhi, a distant cousin, who wrote a little memoir of her own, entitled "Bapu—My Mother," in which she tells how Gandhi tried to be both a father and a mother to her. It seems that in 1940, when she was twelve years old, her mother, who was dying, asked Kasturbai to be a mother to Manu, and Kasturbai took her in. When Kasturbai was on her deathbed, four years later, she asked Gandhi to be a mother to the girl in her place. Gandhi took Kasturbai's last wish very seriously. He came to have a motherly interest in the girl's physical development, and in the minutest details of her life. He told her how to wash her hair, how to wear her clothes, what, how much, and how often to eat. He took charge of her religious education, teaching her the Bhagavad Gita and the pronunciation of the difficult Sanskrit words. She cooked for him and served him his food. She washed his feet and massaged him. She read him the newspapers, and kept a diary in which she recorded the minutest details of *his* life. At first, she slept by his pallet, and doesn't seem to have minded when he woke her up in the middle of the night to talk. When she was about nineteen, she started sleeping in his bed, and that, she implies, happened in Noakhali. But, discreetly, that is all she does say about the brahmacharya experiments in "Bapu—My Mother."

Manu died young, in 1969, but Abha Gandhi—the wife of Gandhi's grandnephew Kanu—who was about the same age as Manu, and who many Gandhians say in private was even closer to Gandhi than Manu was, is still alive. Gandhi liked to call the two girls his "walking sticks''; toward the end of his life he was almost invariably seen walking with his hands resting on their shoulders—as he was when he was assassinated, on the terrace of Birla House, in Delhi. Abha is in Ahmedabad visiting her elder sister, Mrs. Vina Patel, who lives in one of the old houses connected to the Sabarmati Ashram. At the time I stop by the house, some women are sitting sewing on a large wooden swing on the veranda while at their feet two boys are shelling a big pile of peanuts.

One woman gets up and comes forward to greet me. She is short and plump, with black curly hair pulled back in a bun but straying loose, and has a round face with large eyes behind spectacles with black half-rims. She is wearing a white sari with a hand-stitched blue border and a white choli sparsely scattered with mirrorwork, and she has a red bangle on each wrist. She has small feet and hands, and her voice is light and sweet. She is Abha.

Sewing in hand, Abha takes me inside, to a room that has exposed rafters supporting a high tiled roof. A few of the tiles are made of opaque glass and act as small skylights. There is a divan with a muted gold-and-purple cover, the colors set off by bright-green cushions; a table spread with a sheet of plastic; and a built-in cupboard holding a large old radio, dishes, a Staffordshire dog, and other knickknacks. On the walls are pictures of various Hindu gods and goddesses and swamis, and one photograph of Gandhi spinning.

"My husband and I now manage the Kasturbai Ashram, some distance from here," she tells me in colloquial Hindi, going on with her sewing. "We started the ashram in 1956, in the summer residence of the raja of Rajkot, with the help of the Gandhi National Memorial Trust. The summer residence is one of the places where Ba was imprisoned for her part in the satyagraha campaigns. It's one of the few memorials to her."

Abha presents me with an ingenuous leaflet about her ashram:

> AT PRESENT ONE CAN SEE
> the summer-resort of a Native Ruler
> is changed into an
> 'ASHRAM'
> DEDICATED TO THE CAUSE OF
> RURAL UPLIFT

AND AMONGST ITS OTHER
MANY-FOLD
ACTIVITIES IT INCLUDES THIS
KASTURBA AROGYADHAM
(HEALTH CLINIC)
which endavours day and night

for

Physical, Intelectual [*sic*], Educational, Economical, Social & Cultural uplift of the Villages and especially for the Prevention and Eradication of diseases from Villages through Medico-Educational Programme and serves the surrounding 30 Villages since 6 years through:

•Maternal & Child Health Centre
•T. B. Clinic (With X-Ray plant)
•Indoor 8 bed Hospital
•Mobile Health Unit for villages
•General out-door patient department
•Opthalmic department.

"When Bapu was taken away from us forever, all I could think about was dying," she says. "After he was shot in front of my eyes, I couldn't speak for six months, but I went back to Noakhali and threw myself into his work. One day, a child came up to me and asked me something, and suddenly I found I could talk again. But it was some time before I was able to talk easily. No one can give me the love Bapu gave me. I think of him all the time."

"How did you become Gandhi's constant companion?" I ask.

"Through my father," she says. "He originally became interested in Bapu's career through the newspapers and took up wearing khadi and the Gandhi cap. One day, he wore his Gandhi cap to work—he was a jailer in Calcutta—and his superior upbraided him. He resigned. That was in 1930. We all went back to our village in Bengal to live. It was very difficult for us to make ends meet. There were eight of us children, and my father took part in Bapu's civil-disobedience campaign against the British salt laws, in 1930, and was arrested—he had to spend some time in jail. All along, my father had been corresponding with Bapu, and when Bapu came to Bengal for a conference in 1940 my father took us all to meet him. My father told Bapu that he wanted to send me to the Sevagram Ashram for my education. Bapu inspected me and agreed. I was twelve at the time. In the ashram, I noticed that Bapu always used two children as his walking sticks. I wanted to be a walking stick, but I used to lag behind, because I was shy. Bapu saw through my shyness right away and called me to his side and started using me as a walking stick. Eventually, I was doing everything for him, but if Manu or any of the other sisters were there, we divided the tasks."

I ask her how the sisters got along together.

"We took pains to keep up good relations," she says. "Also, we were good at doing different things. Manu was good at taking notes for him; I was good at cooking and washing. Bapu never wanted his clothes ironed, but I kept them washed and neatly folded. I loved taking care of him—it gave me a lot of happiness, of the kind that a mother gets from tending her child. Bapu often said, 'You are like a mother to me.' Once, I was bathing him and he asked me to hurry up. He had an appointment. He told me to hurry up three times, and I said, 'You are a renowned mahatma and yet you are so impatient, like any other common mortal. What does it matter if you're a little late?' Bapu laughed. 'I like your spirit,' he said. 'Only a mother would dare talk to her child the way you talk to me. They call me Rashtra Pita; they should call *you* Rashtra Mata.'" Rashtra Pita means "nation's father," and Rashtra Mata means "nation's mother." Gandhi used to refer to Kasturbai as Rashtra Mata. "I was so childish then. When I think of it now, I feel very bad. Bapu and I used to quarrel all the time."

"What did you quarrel about?"

"We often had clashes of will. Bapu left me behind in Noakhali to carry on his work, and I got a very bad case of dysentery. No medicine seemed to help, and Satish Chandra Das Gupta, who was looking after me, wrote to Bapu and said he was sending me to Calcutta for treatment. When I got there, I received a letter from Bapu saying that he felt responsible for my condition, because he had taken me to Noakhali, and that if I wanted to I could go to him in Delhi. I wrote back, 'The question is not what *I* want to do but what *you* want me to do.' He answered, 'All right—you win. *I* want you to come to Delhi. You are a very willful girl.' I went. How sad he was in Delhi! Noakhali had disturbed his peace of mind along with his routine. I said to him, 'I'm with you all day long and you don't so much as smile, and then in the evening Jawaharlal Nehru comes and you laugh with him the whole time.' Bapu said, 'You're such a foolish girl to be jealous of Jawaharlal. Don't you understand that I laugh and joke with him so that we won't cry?' "

I ask her about the brahmacharya experiments.

"It was common knowledge that Sushila Nayar often slept next to Bapu. He first asked me to sleep next to him when I was sixteen. I thought he just got cold at night and wanted me to sleep with him to keep him warm. So I did now and again, with my clothes on. But two years later, in Noakhali, I began sleeping next to him regularly."

"Did you still wear your clothes?"

She hesitates, and finally says, "He did ask me to take my clothes off. But, as far as I remember, I usually kept my petticoat and choli on."

"But what about him?"

"I don't remember whether he had any clothes on or not. I don't like to think about it."

"How did you feel about it?"

"It was nothing."

"Didn't your husband mind your sleeping with Gandhi?"

"He did mind, and he went to Bapu and told him that if he wanted someone to keep him warm, his—Kanu's—body was warmer than mine. He said that he had more vitality, more energy—was healthier all round."

"What did Gandhi say?"

"I think he said he wanted me as much for the brahmacharya experiments as for the warmth. He said our sleeping together was a way of testing that he was as pure in mind as he was in body, as free from lustful thoughts as he was from physical desire. There was a lot of hubbub among the men about the experiments, and Kanu and the other men met with Bapu and said, 'Bapu, you are a renowned mahatma. There is no need for you to test yourself in this unseemly manner. Anyway, such a test would be more appropriate for a virile young man.' Bapu heard them out but said nothing and continued with his experiments."

"What did Kanu say?"

"What could he say? I had always spent all my time looking after Bapu, and Kanu took care of himself. He was Bapu's typist and photographer, and he kept himself very busy. God has given Kanu a strong constitution. He's never needed much looking after."

Dr. Sushila Nayar was Gandhi's personal physician. Although she received training in Western medicine and served for five years—between 1962 and 1967—as the country's Minister of State for Health, she is one of Gandhi's most orthodox disciples, espousing such causes as legal prohibition, and abstinence as the only morally acceptable method of birth control. She lives in a rather bleak area on the outskirts of Delhi. She turns out to be a short, stout, round-faced woman of about sixty. She has graying black hair with reddish tints, and she is dressed in a crumpled white khadi sari with a yellow border and a white khadi choli with a faint green print. Her combined living room and dining room, where we sit and talk, is lined with glass-fronted cupboards in which miscellaneous china, dolls, statues, and books are crammed. In one corner is an old refrigerator, with a very loud motor. There is a woodcut of sandalled feet, probably Gandhi's, on one wall, and numerous photographs of Sushila all around—with Gandhi, with Nehru, with a statue of Buddha.

"I believe, as Bapu did, that if you are a brahmachari and live in harmony with the laws of nature you will not fall sick," she says. "If you do fall sick, you should first use natural, simple remedies—nature cures. A good night's sleep for high blood pressure, fasting for dysentery and flatulence. That's what Bapu did. If you get desperately sick, however, and the simple, natural remedies don't work, then it is all right to experiment with modern medicines. Bapu was not above taking a little quinine when he was down with malaria. But I wasn't just Bapu's doctor. I was his masseuse, his travelling companion, his secretary. If I was in Bapu's hut and he was talking to a visitor, I took down the conversation. All the secretaries there did, and afterward Bapu picked for publication the version he considered most accurate. He once picked my version over Bose's. I was just a student at the time, and Bose fancied himself a distinguished scholar. He never forgave me and sought every opportunity to malign me after that as 'a hysterical, jealous woman who regarded Bapu as her private possession.' "

I ask her if she knows how and when the brahmacharya experiments got started.

"There was nothing special about sleeping next to Bapu. I heard from Bapu's own lips that when he first asked Manu to sleep with him, in Noakhali, they slept under the same covers with their clothes on, and that even on the first night Manu was snoring within minutes of getting into his bed. Sometime later, Bapu said to her, 'We both may be killed by the Muslims at any time. We must both put our purity to the ultimate test, so that we know that we are offering the purest of sacrifices, and we should now both start sleeping naked.' She said, 'Of course,' and I heard from Bapu's own lips that neither he nor she felt any sexual desire whatsoever. Manu wanted to serve Bapu in Noakhali because it was the worst place possible, full of mortal danger. But long before Manu came into the picture I used to sleep with him, just as I would with my mother. He might say, 'My back aches. Put some pressure on it.' So I might put some pressure on it or lie down on his back and he might just go to sleep. In the early days, there was no question of calling this a brahmacharya experiment. It was just part of the nature cure. Later on, when people started asking questions about his physical contact with women—with Manu, with Abha, with me—the idea of brahmacharya experiments was developed. Don't ask me any more about brahmacharya experiments. There's nothing more to say, unless you have a dirty mind, like Bose."

A man comes in. He has a pear-shaped head, heavy jowls, short white hair, and white stubble on his chin, and is wearing a white khadi kurta and dhoti.

"That's Lalaji," Sushila says. "He lives with me, answers my telephone, and helps around the house."

Lalaji cackles in agreement, but he doesn't say anything.

I ask Sushila why she, like many other women who spent their youth around Gandhi, has never married.

"I don't know about the others, but I was once engaged to Dattatreya Balkrishna Kalelkar's son," Sushila tells me. "He wanted to marry right away, but I wanted to wait, and first serve Bapu and the country. Then he said something very nasty. He said, 'All you Gandhiites profess these ideals about service, but you really just can't tear yourselves away from your lord and master. You all bask in his reflected glory. Well, go bask in his reflected hell.' That was the end of our engage-

203

ment, and I never wanted to marry anyone else."

Lalaji cackles but again doesn't say anything.

"But then, for me Bapu was everything," Sushila goes on, ignoring Lalaji. "He was a god. I have always been drawn to the supernatural." She fingers a gold locket around her neck, and adds, "I recently became a devotee of Satya Sai Baba." Satya Sai Baba, who claims to be God incarnate, is enjoying a great vogue in India these days, especially among the well-to-do. One of his favorite miracles is to produce out of thin air twenty-two-karat-gold lockets with his picture inside, which his devotees wear as talismans.

Just how Kasturbai felt about being a brahmachari wife is not known. She left no record herself, and there is very little written about her, but Gandhi often speaks of their quarrels and periods of estrangement in the early years of their marriage. Gandhi, who was his own best prosecutor, says that in those years he could be quite brutal to her in pursuit of what he believed was virtue. In the later years of their marriage, he says, she conquered what he considered to be her willful, obstinate nature and adapted herself completely to the demands of his life and work. "What developed the self-abnegation in her to the highest level was our brahmacharya," he wrote after her death. "From 1901, Ba had no other interest in staying with me except to help me in my work. . . . As a woman and wife she considered it her duty to lose herself in me ever after."

Gandhi believed that sexual intercourse was a religious duty purely for the purpose of procreation but that service to society was a higher religious duty than procreation. He therefore advocated that his married disciples take a vow of brahmacharya as soon after they had completed their families as they could—which was what he had done—and that those who had never married and wanted to dedicate themselves totally to service to society eliminate sex and marriage altogether. Some of Gandhi's brahmachari disciples, however, met and fell in love in the course of their service and, without abjuring their vows of brahmacharya, started living together in what they called a "spiritual marriage" or "spiritual family," insisting that they were carrying out, in

Gandhi's tradition, further experiments in the practice of brahmachar-ya—further explorations of the purity of sacrifice. From a Western point of view, such connubial arrangements may seem bizarre, but they are not uncommon among Hindus.

J. B. and Sucheta Kripalani are perhaps the most eminent of Gandhi's disciples who entered into a brahmachari marriage. (Sucheta is also known to have participated in Gandhi's own brahmacharya experiments.) When I meet them, Kripalani is in his late eighties and Sucheta is in her late sixties. They live in a new gray concrete house near Qutab Minar, the old Muslim tower on the outskirts of New Delhi. The house is built in the boxy modern style typical of New Delhi but has cleaner, more elegant lines and is beautifully furnished in the best of Indian contemporary design, accented with carefully selected pieces of folk art—old statues, pottery, wall hangings. It could be the home of a wealthy, sophisticated young couple.

"The house belongs to the missis," Kripalani tells me quickly, as if he were merely a guest. "It was furnished this way against my wishes. I try to keep to as many of my old ashram habits as I can. I don't use a fan, but now I do allow my clothes to be washed and my food to be cooked. In the old days, I did everything myself, but now the missis pampers me." His voice is rather weak, but his manner of speaking is emphatic. Like Gandhi, he wears nothing but a simple white dhoti. His body is withered and emaciated. He has a sunken chest sprinkled with a few white hairs, and elongated breasts. His head is rather delicate, with thin, fine grayish-brown hair worn somewhat long, and he has small eyes with large pouches underneath, and a nice smile. He seems to have all his teeth. He gives an impression of frailty but is actually quite spry.

"I have a brother who is a fairly well-known artist and designer," Sucheta says. She is a plump woman with graying black hair in a short, businesslike cut, and has a round face with large eyes and a small nose. She is wearing glasses with brown frames, and a white khadi sari with a patterned blue border. "He designed all our furniture. We were able to afford good things because Kripalaniji inherited a considerable amount of money from his family and we were able to save quite a lot of the money I earned. I also managed to make some wise investments."

I ask them if they were brahmacharis before their marriage, and, if so, how they came to marry and whether they have continued to be brahmacharis throughout their marriage.

"We've always been brahmacharis," Kripalani says. "When we married, in 1936, I was in my late forties and Sucheta was in her late twenties, so she was not exactly a child bride. In fact, she had already been a professor for six years at the Hindu University at Benares."

"I haven't taught for many years now," Sucheta says. "We were both members of Parliament from 1946 on. We were originally elected on the Congress ticket, but Kripalaniji left the Congress in 1951 to form what became the Praja Socialist Party, which I then joined. But we have both long since retired from politics, and I'm just an administrator. I run a clinic and a school for poor girls."

Kripalani puts on thick glasses and starts reading a book, which he holds close to his face.

"We met through Bapu," Sucheta goes on. "I was one of Bapu's volunteers in Bihar after the earthquake there in 1934. So was Kripalaniji, but he had been working for Bapu for fourteen years before that. For me, it was love at first sight. I felt that Kripalaniji's gentle personality and my forceful, idealistic nature would make a good combination. When Bapu heard of it, he said, 'If you marry him, Sucheta, you will break my right arm. You must give him up. His life is dedicated to our struggle, and you wouldn't want him to be diverted from it, would you?' I said, 'Why do you think our marriage would take him away from your work? Our marriage will simply enrich your work. You will have two dedicated workers instead of one.' We had this argument again and again over several months. I was a very stubborn woman, but Bapu was a very persuasive man, and I finally gave up any idea of marrying Kripalaniji. But then Bapu insisted not only that I renounce Kripalaniji but that I marry someone else. That was too much, so Kripalaniji and I got married after all. Bapu gave his consent grudgingly but withheld his blessing."

"I get the impression from what you say that Gandhi mostly pressured you, rather than Kripalani, against the marriage," I say.

"Bapu thought that Kripalaniji was a confirmed bachelor and that I was the one goading him into marriage," she says. "He wanted all his close associates and workers to be brahmacharis, because he felt that married people could not be intensely single-minded about the Constructive Programme and the freedom struggle, about our service to society. We agreed. So even though we got married, from the very beginning we continued to be brahmacharis, as Bapu wanted us to, and lived like companions—like brother and sister."

"If you were both going to be brahmacharis, why did you want to get married at all?" I ask.

"We wanted to live together, and we knew that if we weren't married, this would cause a great scandal," she replies. "We've been relatively happy, but in some brahmachari marriages I know, the wives have really suffered. Some went half mad with frustration. But I kept busy in the freedom struggle."

Suddenly, Kripalani puts aside his book and launches into a tirade against the present-day rulers. "There's no difference between the British and their Indian successors. More than twenty-five years after independence, the poor are worse off than they were before. When Bapu talked about service to the country, better conditions for the poor, he didn't mean TVs, radios, and cars for the middle classes. He was talking about the basic requirements for physical life—two square meals a day, clean clothes, and shelter. What was the use of brahmacharya and the freedom struggle and all our going to jail?"

Raihana Tyabji, a disciple of Gandhi who is herself a famous brahmachari, has also become famous in India as a self-styled psychological consultant and spiritual healer for brahmacharis, among others. On occasion, because she had a haunting, soothing voice, she was the solo hymn singer at Gandhi's prayer meetings. By birth and upbringing she is a Sufi Muslim, and by inclination and choice a Vishnuite Hindu. In the foreword to a small book she wrote called "The Heart of a Gopi," published in 1936, she says that for three feverish days she became a *gopi,* "possessed" by the spirit of Krishna, who is the voluptuary incarnation of Vishnu, and who often appears in the guise of a cowherd playing a flute and dallying with milkmaids. She claims that during those three days she wrote the entire book, in English, in a fit of automatic writing. As the story opens, it appears that the world is at war and that the narrator, one Princess Sharmila, is Raihana herself. For her safety, she has been given in marriage to an actual cowherd, who takes her to his home in Krishna's mythical dominion, on the banks of the sacred river Jumna. There she is swept up into the romantic world of Krishna and his milkmaids. She becomes alienated from her husband as her senses are gradually awakened and excited by visions of Krishna.

Krishna plays with her. He lurks behind every bush. He steals her clothes and her milk vessels. He is the air she breathes, the ground she walks on, the river she bathes in, the sari she wears. She writes:

Near that great tree with flame-colored blossoms I stopped, my feet weighted down so that I could not lift them, my senses swimming. Then said a deep, golden voice, "Sharmila!" . . . It seemed a blue sun arose in the heavens. . . . And before my eager eyes stood a form celestial—so beautiful, so unutterably beautiful. . . . And then, before my eyes that incarnation of divine beauty began to shine with greater and with greater brilliance, until there stood before me a Form made, from head to foot, purely of dazzling blue light, like blue lightning chiselled and molded to the semblance of the human body. Whereat mine eyes closed, and my breath left me, and I sank quivering to my knees, my arms upflung before my aching eyes. "Enough, enough. Oh thou Marvellous One, Oh Thou Uttermost of beauty and of light!" I cried. "Mine eyes are dazzled, my heart broken with Thy blinding, blinding loveliness! Have pity, Lord, or I shall die, here, at Thy Feet, slain by unendurable ecstasy!"

In the end, Sharmila persuades herself—and her alarmed husband and in-laws—that love for a god need not interfere with love for a man. It is not so easy for her to persuade the reader, because she describes her mystical passion mostly in the language of earthly passion, even though she does attempt to make her outpourings seem innocent by portraying her Krishna as a ten-year-old boy.

It is hard to know what Gandhi thought of the book. He makes only one tantalizing reference to it, in a letter to Raihana's father, saying, "Please tell Raihana I began Gopi's diary." He did, however, have a special fondness for Raihana and for her singing. He once wrote, in reply to a letter in which she asked if she could stay with him at Sabarmati Ashram, "I should prize your presence even if you had not that rich melodious voice. What I prize is your goodness, which can act without speaking. It is like the fragrance of a sweet flower. It does not need any movement and yet the fragrance is all pervading and unmistakable, and it survives for a while even after the flower is withdrawn. How much longer must the fragrance of goodness last even after the body is withdrawn?"

Although Raihana has been in seclusion for many months, she has agreed to see me. She is in her seventies when I visit her, and lives in a gray concrete house near Gandhi's Cremation Ground, in New Delhi. The front yard is a tangle of weeds and bushes. On the front door is this sign:

> Ma in retirement
> No Entry
> NO APPOINTMENT

(Holy women are often known as Ma.) I walk around to the back of the house and come upon a youngish man and an old woman, both bent over inspecting a cornstalk. As soon as the old woman sees me, she makes off for the house.

I introduce myself to the man, who says, "I'm Shamsi. I came to Ma with neurotic complaints. She cured me and adopted me as her spiritual son." He has a shock of dark-brown hair, cut short and standing straight up from his head, and large eyes in a round, boyish face, and he is wearing a tan cotton kurta and white pajamas. He takes me into a stiflingly hot room, filled with Muslim and Hindu artifacts and smelling of burning incense and rotting guavas, where the old woman now reclines on a wooden bed. She gives a high, cracked laugh, jumps up, and embraces me. "I am Raihana," she says, and adds, to my surprise, "In my last incarnation, we were lovers—I danced to your violin throughout Europe. But now we meet as mother and son. Come and tell me about your researches on Bapu."

She lies back on the bed and takes snuff. She is small, potbellied, and rather forbidding. Her mouth is sunken and toothless, her nose large, and her chin pointed. Her eyes are dark and bulging, seemingly all pupil, her hair is gray and unkempt, and her skin is startlingly white—the result of the pigment deficiency known as leucoderma, which has ravaged her whole body. She wears a short blue sari knotted at the shoulder over a shapeless gray khadi dress.

"I could tell you things about my various incarnations that would make your flesh crawl," she says. "My leucoderma was the result of my recklessly indulging my sexual appetite in previous incarnations."

"*La ilaha illal 'lah, Muhammad Rasul Allah* ["Allah is one God, and Muhammad his greatest prophet"]," Shamsi murmurs as he kneels down, stands up, bows, squats, and prostrates himself, striking his forehead on the floor. "*La ilaha illal 'lah, Muhammad Rasul Allah.*"

"My devotional calling in this life is to treat neurotic patients of all kinds—brahmacharis who have neurotic problems and non-brahmacharis who have neurotic problems," Raihana continues. "But too many patients were coming. Their consciousnesses were assaulting my consciousness, and retarding the beating of my heart, and disturbing my stomach. Two years ago, I developed a most ferocious pain in my left leg. It was then that Lord Krishna appeared to me and said, 'Raihana, the pain in your leg is the result of your sitting cross-legged all these years late into the night listening to neurotic patients. The wind in your stomach has been denied its natural channel and has got trapped in your leg. But this is your final pain, the last payment for the sins of your past lives. You can now enter death consciousness.' I immediately went into seclusion, and I've been lying in this room ever since. All I know about life consciousness is that I eat and I sleep. I'm told, my son, that I eat chapattis and mushrooms and lentils and rice and toast and butter and cheese and porridge and sweet halvah and savory patties. But I taste nothing. I'm told, my son, that I sleep by day and am awake by night. That must be so, but I cannot tell."

At the first opportunity, I ask her about her relationship to Gandhi.

"I met Bapu at a grand dinner given by a cousin of mine, in Bombay, just after he arrived from South Africa. I was in my teens. I caught a glimpse of him in the midst of silks and brocades, frills and sparkling jewels. He was dressed in a coarse khadi dhoti and looked like a small-time tailor who'd wandered in by mistake. I lost my heart to him. He became my father, my mother, my girlfriend, my boyfriend, my daughter, my son, my teacher, my guru."

"*La ilaha illal . . .*" Shamsi intones.

"When I was getting ready to go to his ashram, he sent word that he could imagine that I was not used to squatting over a trench latrine without a proper seat, so I should be sure to bring my own pot and commode. When I got off the train at the railway station, the biggest thing I had with me was this commode, and I arrived at the ashram in a tonga with the commode prominently—I might say royally—perched on top of my luggage. It exhibited my latrine problem for everyone to see, and I became known as the lady with the commode. You can imagine how silly I felt—how chastened. Bapu had assigned Bibi Amtus Salaam to clean my pot. One morning, she didn't turn up. I waited and waited, and finally decided to do it myself. For a Tyabji to carry a pot of filth—my son, my son! Bibi Amtus Salaam saw me and came running after me. 'What are you doing? What do you think you're doing? You are a Tyabji.' She grabbed hold of the pot, and we struggled over it for a while. 'Bapu will be very angry,' she said. 'He's told us that we must do it until you become spiritually attuned to the holy task.' I let go. I really didn't like ashram living, but because of Bapu I learned to go anywhere, sleep anyplace, eat anything. Sex was another matter. Bapu wanted a standing army of brahmachari volunteers pledged to ahimsa and satyagraha. He insisted that if a brahmachari developed his consciousness far enough, sexual desire would disappear. Yet Bapu's brahmachari soldiers were mostly virgins or newlyweds, and the more they tried to restrain themselves and repress their sexual impulses and fill their consciousness with the satyagraha movement, the more oversexed and sex-conscious they became. I often told Bapu that there was a great difference between repressing libido and outgrowing it, and that the only way to outgrow it was to give free rein to it—to indulge it and satiate it. But he wouldn't listen. Because of my sexual indulgences in previous incarnations, I was, of course, as sexless as a stone. Bapu knew that, but he still worried about the extent of my brahmacharya experiments with men, even though they are in the ancient yogic tradition. He scolded me once for sleeping naked with one of my patients. The patient had lost his wife, and his sexual desire had reached such a feverish pitch that he lusted after his own daughters. I slept with him naked continually for a week, with wonderful results—he was completely cured. Later on, Bapu himself tried brahmacharya experiments with women, and he, too, had wonderful results."

"La ilaha illal 'lah, Muhammad Rasul Allah."

She closes her eyes and murmurs, "Lord Krishna is speaking to me. What a dashing figure you were in your previous incarnation! Your violin virtuosity would have inspired Paganini. But because you recklessly broke the hearts of us passionate, romantic girls, you are now saddled with your present tawdry incarnation."

Living in the same house as Raihana are two other Gandhians—Raihana's brahmachari "spiritual sister" Saroj Nanavati, and their well-known brahmachari "spiritual father," Dattatreya Balkrishna Kalelkar. Like many of Gandhi's disciples and brahmachari converts, Kalelkar had had a violent past. As a student at Fergusson College, in Poona, from 1904 to 1907, he had belonged to several clandestine revolutionary organizations working to overthrow British rule, and he had eventually been forced to take refuge from the British police in the nearby princely state of Baroda, where he became headmaster of a secondary school. The Maharaja of Baroda closed the school down in 1911 for "seditious activities." The Maharaja was eager to get back into the good graces of the British authorities, who had viewed him with suspicion since the Delhi Durbar earlier that year, when he refused to walk backward, in the manner of other Indian princes, in obeisance to George V. From Baroda, Kalelkar went to the Himalayas. He abandoned his revolutionary career and began a search for moksha, or salvation from the bondage of finite existence. When he returned to the plains, after reportedly walking for three years, he was taken for a holy man. He proceeded to Santiniketan, the school founded in Bengal by Rabindranath Tagore, in order to further his studies in Hinduism. It was there that Kalelkar met Gandhi. In 1917, he became a brahmachari and went to live for a time with Gandhi in his ashram, becoming one of his chief disciples. He has been engaged in the Constructive Programme for more than fifty years.

I find Kalelkar, who is now in his late eighties, lying on a cot in a musty closed room adjacent to Raihana's, his head propped up by two pillows. He has silvery hair hanging almost to his shoulders and forming a prominent widow's peak on a wide, furrowed forehead. He also has a long beard, reaching the middle of his exposed chest—for, except for spectacles, he is wearing just a dhoti. His face is bright, and there is a rakish air about him. Saroj, a maternal-looking woman with a beatific smile, is slowly massaging his feet.

"I met Kaka-Saheb through Sister Raihana," Saroj tells me, referring to Kalelkar. "Kaka-Saheb used to travel to Baroda on Bapu's work and always visited Sister Raihana's father. Sister Raihana and I both came from very good families and we were very close. Sister Raihana's father was a judge, and my father was in the Indian Civil Service. After Kaka-Saheb had finished talking business, Sister Raihana would catch hold of his hand, take him to her room, and sing *bhajans* [hymns] to him. The *bhajans* were about Krishna making merry with his milk-maids, and came to her spontaneously. I sometimes joined them. My father died in 1922, and I began having a recurring dream in which Kaka-Saheb came to me and said, 'Saroj, I am your father. Be with me always.' I told Sister Raihana about the dream, and she said, 'He is our father. Let us both accept him as our guru and go with him.' Sister Raihana had just lost her father, too. That's how the two of us came to live with Kaka-Saheb in his spiritual family.''

Kalelkar has been listening good-humoredly, and now he says, "There's nothing unusual about such arrangements among Bapu's brahmacharis. They're quite common, in fact, though many brahmacharis also go on living with their wives. I was married and had children before I became a brahmachari. One of my sons was once engaged to Sushila Nayar. I continued to sleep with my wife until she died, some years ago. I embraced her, I kissed her, I fondled her, but I had to deny her the ultimate satisfaction of sexual intercourse. 'The greater the temptation, the greater the renunciation,' Bapu always said. I have to admit that I myself often felt torn between my duty to my wife and my duty to my vow of brahmacharya, because part of me believes that sex is an appetite, like eating, that should not be denied.''

"It seems that the more a Gandhian tried to get away from sex, the more he was trapped by it," I say.

"I don't agree," he says. "Bapu used to tell a story about a European girl in South Africa—I forget her name. She was young and was living with Bapu as a member of his family. She suffered from headaches, and no medicine seemed to help. When she told this to Bapu, he said to her, 'You must be constipated. I'll give you an enema.' As he was preparing the syringe, she undressed and came up to him and embraced him. Bapu asked her, 'Do you take me to be your father or your paramour?' She blushed with shame and backed away. Bapu was not the slightest bit disturbed in body or mind, and proceeded to give her the enema. Then he made her confess her transgression to friends and family, and saw to it that they respected her for her truthfulness. The few times in his brahmachari life when he did feel sexual excitement, he felt that public confession was the only way to expiate his sense of sin. I myself completely approved of his brahmacharya experiments, although I never agreed with him that sleeping with Manu in Noakhali was the ultimate test of his purity, because Manu was like a granddaughter to him. But then he didn't really need to experiment, to test himself, because his relationships with women were, beginning to end, as pure as mother's milk.''

Revolution: The Constructive

Programme and Its Mahatmas

THE EDITOR OF "THE COLLECTED WORKS OF MAHATMA GANDHI,"
K. Swaminathan, recently told a visitor that Gandhi had no use for
government as it is conventionally defined. "If Gandhi had wanted to
run the government, he could have done so for the asking at independence," Swaminathan said. "But he handed over the country to Nehru,
who was an aristocrat, who had never lived in a village, who knew
nothing about farming, so that today Gandhian ideas are completely
forgotten by our government and society at large. Gandhi felt that
ninety per cent of our people didn't need to be governed. The only
people who needed to be governed were the top five per cent, made
up of the avaricious, the hoarders, and the black marketeers, and the
bottom five per cent, made up of the common thieves, the murderers,
and the gangsters. The rest were fit to manage their own affairs in the
villages, because they were godly men and women, the custodians of
ancient Indian wisdom, of India's morality and religion."

Gandhi put all his emphasis on agrarian rather than industrial
development, to achieve social and economic regeneration at the grassroots level through such simple self-help measures as growing cotton
and spinning yarn. This was his Constructive Programme—his revolution. Thousands of Constructive Workers, in all parts of the country,
dedicated themselves to it, each in his or her own fashion. Many of
them are still alive. What kinds of people are they? How do they reflect

Gandhi's work and spirit? What kind of lives do they lead now? Seeking answers to questions such as these brings me to the last leg of a journey that has turned out to be somewhat reminiscent of Captain Marlow's in Joseph Conrad's story "Heart of Darkness": "To him the meaning of an episode was not inside like a kernel but outside, enveloping the tale which brought it out only as a glow brings out a haze, in the likeness of one of these misty halos that sometimes are made visible by the spectral illumination of moonshine."

G. Ramachandran was recently made the chairman of the Khadi and Village Industries Commission, which had been established by the central government in 1956 to foster the production of khadi, and which is the most important part of Gandhi's Constructive Programme being carried on in India today. Ramachandran is in Delhi, staying in one of the guest rooms of the Gandhi Peace Foundation.

When I go up to his room, a dishevelled man with a striped towel thrown around his neck peeks out through a crack in the door. He is Ramachandran.

"As they say in French, you catch me deshabilly," he says. He lets me in and quickly retreats to the bathroom. His room, which has gray walls, a bed covered with a paisley spread, a built-in desk with bookshelves, assorted chairs, and a Formica-topped card table with a copy of Speer's "Inside the Third Reich" on it, could be straight out of a college dormitory. Ramachandran reappears wearing a freshly laundered khadi dhoti and a long white khadi kurta with close-fitting sleeves. He is a rather short and heavy man in his late sixties, with a fringe of white curls above large ears. He has a high, rounded forehead, small eyes with heavy lids, a long, pointed, bumpy nose, a tiny, bristly mustache, and a small, somewhat prim mouth.

"Except for khadi work, our government has rejected Gandhi's Constructive Programme as unsuited for modern, industrial India, but my wife and I are trying to keep it alive in all its multifarious aspects in South India, in Madurai," he says. "How I wish you and I could have met there. We set up a model Gandhian village, Gandhigram, in 1953, and now we have our own schools, a university, medical services, a cooperative farm, and a bank—all based on Bapu's principles."

I ask him how he became one of Gandhi's Constructive Workers.

"I was a young fellow of seventeen," he says. "The princely state of Travancore, where I was living, was convulsed by revolutionary activity. It was the early twenties, when Bapu and his Constructive Workers were lighting fires everywhere, and in Travancore the lowly, downtrodden untouchables suddenly started walking on roads that for centuries had been reserved for high-caste Hindus. The Maharaja arrested hundreds of them. Bapu arrived, and the untouchables organized a rally to hear him speak. My parents wouldn't give me permission to attend it, but I slipped out of the house without their knowledge and got my first look at Bapu from a distance through a tremendous crowd. That was enough."

"What impressed you so much?"

"The crowd was chanting *'Mahatma Gandhi ki jai!'* but as soon as Bapu raised one finger they fell silent. He could control vast crowds, sometimes numbering millions, just by raising his finger. The magic of the man's finger was what affected me."

Ramachandran, who has small, nervous hands with thin fingers, raises his right hand and holds up his forefinger. "The crowd expected Bapu to attack the Maharaja, but practically the first thing he said was 'I've come here on a pilgrimage to help the Harijans gain their self-respect, but I've also come here to pay my respects to your great Maharaja.' You could see that the people were stunned and were beginning to turn hostile. They would have stoned him, but Bapu was able to control them with his magic finger. Within a few days of the rally, Bapu had persuaded the Maharaja to allow the untouchables to walk on the roads. That's my favorite fable for our times. But no one listens to me."

It's hard to know just what he has in mind as the moral of his story, but as he talks on, it becomes clear that, at a time when most people see more virtue and value in the soft, mill-made cloth now sold throughout the country, he, as chairman of the Khadi Commission, devotes his energy to travelling from city to city lecturing on the virtues and values of making and wearing homespun.

Maurice Frydman is a Polish-born engineer who lived and worked with Gandhi off and on in the Constructive Programme and became known for his research on Gandhian, or village-centered, economics—for working on such inventions as the perfect spinning wheel and the most enduring mud hut, and for writing such pamphlets and articles as "Micro-Technology and Micro-Energetics," "Sound Money: Wheat Money," and "Right Eating." He now lives in an old building in a pleasant residential area of Bombay. Wooden stairs leading to his flat, on the second floor, smell of disinfectant. From a sign on the door it appears that Frydman is not the principal occupant but shares his quarters with a variety of people and organizations, in his own version of an ashram. It reads:

Hiralai B. Petit
Maurice Frydman
Bharatananda
Magdalene A. Pinto
Indo-Polish Library
Kh. and Village Industries
Tibetan Refugees
Pascual Fernandez
Martha Gois
Rita Pinto
Lawrence Pinto

When I knock on the door, I think I hear a voice bid me enter, and I walk into a large, stuffy, noisy, cluttered room. There is no one to be seen, but from behind a wooden partition come the sounds of people laughing, singing, and whistling, along with the strains of Bach's Double Concerto, the clatter of a sewing machine, and a boyish voice with a strong English accent saying, "I l-l-l-love you. I l-l-l-ove you." The room contains two large Indian-Victorian settees with khadi cushions, an ornate dining table with seven chairs around it and a crystal chandelier hanging over it, some intricately carved wooden screens, and two marble statues of little girls—one demurely reading a book and the other coyly holding up her skirt.

"Hello!" I call out. And a small, thin old man with a slight hunch, a large head, thick white hair, and eyeglasses with clear frames shuffles into the room from behind the partition, followed by a short, heavy old woman with close-cropped white hair, thick glasses with black frames, and a big cane. He is dressed in a white khadi kurta and matching trousers with black shoes and white socks, and she in a waist-length white choli and a yellow sari worn Gujarati-peasant style—coming over the right shoulder from the back and tucked in at the waist. The man walks toward me and says, over the din, "I'm Maurice Frydman. Bharatananda is my Hindu name. And this is my lady companion, philosopher, friend, guide, and benefactress, Miss Petit. You must have heard of the Bombay Petits—the Petit Library, the Petit Institute, the Petit Hospital, the Petit Parsi Girls' Orphanage, the Petit this, the Petit that. She's that family. It all started with a little Parsi ship chandler and a French sea captain who called him 'Petit.' The name stuck."

I ask Frydman about the other names on the door.

"It tells the world who we are, what we're interested in, and who stays with us," he says, with a mysterious air.

Miss Petit, who has not been paying much attention, rouses herself to say, "Mr. Frydman talks too much."

"We're perfect complements," Frydman goes on. "I'm a talker. She's a doer of good deeds. She also happens to be a marvellous medium, you know. If you like, she can make contact with Gandhi for you, and you can talk to him directly. But I should warn you she always thought I wasted my time with Gandhiji. He wasn't spiritual enough for her"—a crescendo from Bach almost drowns him out—"but she's a very obstinate miss. I've been trying to marry her for years, but she's not much interested in that."

Miss Petit abruptly leaves the room. The din beyond the partition continues unabated.

I ask him how a Polish engineer became an Indian Constructive Worker.

"That's a long story," he tells me. "I was born in Poland in 1901, into a poor family. I never knew my father—he died before I was born—but my mother managed somehow to put me through a university, where I studied electrical and mechanical engineering. During the Depression, I went to Paris in search of work. One day, I happened to be at the Gare de Lyon. A crowd had gathered, and I joined it to see what was happening. A train pulled in, and a little half-naked man, all luminous and shiny like burnished gold, got off. The police tried to hold people back, but this remarkable, godlike man stepped right into the thick of things, greeting and blessing everyone. It was my first glimpse of Gandhiji—Gandhiji in action. It was a rapturous experience. I might say a mystical experience. I subsequently learned that he was on his way home from the Second Round Table Conference in London. My sweetheart and I came to India a couple of years later in search of mystical experiences. She contracted typhoid and died within three months. I stayed on, and studied philosophy with the Yogi Ramana Maharishi, in South India. Miss Petit and I were fellow-disciples—that's how we met—and she's been my benefactress ever since. I went to Gandhiji's ashram in search of more spiritual enlightenment, and he asked me if I could build him a light, portable spinning wheel. I made a simple eight-spindle spinning wheel. He said that it looked too complicated—that he needed something much simpler for Indian villagers. 'But a simpler spinning wheel wouldn't give you the output,' I said. 'I don't care about the output. I want everyone to be employed,' he said. He believed that the work available in any society was limited and static, and that if one person produced more than his share, it would cut into the work of another person. I, as an engineer, had a dynamic view of work and society. We didn't see eye to eye on practical matters, although I embraced him as my guru."

"But you go on working on Gandhian projects?"

"Yes, when I'm not busy with spiritual matters. Just now, I'm trying to convert the mountains of cornhusks that Indians throw away into food for children. I've already published a paper on food from watermelon waste." He falls silent and seems to listen for the finale of the Bach.

After the record has finished, I ask him if he misses Europe.

"Not at all. When I see European faces now, they seem bleached and full of anxiety. They don't have the Indian spiritual heritage."

As I'm leaving, he calls after me, "Do come back if you want Miss Petit to arrange an interview for you with Gandhiji!"

Gandhi had a long succession of foreign disciples, the best-known being Albert West, Henry Polak, Hermann Kallenbach, C. F. Andrews, Verrier Elwin, and Madeleine Slade. Madeleine Slade, the daughter of an English admiral, is about eighty when I visit her. She says in her autobiography, "The Spirit's Pilgrimage," which was published in 1960, that she was a solitary child, whose chief companions were animals, trees, and plants. When she was about fifteen, her father brought home an Angelus pianola and some rolls of music. None of the music made any impression on her until she happened to listen to a Beethoven sonata (Opus 31, No. 2), after which Beethoven became her chief companion: she spent her time listening to every Beethoven sonata she could get hold of. She writes:

> Though I have never had any musical training whatever, yet I *heard.* I was finding something far beyond the music as such; I was contacting the spirit speaking through sound, the spirit of Beethoven. . . . I threw myself down on my knees in the seclusion of my room and prayed, *really* prayed to God for the first time in my life: "Why have I been born over a century too late? Why hast Thou given me realization of him and yet put all these years in between?"

In 1909, the year she turned seventeen, her father was posted to India, and she and her sister Rhona lived there with their parents for two years. The India they saw consisted of balls and formal dinner parties. It made no particular impression on Madeleine, and she considered her time in India a mere interruption of her infatuation with Beethoven. Back in England, she continued trying to learn to play the piano, which she had begun studying in India, but she had no aptitude for it. She prayed ardently for guidance on the best way of serving Beethoven, but none was forthcoming. Finally, after the First World War, she sought inspiration on the Continent, where she visited Beethoven's birthplace, in Germany, and his grave, in Austria. She says that in those sacred places she felt a throb of "infinite longing" but came away no wiser about how best to serve Beethoven. She organized concerts of Beethoven's music in London. She went to France to learn French so that she could read a much talked-about novel by Romain Rolland, "Jean Christophe," which was based in part on Beethoven's life. She tried to meet its author, and eventually, in 1924, caught up with him in Switzerland, only to be told by Rolland about a new book of his, on a man called Gandhi, whom Rolland regarded as "another Christ." Later, when she read the Gandhi book, it struck her that all the time she had been destined not for Beethoven but for Gandhi— that Beethoven had simply been God's way of bringing her to Rolland, so that he could point the way to Gandhi. She resisted her first impulse, which was to rush off to India and find Gandhi at once. Instead, she decided to spend a year training herself for a life in India with him— sitting and sleeping on the floor, wearing frocks of khadi, studying translations of Hindu scriptures, taking language lessons, working at the spinning wheel, eating vegetarian fare, abjuring alcohol, faithfully reading *Young India*. During that time, she wrote to Gandhi, and he replied that if after her year's training she still felt she wanted to come to him he would be glad to have her do so.

Some months later, she arrived at Gandhi's hut at Sabarmati Ashram. She was thirty-three. "A slight brown figure rose up and came toward me," she writes of her first meeting with Gandhi. "I was conscious of nothing but a sense of light. I fell on my knees. Hands gently raised me up, and a voice said: 'You shall be my daughter.'" She was accepted as a member of the ashram and given the name Mirabehn.

The finest feature of her appearance was her hair, which was long, thick, and dark. As a mark of her devotion to Gandhi and to the ascetic life, she decided to have it all cut off. The women residents were shocked at the suggestion. They themselves had never contemplated such an extreme step, and they told her that with a shorn head she would only succeed in making herself more conspicuously different from them than she already was. But Mirabehn was adamant, and Gandhi did the job. "Bapu quite simply cut off my hair with his own hands, and gave me a loving slap on the back when I bowed down at his feet for blessings," she writes. Mirabehn's zeal, however, soon got on Gandhi's nerves—or so it appears from letters he wrote to her at this time—and within a year he found an excuse to send her away to Delhi, ostensibly to learn Hindi. From that time on, she mostly lived away from him, staying in other ashrams and serving as a Constructive Worker in schools and villages in various parts of India.

He says in a letter to her that whenever she went back to stay with him her mere presence irked him, and, no matter what she did and no matter how hard he tried to control himself, they always quarrelled. After one such stay, he wrote to her:

All the time you were squandering your love on me personally, I felt guilty of misappropriation. And I exploded on the slightest pretext. Now that you are not with me, my anger turns itself upon me for having given you all those terrible scoldings. But I was on a bed of hot ashes all the while I was accepting your service. You will truly serve me by joyously serving the cause. "Cheer boys, cheer, no more of idle sorrow."

In other letters, he admonishes her "to be a perfect woman . . . to shed all angularities"—her nervousness, her shyness, her dependence on him. He is solicitous about her weight and the regularity of her bowel movements. He says he is "haunted" by her in his sleep, and invites her to write to him about matters she would not mention to anyone else. She does just that. For example, she writes to him about encountering discrimination from orthodox Hindus during her menstrual periods. She says that she is revolted, because in the ashram in which she happens to be staying she and the other women are expected to live in rags, in miserable quarters, during menstruation. They are considered unclean and, for all practical purposes, untouchable, so they are not only segregated but also forbidden to go near places where food is being prepared or served. He sympathizes with her complaint, and agrees that women should not be treated in such a manner. Yet he tells her, "It should not be 'revolting' to you to accept such untouchability. On the contrary, you should impose it on yourself or accept it with grace and cheerfulness without thinking that the orthodox party is in any way unreasonable." He feels that the tradition of "this monthly untouchability" arose because of "man's inability to curb his beastly lust." But she insists that she is neither lustful nor the object of anyone's lust. After all, she is a virgin. They reach an impasse, and all that Gandhi can say is that such untouchability has never been compulsory in any of his communities and that anyway she will soon be leaving her orthodox ashram.

Gandhi's American biographer Louis Fischer writes:

> The women in the Mahatma's entourage . . . loved Gandhi, and he loved them. It was a father-daughter relationship of more than usual warmth and interdependence. Miss Slade became physically ill on a number of occasions when she was separated from Bapu or when she was worried about his health. Her bond with him was one of the remarkable platonic associations of our age. He often said to her, "When this body is no more there will not be separation, but I shall be nearer to you. The body is a hindrance."

On the whole, Mirabehn bore the vicissitudes of Indian life at that time stoically, although when she was away from Gandhi she felt restless and unfulfilled. She was ravaged by disease—malaria, dysentery, typhoid—and spent a total of three years in jail for her part in the satyagraha campaigns. Eventually, Gandhi gave her money to found her own ashram, which she did at the end of 1944. She set up a sort of laboratory for experiments in agriculture and animal husbandry on ten acres of land in what were then the United Provinces, in northern India, but after a couple of years she turned the land over to the government and moved the animals farther north, into the hills by the Ganges, where she founded a second ashram, naming it Pashulok, or "animal world." She spent some time travelling through the neighboring forest on the back of an elephant, looking for open grazing land and collecting old, decrepit bulls and cows and buffaloes and taking them to Pashulok.

After Gandhi's death, Mirabehn felt that the government and people of independent India, even the other Constructive Workers, completely forgot what Gandhi had stood for, including his insistence that the first task of any truly democratic government was to help the people feed and clothe themselves. She therefore left a third ashram, which she had founded in the early fifties, and tried to revive his memory single-handed. She took a horse and for months at a time rode through the countryside speaking to villagers about Gandhi and his Constructive Programme in her limited Hindi or through inexperienced interpreters, only to be confronted with incomprehension and unresponsiveness.

One day, completely broken in health and spirit, she found herself once again reading about Beethoven, and once again it was a book by Rolland, "Beethoven—Les Grandes Époques Créatrices," which, she says, had remained forgotten and unread in a trunk. "Yes—it was the spirit of him from whose music I had been separated for over thirty years that I heard and felt, but now with new vision and inspiration," she writes. "I became conscious of the realization of my true self. For a while I remained lost in the World of the Spirit, and when I finally came back the former tension and restlessness had passed out of me." So it was that in 1959, eleven years after Gandhi's death and thirty-four years after she had arrived at Gandhi's ashram, she left the country, to find rest and repose in the more temperate climate of Europe and to follow what she once more regarded as her true calling—serving Beethoven.

In order to meet Mirabehn, who is now, in a sense, Madeleine Slade again, I go to Austria, where she has been working on a biography of Beethoven almost continuously since she rediscovered him. She is living in Vienna when I visit her, with the Indian Ambassador to Austria, Vishnuprasad Chunilal Trivedi, and his wife, Devika. The Ambassador's residence is a solid-looking house on Spitzergasse, with rosebushes and lime trees in the front garden. The door is opened by Miss Slade's Indian servant, Brahmachariji (her name for him), whom I feel I know from the description she gives of him in her autobiography. He is a rugged-looking man in his middle forties with a black beard, and still looks "as if he had stepped out of a painting of the Apostles," in Miss Slade's words.

Brahmachariji falls at my feet, coughing repeatedly and muttering in broken English, "Sahib, I having a wife and four children back in my village. Must seeing them. Please help. Memsahib saying I am attaching to her because of karma, but already spending twenty-one years in Memsahib's service. Now, must seeing family. Help, please!"

It seems that Brahmachariji sees in every Indian visitor he meets a chance to get home, but at the same time it seems that he is resigned to the idea that nothing will come of his plea, because immediately after making it he gets up and without more ado leads me upstairs and into a little room where a tall, imperious-looking woman with severe features and a defiant expression is sitting on a narrow bed strewn with papers. She has shoulder-length gray hair, and wears glasses and a black wool dress. She gets up, picks up a walking stick beside the bed, and comes forward to receive me somewhat reluctantly, as if she didn't like to be bothered.

"I fell," she says, holding up her right arm, which is in a cast. "I don't see very well, because I've had cataracts for the last few years." Her voice is upper-crust English.

She sits down on the bed again and busies herself with tea, which Brahmachariji has brought in on a tray, with some little cakes, and put on the bedside table.

The room is simply furnished, with a couple of wooden armchairs and a large table covered with a blanket, on which are a typewriter, a fat English-German dictionary, a copy of Plutarch's "Lives," a copy of "Beethoven—Les Grandes Époques Créatrices," and a book of Beethoven's letters. On the walls there is only one picture—a small portrait of Beethoven. Birds fly in and out of the room and feed on birdseed that has been set out for them on the windowsill.

"The birds come and peck at the manuscript," she says. "I like their company. In fact, I have always preferred the company of birds, horses, and cattle to that of my fellow-men, who are busy despoiling our planet."

I try to draw her out on the subject of Gandhi, but her answers are vague. She speaks of him in the most general and abstract terms as a great hero of history, comparing him to Socrates, Christ, and Beethoven.

"How is it that you were so readily able to substitute Gandhi for Beethoven and Beethoven for Gandhi?" I ask. "Surely what distinguishes the hero from the rest of us is his extraordinary individuality?"

"They were much more alike than anyone supposes," she says. "My book on van Beethoven will show that. They both believed in God. They both had great spiritual power. And don't think that van Beethoven wasn't political. He read the newspapers and followed Parliamentary debates in England. Please don't ask me any more about Bapu. I now belong to van Beethoven. In matters of the spirit, there is always a call. After my years in India, I came to Vienna in search of van Beethoven and visited every house in Vienna in which he had done anything at all. Then I realized that I could find my inspiration to write about him only where he had found his most important inspiration— in the forest. They still have forests here and understand that forests are necessary for man's well-being. I went to Gaaden, a village deep in the forest, mentioned in a note of van Beethoven's, and lived alone in a farmhouse there for next to nothing. It was very primitive. There was no running water, and a pigsty some distance away was the only sanitary facility. I soon realized that I couldn't do all the chores alone and devote myself to van Beethoven's music, so I sent for Brahmachariji. We had nice times together. We fetched water, cut down trees, and chopped wood. We went for long walks and gathered mushrooms and flowers. For the first five years, I didn't write a sentence. I just listened to van Beethoven's music—I had brought along my gramophone—and wandered around the forest waiting for inspiration. Then I wrote and wrote and wrote, and now I have hundreds of pages. But no one wants them. All the publishers say that my kind of inspirational writing is out of style. Will you have one of these little cakes?"

Brahmachariji brings in some hot water and skulks away.

"Brahmachariji and I stayed in Gaaden for nine years. The Trivedis heard about us, and when they saw the conditions we were living in they offered us a room in their house. That was two years ago, and we've been living here ever since."

I try to bring the conversation around to Gandhi again. "Do you keep in contact with any other Gandhians?"

"Not much," she says. "Some time ago, I think, I had a letter from Pyarelal, asking me some questions for his biography which he said only I could answer. But I can't be bothered to write letters anymore."

"Have you given up all the old Gandhian ways?" I ask. "Do you ever wear khadi or do any spinning? Are you still a vegetarian?"

"Those things are not suited to European life," she says. "Even in India, when I was in the Himalayas with my animals, I started eating eggs to fortify myself against the cold, and as soon as I got to Europe I started eating meat. But I stick to chicken and fish, because they're easy to digest, and I eat at what seem to Europeans like strange hours, because I go to bed early and wake up early. That's the only thing that has really stayed with me from my time in India."

Gulzarilal Nanda is the best-known Gandhian in national politics today. He was the Acting Prime Minister and one of Indira Gandhi's main competitors for the post of Prime Minister when she acceded to power, in 1966. He has held several Ministerial portfolios in the central government, and is, in his way, as influential as Morarji Desai, the only other powerful Gandhian currently on the national scene. Nanda lives in a large pink house, set back from the road and enclosed by a wall, in one of New Delhi's wealthy residential areas. I wait for him in a large, bare, and rather impersonal living room, furnished with two daybeds, a couch, and several armchairs, all with yellow-and-white slipcovers. There is a picture of Nehru on the mantelpiece and a large bust of Buddha in one corner, and set out on the coffee table are books with such titles as "Chariots of the Gods," "Was God an Astronaut?," "Spiritual Crisis of Man," and "Fifth Dimension."

Nanda comes in. He is a thin, rather furtive-seeming man with a slight stoop. He has an oblong face, small features, and black hair and a black mustache, which seem to have been dyed. He is seventy-four years old. He wears a long white khadi kurta, white pajama trousers, a white Gandhi cap, gold-half-rimmed spectacles, and pegged wooden clogs of the kind that Gandhi wore. He is accompanied by a tall, black-haired man, also dressed in a white kurta, pajamas, and cap, whom he introduces as his secretary, and who settles down with pencil and paper to take notes on the conversation.

"Gandhi was my social and political mentor," Nanda tells me, leaning back wearily on the couch. "I first got involved with him as a result of my work in the textile union in Ahmedabad, and I became his chief lieutenant in the trade-union movement. The whole trade-union movement in India was shaped by Gandhi's idea that a worker should not economically blackmail his employer but appeal to his spiritual self to secure higher wages and better working conditions. But few today even pay lip service to this or any other idea of Gandhi's."

"For many years, you had a powerful position in the government," I say. "Did you ever try to make any elements of the Constructive Programme law?"

"Gandhi's Constructive Programme depended on individual effort. And, anyway, what can you do when the government is bent on Western science and industrialization? I myself have left politics for higher things."

He seems ill at ease, drumming his fingers on a book and slapping his clogs against his heels.

"What are those higher things?" I ask.

"Astrology," he says, sitting up and becoming animated. "I study it with Pandit Haveliram. He sees everything in the world—past, present, and future. Throughout the time I was in the Cabinet, I consulted him before making any important decision. People like Pandit Haveliram have no need for power themselves. They are interested only in the occult. Now he comes and sees me every day and reads the 'Arun Sangita' to me. I have been reading it with him for fifteen years, and new sections keep coming and coming."

"What is it?" I ask.

"It's the Book of Books."

"What would Gandhi have thought about all this?"

"He would have approved. I once read him a book about the world future by an American astrologer and palmist who was very well known in the twenties, and he was very excited by it. Here comes Haveliram." He raises his voice. "Haveliram, come in, come in! What are you going to read to me today?"

Haveliram is a fat, sweaty man with thin dark-gray hair, one wet curl of which is plastered to his forehead. He has small eyes with large, puffy bags under them, and heavy jowls. He wears a white dhoti and a limp white kurta, the pocket of which sags under the weight of pens, glasses, and papers. He has a sacred red thread on one wrist and a silver watch on the other. He is carrying several sheets of paper. They are about eight inches long and four inches wide, and are yellowish-brown with frayed edges. Holes have apparently been eaten in them, and the script is faded and difficult to read. They are the day's pages from the "Arun Sangita."

"Tell our friend about the Book of Books," Nanda says, pointing to me.

"Out of the horoscope I get a number, and out of the number I get a life," Haveliram says. "I cast a horoscope from a person's time and date of birth, and then am able to calculate the number of the page in the 'Arun Sangita' on which his life is told. Each leaf has a number at the top." Haveliram has an odd, high-pitched, nasal voice, and he seems to suffer from a slight palsy. As he speaks, he trembles and his head shakes from side to side.

"In addition to the section on individual lives, there are numerous other sections," Nanda says. "Sometimes at the end of a life of an individual there is another number, referring to a passage in a more philosophical section, for further enlightenment. And sometimes at the end of that passage there will be yet another section, and it just goes on and on in this way, leading to deeper and deeper knowledge."

All the time Nanda is talking, Haveliram emits low moans.

"If the book is so old, how can it tell about people not yet born and countries not yet dreamed of?" I ask.

"The Book has everything in it," Haveliram says. "But you have to know the code. America, for instance, is called Kumari Deep, or 'golden land.' It is also referred to as the 'virgin continent.' Germany is known as Ari Yamanan and Israel as Patik Ram."

"The Book is very specific," Nanda says. "It predicted Johnson's victory over Goldwater. When Chou En-lai came here, the Book said, 'Brother-Brother is going on, but beware of this man from China. He has eyes on your territory.' Soon after that, there was a Chinese attack on India. The Book gives formulas for making atomic bombs. A Ph.D. in physics came to see me one day, and Haveliram read the Book's

228

formula out to him. The physicist couldn't follow the intricacies of the formula, but he said it was right in the main."

"What did it say?" I ask.

"Oh, something about generating a worldwide thunder with uranium and lemon."

"Then why didn't someone make a bomb from the Book long ago?" I ask.

"Someone did, and there was an atomic holocaust in ancient times. Now there is only one copy of the Book, and I have it," Haveliram says.

"How do you come to have it?" I ask.

Haveliram leans back on a daybed against a round white pillow, tucks his feet up, and bunches up his dhoti, baring his knees. He then launches into the story of how the leaves were found, sometimes slapping his knees for emphasis. He is a good storyteller, with the gestures and sense of timing of an accomplished performer. The story is a long rigmarole, with lots of local color and folk history. It has numerous narrators, all far removed from anyone who might have witnessed the actual events, and encompasses endless generations of people, improbable coincidences, and great calamities.

Nanda listens with intense interest and the credulity of a child, frequently asking, "Then what happened? Then what happened?"

"Then . . ." Haveliram invariably says, pausing to catch his breath before taking up the story. Like Gandhi's disciples talking about their guru, Nanda acts at times like Haveliram's son; at other times, he acts like a person with a stake in his protégé's performance, and looks at me to see if I'm enjoying it as much as he is.

It seems that a hundred or two hundred years ago—it's never quite clear which—it was put about that a certain woman recently widowed had been left dozens and dozens of bulging gunnies, and since people's wealth used to be measured by the number of bulging gunnies they owned, the widow was judged to be very wealthy, even though her husband had been only a poor scholar. A notorious band of dacoits, hearing about the widow and her wealth, arrived at her house in the dead of night with thirty-six camels. They murdered the widow, loaded the gunnies on the camels, and set out for their camp in the forest. Now, it happened that that same night the local nawab had been married, and his wedding procession, including richly caparisoned elephants, camels, and horses, bumped into the dacoits and their train. In the ensuing melee, the dacoits were routed. They fled with their camels but left the gunnies behind. The nawab posted some strong guards on the highway and continued on his wedding route, but instead of returning for the precious gunnies he dallied for a while with his bride. Then Haveliram's great-grand-ancestor heard about the treasure under guard on the road. He seems to have had masterly powers of persuasion, for he prevailed upon the guards to carry the gunnies on their backs to his house, where they all planned to share the loot. When they finally opened the gunnies, they were shocked to discover that the gunnies were filled with nothing more valuable than sheets of paper covered with mysterious writing. The guards took to their heels, and the great-grand-ancestor was left with a houseful of mysterious papers on his hands. Knowing that his entire family would be put to death if the nawab discovered them in his possession, he tried to get rid of them. At that point, God Himself appeared from the Heavens and revealed to him that the papers were the Book of Books and how to decipher it. He was at first afraid to make use of his power, but one day he predicted the death of a young boy. That was the beginning of his fame and fortune.

The long and short of it was that after several more generations of dacoits, murdered widows, ambushes on lonely roads, intrigues, and revelations, and much besides, the Book fell into the waiting hands of Haveliram.

Each Constructive Worker I meet seems to take refuge in his or her own way from the despairing task of coming to grips with Indian poverty without Gandhi—Ramachandran resorting to the bureaucracy, Frydman to spiritualism, Miss Slade to Beethoven, and Nanda to astrology. But at least three Constructive Workers—Vinoba Bhave, Satish Chandra Das Gupta, and Abdul Ghaffar Khan—continue to do battle for Gandhi's ideas and ideals, undaunted by Gandhi's absence. These men are Gandhi's real heirs—mahatmas, or "great souls," in their own right.

Gandhi considered Vinoba Bhave the purest and most uncompromising of his workers. Vinoba became a brahmachari when he was twelve, never married, never formed any other worldly attachments, and never held any political office. He joined Gandhi's ashram at

Ahmedabad in 1916, when he was twenty-one, and thereafter devoted himself to religious scholarship, satyagraha, and the Constructive Programme. In 1951, three years after Gandhi's death, when it seemed unlikely that land reform would ever be effected in India, because the new ruling classes were property owners and were committed to the inviolability of property rights, Vinoba launched the largest and in some ways the most heroic experiment ever undertaken in the Constructive Programme—the Bhudan, or Land Gift, Movement. He walked from village to village, covering about ten miles a day, and held public meetings in which he solicited land from landowners for the landless by contending that God's earth belonged not to individuals but to everyone, and that the landowners' acceptance of this principle was the essential first step in creating Gandhi's just society. Within the first three years, he and his followers succeeded in collecting four million acres of land, but much of it proved to be barren or rocky, with scarcely a blade of grass on it, or in such odd parcels that it could not be cultivated. Still, over the next thirteen years or so the Bhudan Movement became a rallying point for all workers in the Constructive Programme.

In the mid-sixties, Vinoba retired from the world to pursue a life of meditation. He now lives in his own ashram, near the town of Pawnar and sixteen miles from Sevagram. The ashram stands high on a hill overlooking the River Dham. In the middle of the river is an ancient white pedestal with a sacrificial urn on it. A concrete ramp leads from the riverbank to the pedestal. Rising out of the river are lavalike black rocks, on some of which, when I visit the ashram, white cows are standing lackadaisically drinking. The ashram, which consists of a fairly large red building, several low white buildings with blue windows and doors, and a vegetable garden, is next to a white temple. Pieces of broken statues of gods and goddesses are strewn about on the ground near the temple.

I wait for Vinoba in a small room with a polished stone floor. It has windows looking out onto the garden, where an old man with a young man at his side can be seen bending over, cutting grass. They presently leave off their task and come into the room, scythes in hand. The old man has a short white beard and mustache; the rest of his face is almost hidden by sunglasses and by a green cloth helmet with earflaps and a chin strap. He is lean and tanned and is naked except for a skimpy khadi dhoti. His manner is somewhat aloof and defiant. He is Vinoba.

"You see, Vinobaji still works in the garden every day. Everyone is amazed that he gets such comfort and solace from cutting grass. It is a form of devotion for him," the young man says. He turns out to be Vinoba's secretary. He has black hair and slightly protruding teeth, and wears black-framed glasses and a white dhoti.

Silent devotees, mostly old men in white kurtas and dhotis, file in and sit on the floor around Vinoba until there is no space left to sit. Two devotees—a pretty young Hindu girl with black hair starting to grow again on her shaven head, and an old man wearing a dhoti and brown-framed glasses—have to stand and peer in through the window.

From the back of the room, a devotee who, in the manner of orthodox Hindus, has a vertical white-and-red stripe on his forehead and has his head shaven except for a long *bodhi,* or tuft of hair, passes a piece of paper to the secretary. The secretary hands the paper to Vinoba and, turning to me, says with a knowing laugh, "Baba likes questions to be submitted to him in writing—he's deaf. But he's a great linguist. He knows many foreign and Indian languages, so you can submit your questions in any language you like." Baba is an honorific for an old man.

Vinoba has a cough, which he controls by pressing his thumb on the base of his collarbone. The secretary gives him some medicine in a small glass. Vinoba drinks it, belches several times, and makes a little squeaking sound in his throat. Then, pointing to the devotee who handed in the question, Vinoba says to the company generally, "If he had read my book 'Talks on the Gita,' he would know the answer to his question." He slaps his feet down for emphasis. Pointing to me, he continues, "He's Indian, but he lives abroad." His slow, soft voice suddenly acquires a sharp edge. "Perhaps because he doesn't have to wrestle with Mother India's poverty there."

I ask him why he himself has given up wrestling with India's poverty.

"I'm a very old man," he says sadly. "I must prepare to meet my God."

"What impression did Gandhi make on your life?" I ask.

"I did not let him make any impression on me," he replies. "Impressions are transient. Only understanding is permanent. Gandhiji had a statuette of three monkeys in his hut from which we understood that

232

in order to find truth we must neither hear nor see nor speak evil. So far, thanks to the onset of deafness, I've managed only not to hear evil."

Everyone laughs a little uncertainly at his joke.

I ask him what the ultimate outcome of the Constructive Programme will be.

"Long before I retired from the world, our government had swept aside most of the nascent elements in the Constructive Programme as it scrambled to industrialize the country on the Western model," he says. "But, I tell you, the effects of the work of the Harold Wilsons and the Harold Bilsons and all the other secular 'sons' of Socialism are short-term. The effects of the Constructive Programme will be long-term. Gandhiji's spiritual Socialism is in eclipse right now, but it will triumph in the end."

Satish Chandra Das Gupta, a chemist and chemical engineer who renounced his profession in 1921, when he was forty-two, in order to take part in the Constructive Programme, now also lives in his own ashram, with his own disciples, in what is perhaps the poorest area of India—the Bankura District of West Bengal, settled mainly by tribal peoples, most of whom are considered untouchable, and many of whom leave the district to join wandering orders of mendicants or holy men.

To meet Satish Babu, as he is affectionately known, I take an overnight train from Calcutta to the new steel town of Durgapur, where I hire a taxi and drive twenty-eight miles southwest to Bankura, the headquarters of the district, and the nearest town to the ashram. On either side of the road are paddy fields. It is just after the monsoon rains, and men and women, up to their knees in water, are planting seedlings and driving teams of bullocks yoked to upright plows, which move across the watery fields like ships' masts. Four-foot-high clumps of green jute, bearing yellow flowers, mingle with the rice plants, and the jute and rice occasionally give way to patches of reddish clay soil or scrubby jungle—a tangled green undergrowth dotted with a few tall trees and some lavender-colored wild flowers similar to morning glories. The villages along the way consist of little more than thatched mud huts, a few palm trees, and sometimes a mango grove. Here and there, bunches of large green leaves are hanging from the eaves of the mud huts, and on the ground in front of the huts are neat rows of unhusked rice—all put out to dry. The last stretch of the road runs alongside a small river and is under a foot of water, in which people are washing clothes and bathing.

Bankura is a rather desolate small town. The main street is almost completely blocked by a tractor pulling an open wagon loaded with refuse. In addition to the grain market that is the raison d'être for this sort of town, there are a few stalls selling the dried green leaves—to be used as plates—and, of all things, life-size clay horses. It seems that the sale of these horses, along with subsistence rice farming, is the district's main source of livelihood, although the town does boast a small fleet of jeeps to take district officials into the remote interior. Since the road to the ashram, which is another twenty-eight miles away, is not negotiable by car, I hire one of the jeeps to continue my journey.

The land becomes increasingly barren. There are fewer paddy fields, and the earth mostly looks seared in spite of the monsoon rains. The domestic animals seem to be scarcely alive; the cows and horses are small and emaciated, and the pigs and goats are tiny runts. The people are noticeably dark-skinned, and are skimpily dressed. They watch impassively as the jeep bumps along over stony ground or squelches through mire. The road skirts a low hill that in profile looks something like the back of an elephant, and comes out onto a wasteland of dry, crumbly red soil relieved only by a few patches of grass or rice and a line of thatched mud huts. This is Gogra, the last hamlet before the ashram, and is as far as the jeep will go.

I get down, jump over a ditch, and continue on foot for a couple of miles to the ashram, which appears to be merely a series of rice fields in various shades of green—that is, various stages of cultivation—and a straggly line of mud huts. A large, lacy tree shades the front of the sturdiest-looking hut, which has a red tile roof, and windows barred to keep out bats and predatory birds. Inside the hut, an elderly man, flushed and perspiring, lies heavily on a wooden charpoy. He is Satish Babu.

"I have just made the four-mile walk to Gogra and back," he tells me, not getting up but dispelling any notion that he might be ill. He slips a set of false teeth into his mouth with scarcely a pause in his talk. "I do the four miles in fifty-three minutes, and I'm ninety-three, friend. Night and day, I try to live as the Mahatma lived. I go for a long walk, as he did; have a good long massage to keep my circulation toned up, as he did; eat sparingly, as he did; make a nuisance of myself to the authorities with my writing, as he did."

He sits up and pulls energetically at his toes. He is wearing a white dhoti and no shirt; his arms and stomach are a bit withered, but he seems remarkably well preserved. He is bald, wears brown-rimmed spectacles, and has blue eyes with large pupils; a small mouth; and a chin covered with white stubble. On the charpoy, near his head, is a little bamboo tray holding a hand fan, a book, pens and papers, and a clipboard with a page of two neat columns of cramped writing. A table on which are a stack of file folders and a covered typewriter stands at the foot of the charpoy. On the walls are a number of soil maps, a photograph of Gandhi spinning, and several shelves of books, medicine bottles, and miscellaneous objects. There is a garland of wild flowers woven with sheaves of rice around the photograph of Gandhi.

"I'm writing a story on population control for a Bengali newspaper," Satish Babu says, tapping the clipboard. "Like the Mahatma, friend, I believe that the only honest way for our people to conquer the population problem is to restrain themselves, and not use these satanic diaphragm things. I came to the conclusion long ago that it was impossible to be an honest man in society as it was." He points to Gandhi's photograph. "It was then, friend, that I met the Mahatma. I knew right away that this man lived by truth and truth alone, that he was a mountain-high man. I shook and shook with emotion." He throws back his head, rolls his eyes, and flails his arms about. One imagines that he could be a great actor or a powerful dictator. "He became my guru, my god, my religion, and I threw myself into his Constructive Programme—selling khadi and setting up cottage tanneries for untouchables."

"How did you come to have your own ashram?" I ask.

"I came here during the famine of 1966," he says. "Thousands of our countrymen were dying of hunger, and everyone was crying out for more and more American aid. But had not the Mahatma always said that foreign aid was colonialism, enslavement, and strangulation?" He becomes very agitated. "What was wrong with us Indians, that with so much land and rain we had been dying of hunger since the beginning of time? In the name of God and the Mahatma, I took up the challenge. I had heard that in Israel they were able to grow three crops a year on desert land. Here in West Bengal alone, we had two thousand square miles of barren land, on which nothing had ever grown and on which it was supposed that nothing ever would. So I came here with a handful of disciples, took ten acres of this barren land, and began experimenting with reclamation and cultivation. That was seven or eight years ago, and, friend, if the results of my experiments were generally applied, all the proverbial deserts would bloom. I was just reading that our central government's budget for this year is almost forty-four billion rupees. If they adopted my methods and reclaimed and cultivated all the barren land in India, they could have a budget of two hundred and fifty billion rupees—almost six times as much. From being one of the poorest countries in the world, we would become one of the richest. We wouldn't know what to do with our wealth, we would be so rich. But I can't get anyone to listen to me, let alone get anyone in the government to try my methods. Can you understand why I am going mad? I'm going mad because I can't get anyone to listen to me."

I know all too well from my journey in search of Gandhi that men of good will here—even when they served their apprenticeship in Indian reality under Gandhi, who knew more about it than anyone else—often take refuge from that bleak reality in utopian or visionary schemes, but, remembering that Satish Babu was trained as a scientist, I ask him to tell me precisely what his experiments consist of. Whereupon he jumps off the charpoy, tucks his dhoti around his knees, slips black sandals on his feet, wraps a white shawl around his shoulders, seizes a long, stout staff, and sets off at a very fast pace. From the back, he has an uncanny resemblance to Gandhi—the shawl, the sandals, the staff, even his bearing and the shape of his head. He leads the way along a narrow grassy path, through clusters of butterflies, to the highest point of his land, below which can be seen, in the middle of the wasteland, the ashram, with its cultivated fields.

"When I took possession of this land, I asked myself, 'Why has all this land been barren since time out of mind?'" he says rhetorically. "Why, friend? Well, I can now tell you why. I concluded it's because the soil is so crumbly. Almost all the rain drains away as soon as it falls, and we get something like sixty inches of rain a year here. 'What happens to all the water? Where does it all go?' I asked myself. 'Does it go out to sea? Or does it stay underground? If so, why doesn't it come up at some point?' I wrote off to the archeologist in charge of the government excavations on Susinia Hill—what the villagers call the

Elephant Hill. You must have passed it coming here. I told him about my project and asked him if they had discovered any water in their digging and what they could tell me about the subsoil. He wrote back saying, 'Give up your project; there is no water.' I consulted waterfinders, who said there was an inexhaustible supply of water here deep underground, so I started digging, at my own expense. I went on digging and digging for three months, and then I came up against layers of rock. I wrote to the government archeologist again, and said, 'Help me, help me, I'm on the verge of finding water.' He wrote me another stern letter saying, 'Give up your project; there is no water.' To break through the rocks, I needed power compressors, but I had no money, so I had to do everything by hand. I begged and begged until my friends got me some dynamite, and I blasted through the layers of rock. And, sure enough, I found water, plenty of water, water in plenty, which I could pump out by sinking a very deep well. That's it, over there."

He points to a nearby well, above which hundreds of dragonflies hover, and goes on, "But how was I to use this water? How was I to get the soil to retain some of it long enough to grow something? It came to me like a dream: if I could isolate some of the clay from the soil and mix the clay with water, I would get a colloidal suspension that would seal the surface and hold the rainwater there. With what little money I could raise, I hired some laborers. First, we marked off this land into plots and built up several of the plots into terraces, moving the earth we needed in head loads and shaping the ridges with our own hands. Then we flooded the terraces with water from the well, so that we could plow. We hitched up the bullock teams and plowed and plowed and plowed, in order to separate the various lateritic materials—clay, sand, stones. We removed the stones with rakes and wire mesh, and mixed the clay—which, being the smaller particles, was in suspension on the surface—with more water. We added some cow dung as compost, spread it evenly over the terraces, and planted rice. The colloidal clay did seal the surface so that the water stood on it, just as I had thought, and we were eventually able to harvest the first crop ever grown on this barren land. And the beauty of this experiment in land reclamation and cultivation was that it was all done by manpower, bullock power, and dung power—resources we Indians possess in abundance."

The method seems slow, primitive, and back-breaking—suitable at best for only small patches of barren land. But it is, of course, completely Gandhian in that it relies only on men and animals and on the simplest of implements and explosives to tap natural resources. Moreover, like Gandhi, Satish Babu, with his work, manages at the very least to sustain hope—no small achievement in this impoverished, desperate land.

As we stand at the end of the path near the well, Satish Babu clutches my hand. He peers up at me, his eyes swimming with tears. "Do you get my meaning?" he says abruptly.

I shake my head, uncomprehending.

Some ashram disciples suddenly appear from nowhere. They press pamphlets about the ashram into my hands and plead with Satish Babu to return to his hut to rest.

"I take care of them and they take care of me," he says, through his tears. "I have thirty people here in my ashram. Where am I to get the money to feed them? You get my meaning?"

I hand over to him twenty rupees, which is all I have in my pocket.

He is obviously disappointed and seems momentarily defeated, but he rallies quickly and thanks me.

Abdul Ghaffar Khan—affectionately called Badshah, or King, Khan—is the patriarch of the Pathans, a group of mountain tribes numbering some thirty million, who live mostly in Afghanistan and in the part of Pakistan that used to be the Northwest Frontier Province of British India. The Pathans are followers of Islam, and most of them speak Pakhtu (also called Pushtu). Throughout the Moghul and British periods, they were notorious for their feuds and their frequent outbursts of violence, even as they were renowned for their martial tradition and fiercely independent spirit. Because their violence was legendary, it was often forgotten that they were essentially a happy, carefree people, who roamed the mountains and valleys singing and laughing, and that although they always had a weapon in one hand, they often had a musical instrument in the other. Attempts to establish political dominion over them amounted to little more than punitive expeditions to their mountainous preserves to impose a semblance of order. Badshah Khan was the first Pathan to embrace Gandhi's principle of nonviolence and teach it to his people—through a society he founded in 1929 and called

238

Khudai Khidmatgar. To become Khudai Khidmatgars, or Servants of God, the Pathans were required to swear that they would never use violence, never take revenge, and never be a party to any feud but, rather, would forgive anyone who wronged them, consider all Pathans brothers, and, using the methods of Gandhi's Constructive Programme, work for the welfare of their people. Mostly because of Badshah Khan and his Khudai Khidmatgars, the Pathans were swept into Gandhi's struggle for independence, and the Khudai Khidmatgars became the most important social and political force in the Northwest Frontier Province. In fact, Badshah Khan became known as the Frontier Gandhi.

After the partition of India, the Pakistani government tried to assimilate the Pathans into Pakistan in the name of political stability and unity. But it failed to get Badshah Khan's cooperation. The Frontier Gandhi and the Pathans had no more use for military rule as it developed in Pakistan than they had had for British rule, and they sought to establish an independent state of their own, to be called Pakhtunistan. The Pakistani government therefore tried to suppress Khudai Khidmatgar by imprisoning Badshah Khan, his family, and his followers. And Badshah Khan, who had spent fifteen years in British jails for his part in India's struggle for independence, spent fifteen more in Pakistani jails for his opposition to the Pakistani government's policy toward his people. In 1964, when Badshah Khan was seventy-four years old, he was finally allowed to leave Pakistan and go to London for medical treatment, because his years in the Pakistani jails—where he was always in solitary confinement—had broken his health. In 1965, he was granted political asylum in Afghanistan, which ever since the partition has been serving as a refuge and a guerrilla headquarters for discontented Pathans from neighboring Pakistan.

I seek out Badshah Khan in Jalalabad, a town near the Khyber Pass, in Afghanistan, where he now lives in a low, nondescript house. He is sitting in a wicker chair in a bare room buzzing with flies, its windows looking out onto a wildly overgrown garden. Beyond the garden is the main road connecting Afghanistan and Pakistan—cutting through the mountains and valleys where the Pathans have always lived. He is over six feet tall and, despite his age (he is in his eighties), has the rugged, powerful military bearing of a proud Pathan. What a contrast he must have made to the small, frail, spindly Gandhi! Badshah Khan's mouth is set in a determined expression, and his forehead is furrowed, but his eyes are gentle and sad. He has short white hair and a short white beard, and he wears a long, loose shirt and pajamas, both dyed dark brown-red—a color that gave the Khudai Khidmatgars the popular name Red Shirts. They had settled on the color because it would show the jungle dirt less easily. He seems indifferent to the flies that settle on him, never bothering to flick them away—perhaps because he has always had to live with them.

"If I'd remained in Pakistan, I would have spent the rest of my life in jail," he says, in mellifluous Urdu. "That is, if I'd managed to survive the illness I had there at the end. To this day, I don't know precisely what made me ill. I was given some medicine in jail, but I don't know whether it didn't suit me or whether it was an attempt by the authorities to poison me. This much I do know—after taking the medicine, I almost died. For twenty-four hours, my whole body was shaken with spasms. The Pakistani authorities must have decided I was as good as dead, because they finally allowed me to go to London for treatment. The doctor who looked after me in London was a Pathan brother. He prescribed a medicine that I still take today. If Allah gives me health, I hope to live to see the oppressed Pathans of Pakistan united and living together in peace and dignity in Pakhtunistan. Whether our Pakhtunistan becomes an autonomous province of Pakistan or a separate nation like Bangladesh is for the Pakistanis to decide."

I ask him how he came to renounce the violence and feuding of his people for the nonviolence and Constructive Programme of Gandhi.

"It all started with my early education, as a Christian," he says. "My brother and I—he was assassinated in 1958 by the Pakistanis—were among the first Pathans to get an education. We went to schools established in our province by British missionaries. My headmaster at the Edwardes Memorial Mission High School, in Peshawar, was the Reverend E. F. E. Wigram. It was said that the Reverend Mr. Wigram worked gratis at the mission school—in fact, gave scholarships from his own pocket. The thought of this Christian gentleman who belonged to a country thousands of miles away devoting himself to the welfare of the Pathans moved me very much. The feeling grew in me that I, too, must one day serve my people. The Pathan mullahs used to go around proclaiming, 'Those who go to mission schools are infidels. They are paid to learn. They will have no place in Allah's Heaven. They will be cast down into Hell with all other infidels.' The mullahs were afraid that education would loosen their hold on the people. We mission-school boys tried to persuade the Pathans that there could be neither progress nor peace without education. Later on, the Reverend Mr. Wigram arranged for my brother to go to England and study medicine. After he went, the good man encouraged me to think about going, too, to study engineering. But my mother wouldn't let me go. At the time, such British laws as there were on the northwest frontier were enforced indiscriminately, and many an innocent Pathan was put away in jail for life. I told my mother, 'I won't come to any good if I stay back here. I, too, should go to England and learn enlightened ways to challenge bad laws.' But she wouldn't hear of it. So I stayed at home and helped get more schools started for Pathan children. After the First World War, the British looked on our attempts to provide education for Pathans as subversive, and arrested all the teachers and workers connected with our schools. As a result, I spent over three years in jail. As a young boy, I had had violent tendencies; the hot blood of the Pathans was in my veins. But in jail I had nothing to do except read the Koran. I read about the Prophet Muhammad in Mecca, about his patience, his suffering, his dedication. I'd read it all before, as a child, but now I read it in the light of what I was hearing all around me about Gandhiji's struggle against the British raj. The British said that Islam was a religion not of peace but of the sword. This just isn't so. They said it because they wanted Hindus and Muslims to cut each other's throats. There was a lot of violence in the Prophet's time, just as there was in Gandhiji's time, but that doesn't mean that the Prophet Muhammad was a man of the sword, any more than it means that Gandhiji was. When I finally met Gandhiji, I learned all about his ideas of nonviolence and his Constructive Programme. They changed my life forever. I wanted to spread these ideas within our community in the name of Allah, so I helped to start Khudai Khidmatgar. We trained volunteers to go out to the remotest Pathan villages to teach our people hygiene and sanitation, better farming methods, and nonviolence. The British took fright at the rapid spread of our movement. They wanted the Pathans to remain divided and unorganized. They burned down our villages, they jailed us and beat us up. All they succeeded in doing was turning a social movement into a political one. We Pathans eventually threw in our lot with Gandhiji and made his struggle our struggle. In 1931, after Gandhiji negotiated the Irwin-Gandhi Pact, most civil-disobedience prisoners were released, but I was not. Gandhiji went to Lord Irwin and said, 'Badshah Khan is one of us Congress workers, and he should be released, too.' Lord Irwin made some such reply as 'You are talking about a Pathan now. You should go to the Northwest Frontier Province and see for yourself what a violent people they are.' But Gandhiji wouldn't take no for an answer, and Lord Irwin, much against his will, eventually did release me. After Gandhiji returned from the unsuccessful Second Round Table Conference in London in 1931, things got sticky again, and we were all put back in jail. We were released in 1934, but I was forbidden to return to the Northwest Frontier Province. Gandhiji invited me to go and live with him, and I did, for three or four months. I used to read the Koran at the prayer meetings. If I forgot my spectacles, Gandhiji would lend me his."

I ask him what future he thinks there is for Gandhi's Constructive Programme—for Gandhiism.

"In India, Gandhiism is dead. Gandhi is completely forgotten. It's the story of Buddha all over again. When I was in India recently, I said in my speeches again and again, 'Why do you not honor your own prophets? Your government does all the things that Gandhi opposed the British for doing—arms itself to the teeth, neglects the villages and the poor, supports a huge, uncaring, remote bureaucracy. The Gandhians among you, with a few notable exceptions, either put all their emphasis on the spinning wheel, as if that were his entire message, or trade on his name for personal aggrandizement. I am your friend, and I cry over your weaknesses. If I were your enemy, I would jeer at them. Gandhiism has more life among us Pathans than among you. At the moment, we are oppressed and politically powerless, and so in no position to do much about Gandhiji's Constructive Programme. But we are holding fast to the principle of nonviolence, even though on occasion our hot Pathan blood has boiled over under the lash of our Pakistani persecutors.' "

"Why do you think the Pathans are more faithful to Gandhi's principle of nonviolence than Indians are?" I ask.

"I can only give you Gandhiji's answer to that question. I once said to him, in the middle of the violence of the partition, 'Your nonviolent movement has ancient roots in Hinduism, going back to Buddha, and has had almost half a century to develop in India under your leadership. You can call on almost limitless numbers of volunteers to help school your countrymen in nonviolence, and yet at this moment you have violence all over the country. We Khudai Khidmatgars began our nonviolent movement only in 1929, and you know how alien nonviolence is to the Pathan temperament and history. The natural response of a Pathan to any provocation is to kill—if necessary, dying in the attempt. Yet the British routinely stripped us Khudai Khidmatgars naked and caned us until we bled, and we tried to endure such indignities without allowing violence to poison our minds.' Gandhiji laughed, and replied, 'Nonviolence is the child not of the cowardly but of the brave. A Pathan is brave, so nonviolence is natural to him. A Hindu is not so brave, so nonviolence is not so natural to him. It takes longer for him to learn.' But, in a sense, everything Gandhiji taught was hard to learn, and even harder to put into practice day after day. Who of us can say, for example, that we ever succeeded in putting into practice the crux of the Constructive Programme—his ideas on sanitation, which were as basic to his teaching as nonviolence?''

Gandhi was appalled. People were urinating and defecating indiscriminately around their quarters; everywhere there were pools of stagnant water and piles of ordure; the few latrines were unclean and neglected; and no one seemed to notice or care. Yet the offenders were not ignorant rustics. They were India's political leaders, staying in a camp in Calcutta for the meeting of the Indian National Congress in 1901. Gandhi pointed to the filth and asked some Congress workers to clean it up. They refused, saying that it was work for untouchable scavengers, not for them. Gandhi would have cleaned up the whole camp himself, but he saw that it was a superhuman task, and had to content himself with cleaning out a single latrine—the one he used.

In all, Gandhi spent twenty-three years in England and South Africa, and he saw Indian filth with the eyes of a foreigner. "If we approach any village, the very first thing we encounter is the dunghill," he writes. "If a traveller who is unfamiliar with these parts comes across this state of affairs, he will not be able to differentiate between the dunghill and the residential part. As a matter of fact, there is not much of a difference between the two." No Indian village made any provision for private or public latrines, and villagers urinated and defecated anywhere, and threw all their household trash out into the lanes and byways, which were often ankle-deep in filth. Yet virtually every villager went barefoot. The cities and towns were no better. Most of them did not have sewer systems, and when they did, the pipes often emptied into rivers where tens of millions of pilgrims went annually to bathe and wash away their sins. The pilgrims showed no more concern about befouling the sacred rivers than they did about befouling the villages and cities from which they came. "What a sacrilege . . . to make the waters of all rivers, which we deify, filthy!" Gandhi exclaimed at one point.

Yet a Hindu was so afraid of spiritual pollution that he never allowed his right hand to come into contact with his own genitals or anus, if he could avoid it. The right hand was reserved for eating and the left hand for touching the sexual organs and for anal cleaning. Any contact with breath, spittle, mucus, sweat, semen, menses, urine, or feces—one's own or anyone else's—was spiritually polluting; so were dead animals; so were women who had had intercourse with other men. The mere shadow or glance of the people who routinely came into contact with such pollution—the untouchables—was polluting. They were the only people who could engage in such work as scavenging and tanning, and who could marry widows. Traditionally, they had to keep their distance from other Hindus. They had to live in separate communities, were barred from all schools and temples, and were not allowed to use certain public roads or certain wells. They had no hope of improving their station in this life, for that was their karma—their destiny, determined by their actions in a previous life. They could aspire to be better born in the next life only by being true to their dharma—their class rules of duty and service.

The whole notion of karma, dharma, different caste roles, and spiritual pollution was part of the Hindu belief that spiritual purification, or union with the Godhead, could be attained only through a cycle of births and rebirths, although temporary remission for some kinds of pollution, such as accidental contact with an untouchable, could be achieved by washing in the sacred rivers or drinking a sacred concoction made from the milk, butter, curds, urine, and dung of cows.

Gandhi, though a devout Hindu, was, like Buddha, a religious and social reformer. He began dreaming of a day when his India would be rid of the scourge of untouchability (by his time, as much as one-fifth of the population of India was made up of untouchables), and would be as clean and healthy as the West. He realized that the insanitary habits of his countrymen were responsible for cholera, typhoid, and chronic dysentery, and, in fact, he came to believe, for most of his countrymen's diseases. He recognized that these habits might be deeply ingrained, as a result of the institution of untouchability, but he insisted that they were the consequence not so much of religion or poverty as of "criminal apathy." In his view, cleanliness was not a luxury to be enjoyed by the rich or a service to be purchased by vast public expenditure but a necessity within the means of anyone who could master the rudiments of hygiene. He believed that an understanding of hygiene was even more important than the spread of literacy. "I know that the fashion is nowadays to give primary education the first place in the work of a municipality," he once said when he was inaugurating a new township. "In my opinion it is putting the cart before the horse. . . . I have not a shadow of doubt that sanitation occupies the foremost place. . . . In fact, sanitation is itself a first-class primary education for men, women, and children." He called for an army of Constructive Workers to volunteer to go out into the villages and drum into people's heads that, contrary to the accepted belief, everyone's religious and social duty lay in his being his own scavenger. Gandhi realized that exhortation alone would have little effect. He therefore wanted his volunteers to base their work on what he believed was the instinctive aversion that everyone had to defecating in public, and, at the same time, to make provision for public lavatories, which, he said, need be no more than ordinary buckets or earthenware pots, to be emptied regularly into a hole dug in the ground for the purpose. If a village was too poor to afford such receptacles, the Constructive Workers could dig a trench and train the villagers to use it and cover their excreta with clean earth. He warned that if the feces were buried too close to the surface they would emit a bad odor, would be dug up by stray dogs, and would become a source of infection; if they were buried too deep they would not decompose properly, because they would be beyond the reach of the sun's rays and of bacterial agents in the topsoil. He gave specific instructions to the Constructive Workers, even to the extent of pointing out that the spot where feces were buried should be protected by thorny hedges, and should not be used again for the same purpose within a year—but it could be ready for plowing in a matter of two weeks, since by that time the feces would have turned into manure. "The question of soiling the feet, whether of human beings or of cattle, can never arise," he writes, "as nothing can or should be sown without the night-soil being turned into good sweet-smelling manure, which one handles freely without any hesitation." He often uses the term "night-soil" for "excrement," as if to emphasize the connection between it and earth.

Gandhi anticipated the farmers' objections that it would defile their land to have excreta put in their fields, and so advised the Constructive Workers to use unclaimed land until the farmers could be convinced of the sanitary and economic value of excreta, which he also sometimes called "black gold." Thereafter, in Gandhi's words, "every farmer will utilize in his own fields the excreta of his own family, so that no one will find anyone else being a burden to him and everyone will go on enriching his own crop." He claimed that for thirty years he had been using the manure made from his own excreta to enrich the crops grown in his ashrams.

The Constructive Workers were to get hold of whatever implements they could find—spades, brooms, pickaxes, buckets, baskets— and set about clearing lanes and byways of the accumulated filth, separating organic and inorganic matter. The organic matter, being suitable for manure, was to be buried in a field. Some inorganic matter could be used for improving a village—by filling in potholes, for instance— and other inorganic matter, for which the Constructive Workers could not think of a use, could be packed down into deep holes on the outskirts of the village every day. The Constructive Workers were also to enclose the village pond. Most villages had only one pond. The villagers bathed in it, washed clothes and utensils in it, washed down and watered cattle in it, and then used its water for cooking and for drinking. The Constructive Workers were to teach the villagers to carry water from the enclosed pond to separate troughs for the cattle, and also into their huts for themselves. The villagers were to be told to do their washing and bathing in their huts, and to keep the water they used for such activities apart from the water they used for cooking and drinking. Finally, they were to tour the riverbanks every morning and clean them up, too. "We do not need to become municipal councillors or have any appointment from any public body and the government in order to do this work," Gandhi remarks.

Gandhi himself was a veteran of many wars for better sanitation, but seldom won more than a skirmish. In 1935, he wrote:

> In Sindi village we are trying to persuade the villagers not to use the streets, to go to the adjoining fields and to throw dry clean earth on their own evacuations. After two months' continuous labor and co-operation of the municipal councillors and others they have been good enough generally to cease to defile the streets. They go to the fields which their owners have been good enough to open for such use. But the villagers still obstinately refuse to throw earth on their own evacuations. "Surely it is *bhangi's* [untouchable sweeper's] work; it is sinful to look at faeces, more so to throw earth on them," they say. They have been taught to believe so. [Constructive] Workers have therefore not to write on a clean slate. They have to rub off what is drawn into the slate with steel points. . . . Age-hardened ignorance cannot yield to a few months' object-lessons.

One of Gandhi's most renowned skirmishes took place in 1915, when he admitted into the newly established Sabarmati Ashram an untouchable family—Duda and Dani, and their daughter Lakshmi. Duda and Dani are dead now, but Lakshmi lives in Ahmedabad. She makes her home in a two-room apartment a couple of flights up a dark stairway, smelling of urine, in a small tenement building. Slum children are camped outside her door, practically blocking it. Her main room has peeling green walls and a brown stone floor, and is furnished with an iron bedstead on which are a green print sheet and several flat pillows. Trunks are sticking out from under the bed, and there is a bedside table with a radio on it, and a couple of chairs. Hanging on the walls are a few calendars, some photographs of Gandhi, and one of Lakshmi herself, sitting behind a desk. Suspended from the ceiling, like a swing, over the bed is a big wooden slab with a large package wrapped in burlap on it—probably a talisman to ward off evil spirits. Through an open door a shiny brass bucket can be seen in the kitchen.

Lakshmi is a gaunt woman with a square face, a wide mouth, gray hair, and small, bright eyes. She has a nervous blink. She wears a brown-and-white plaid khadi sari and a white choli.

"I rent these rooms and live here with my son, who works at the local Khadi Board," she tells me in slightly formal Hindi. "I have a daughter, who is well married and also lives here in Ahmedabad, but I can't persuade my son to marry. He's getting on in years, but he won't marry, because he's confused about his caste. You see, my children's father was a Brahman. Bapu arranged my marriage to him. But people here still hold it against my children that their mother was born a Harijan. Yet my mother cooked for Bapu and he took food from her hands, and it was here in Ahmedabad that Bapu spent so many years trying to enlighten people. Bapu brought me up as his own daughter from the time I was an infant, and after my marriage he sent for me every year, wherever he was, and I went home to him for my annual visit, just like a daughter. There will never be any improvement in the lot of the Harijans or in the Hindus' attitude toward them until everybody adopts Bapu's ashram system of sanitation."

"What was his system?"

"He had worked it out very carefully in the very first communities he established, in South Africa," she says. "Two white-painted buckets were placed under a wooden platform in whitewashed outhouses. We had to learn to squat in such a manner that stool went into one bucket and urine into the other. Bapu thought it was harder to clean the buckets if solid and liquid wastes were mixed. Near the platform were two earthenware jars, one containing clean water and a dipper, the other fresh earth and a long iron spoon. After passing stool and urine, we had to wash ourselves over the urine bucket with the clean water." Paper in any form has always been too expensive for Indians to use for cleaning. "On the wall above the jars was a sign in Bapu's handwriting which said, 'Always leave the latrine cleaner than you find it.' We would take some of the fresh earth from the jar and completely cover up the stool. When the buckets were full, we ashram residents would take turns cleaning them. They were quite heavy, so it took two of us women to carry each one to the trenches in the nearby field. We first emptied the stool bucket and rinsed it out with the urine, swishing it around with a big broom—Bapu had found a use even for urine! Then we cleaned both buckets out with fresh earth and dumped that in the

248

trench, too, and spread cut grass over it. Finally, we left the buckets out in the sun to dry and picked up any empty buckets that had dried out and could be returned to the outhouses. In a few weeks, the trenches yielded rich compost, and new trenches were dug. It was a hard system and required a lot of training. I remember I vomited when I took my first bucket to the trenches. The sight of it! The smell of it! All the flies and insects! For a time, I couldn't eat, I couldn't keep anything down. But Bapu did make allowances. He would start a Brahman out cleaning the cowshed and gradually introduce him to cleaning the ashram's outhouses, in order to teach him that human excrement was as holy as cow dung. He once asked me, 'Can you pass my first test for a good ashramite?' 'What is it?' I asked. He laughed, and said, 'Can I take my lunch to the latrine after you've cleaned it, and eat it there?' I'm not generally a squeamish person, but I said to him, 'Please don't ask me to take such a test.' The thought of eating in a latrine turned my stomach. Even in the ashram, we had outbreaks of typhoid, because careless children, not trained in Bapu's ways, were always wandering about. I remember once Dr. Sushila Nayar arrived at Sevagram Ashram in the middle of a typhoid epidemic. She immediately went on a tour of inspection, and discovered a bit of excrement on the grinding stone used for grinding the ashram's wheat."

Gandhi, practically until the moment of his death, went on talking about the country's abominable sanitary conditions and exhorting his countrymen to become untouchables and so wipe away the stain of untouchability—now asking soldiers to set aside their arms and take up the urgent work of cleaning the country, now telling the government to spend its money for spades and pickaxes instead of guns and ammunition. When he went for his morning and evening walks, he often took a shovel and a bucket with him, and cleaned up the path as he went, telling his disciples that removing the excreta of others was a form of communion, the ultimate act of humility. In fact, he told them, without such communion with the lowest of the low—the untouchables—Hindus could not hope to overcome their caste prejudices. Although, mainly because of Gandhi, the social and religious disabilities of untouchables were officially abolished by the government of independent India, and untouchables were given the right to enter temples and schools, to walk on all public roads, to draw water from all public wells, to go anywhere, and, in effect, to touch anything and anyone, Gandhi died without making the slightest dent in the Hindu attitude toward excreta and sanitation, and, by extension, toward spiritual pollution and untouchability. Since Gandhi's death, the filth has spread and spread, and the lot of the untouchables has not noticeably improved as a result of their new legal status. For example, V. S. Naipaul notes in "An Area of Darkness"—his book about India, the country of his ancestors:

> Study these four men washing down the steps of this unpalatable Bombay hotel. The first pours water from a bucket, the second scratches the tiles with a twig broom, the third uses a rag to slop the dirty water down the steps into another bucket, which is held by the fourth. After they have passed, the steps are as dirty as before. . . . Four sweepers are in daily attendance, and it is enough in India that the sweepers attend. They are not required to *clean.* That is a subsidiary part of their function, which is to *be* sweepers, degraded beings, to go through the motions of degradation. They must stoop when they sweep; cleaning the floor of the smart Delhi café, they will squat and move like crabs between the feet of the customers, careful to touch no one, never looking up, never rising. In Jammu City you will see them collecting filth from the streets with their bare hands. This is the degradation the society requires of them, and to this they willingly submit. They are dirt; they wish to appear as dirt.

Age-hardened ignorance has not yielded at all to one man's lifetime of superhuman efforts and object lessons.

During the celebration of the centennial of Gandhi's birth, in 1969, many Indians, in their tributes to Gandhi, dwelt on how, during his lifelong struggle for freedom and toleration, human rights and human dignity, he had managed to turn people of clay into heroes. "Sometimes I wonder whether we have not become clay again," one participant in the celebration noted, and went on, "The exaltation which a truly great teacher produces in his time cannot last very long. But the teaching and thought of such people have a reach farther than their own time and country. We who were born in Gandhiji's own time and country have a special obligation to cherish his image. More than his words, his life was his message." These summary observations were delivered by the new leader of India, the new molder of people of clay or of heroes—Prime Minister Indira Gandhi, who had become Mahatma Gandhi's political heir three years earlier, the coincidence of their names being one of the ironies of history.

INDEX